MW00414030

a plant for every day of the year

For my parents, who taught me to love writing,
encouraged me to follow my heart,
and so often tolerated my plants taking over.

Clockwise from top left: *Tulipa* 'Spring Green,' *Canna* × *ehemanii*, *Helleborus* × *hybridus*, *Berberis wilsoniae*.

DK

a plant for every day of the year

Philip Clayton

DK UK

Project Editor Amy Slack
Senior Designer Barbara Zuniga
Production Editor David Almond
US Editor Jennette ElNaggar
Production Controller Rebecca Parton
Jacket Designer Eloise Grohs
Jackets Coordinator Jasmin Lennie
Editorial Manager Ruth O'Rourke
Design Manager Marianne Markham
Art Director Maxine Pedliham
Publisher Katie Cowan

Editor Michael Fullalove
Designer Vicky Read
Picture Researcher Sarah Smithies
Consultant Gardening Publisher Chris Young

ROYAL HORTICULTURAL SOCIETY

Consultant Simon Maughan
Publisher Rae Spencer-Jones

First American Edition, 2022
Published in the United States by DK Publishing
1745 Broadway, 20th Floor, New York, NY 10019

22 23 24 25 26 10 9 8 7 6 5 4 3 2 1
001-327582-Oct/2022

Published in Great Britain by Dorling Kindersley Limited

A catalog record for this book
is available from the Library of Congress.
ISBN 978-0-7440-6129-1

Printed and bound in China

For the curious
www.dk.com

This book was made with Forest Stewardship Council ™ certified paper– one small step in DK's commitment to a sustainable future. For more information go to www.dk.com/our-green-pledge

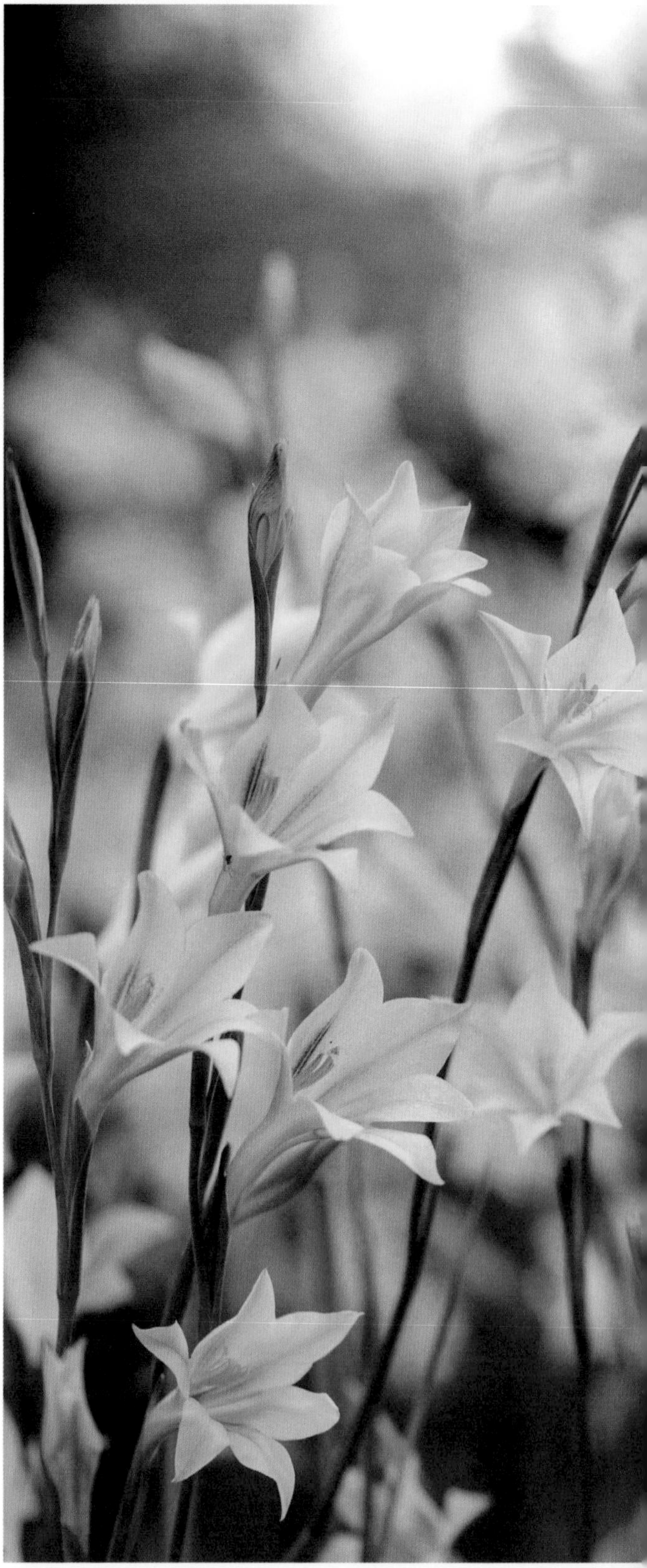

Gladiolus tristis

contents

introduction

People new to gardening are often surprised by how a mild interest in plants can grow into an all-consuming passion. It may eventually become a way of life that's central to all you do, with the power to raise your spirits even when times are hard.

The magic of plants became abundantly clear during the pandemic lockdowns. For many of us during that time—myself included—gardens became places of sanctuary and stimulation, while we also reacquainted ourselves with the charms of those green companions, the houseplants that we share our homes with. Every day I'd see a different plant that lifted my mood. It could be one in my garden, in a pot by the back door, or in the house. Eventually, I started to put images up on social media for others to enjoy, and soon the idea for this book germinated in my mind.

The remarkable force that plants exert is not limited to warmer, sunnier seasons but endures 365 days a year if you grow the right things. What those things are depends partly on the kind of gardener you are, but among the thousands of wonderful plants we cultivate in gardens are stand-out choices that never fail to enchant.

Some of these I grow in my own garden, where successional planting means there is plenty to see every day of the year. By planting successionally, I can cram more plants in, so when bulbs become dormant, the same space is filled by perennials or annuals that grow below canopies of flowering trees and shrubs, exotic bamboos, or bold herbaceous plants. And when the ground is full, I turn to containers.

A bit about my own garden

You might assume I have a huge garden with acres of borders and vast glasshouses. No such luck. My garden is ordinary—at the back of a Victorian end-of-terrace house in Peterborough. It is around 130ft (40m) long, about 25ft (8m) across, and happily walled all round. It also has a plant house made from an old garage with a perspex roof, where I keep more tender plants.

The garden runs east to west, so one wall is hot and sunny, while the other is cool and shaded. These contrasting conditions mean that, despite the plot's limited size, I can grow a wide range of very different plants. The soil is neutral and free-draining, and, thanks to the walls and urban location, it's a sheltered spot, though rather dry and prone to chilly easterly winds in winter.

I keep lots in pots and grow few vegetables, simply because I can't find the space in a garden that's already overflowing with the trees, shrubs, and plants I cherish. It is far from neat or carefully designed (my husband refers to it as a "jungle"), but to my eye, there's order and harmony. I like to encourage wildlife and try not to use chemicals.

Where to buy plants

The gardening books I most enjoy offer personal opinion and that's what I've done in this one. I grow, or have grown, every plant in the book—some several times in different gardens—so I know them extremely well. Among the 365 choices, you'll find some popular plants that are available everywhere. The reason plants like these are widely grown is that they're generally reliable and do well. There are also other plants that are less frequently seen and that you'll need to track down through specialty nurseries. These can be found by searching for them online.

Arranged by season

The book begins with spring, which may seem to go against what I've said about the year-round appeal of gardens, but for many people—myself included—spring is the natural start of the gardening year.

I was tempted initially to assign each plant to a particular date, but I had to admit that in differing sites and differing years, the same plant will peak at different times. So, it seemed better to be less rigid and to consider plants that are suitable for the start, middle, or end of each season (sometimes they span more than one). In short, this is a guide, not a diary. As a rule of thumb then, think of early spring as March, early summer as June, early fall as September, and early winter as December.

Choosing the right plants for you

The plants I've picked cover a wide range: some are tender and need moving indoors for part of the year so are not suitable for every gardener; others need growing with sharp drainage or require the reflected heat from a wall, which are conditions that not every garden can provide.

To help you choose the plants that will thrive in your space, I've listed the conditions each one prefers, as well as the size they're likely to reach when established.

Not all plants have common names, so while I understand that the Latin ones might seem long and scary, they're important, and most people, I find, soon get used to them.

By selecting a spread of choices from the brilliant plants in this book, you can bring excitement to your garden and home every day, be it in the beauty of an individual plant or in the new combinations that are bound to arise. In gardening, a world of life-enhancing fascination and satisfaction awaits.

USDA HARDINESS ZONES

The US is a vast country with multiple climate regions. To help gardeners estimate plant hardiness, the country is divided into zones based on the expected range of minimum annual temperatures. Other factors, including soil type, exposure, moisture levels, wind, and plant health, influence hardiness and should receive consideration.

Zone	Average Minimum Temperature Range
2	–50°F (–45.6°C) to –40°F (–40°C)
3	–40°F (–40°C) to –30°F (–34.4°C)
4	–30°F (–34.4°C) to –20°F (–28.9°C)
5	–20°F (–28.9°C) to –10°F (–23.3°C)
6	–10°F (–23.3°C) to 0°F (–17.8°C)
7	0°F (–17.8°C) to 10°F (–12.2°C)
8	10°F (–12.2°C) to 20°F (–6.7°C)
9	20°F (–6.7°C) to 30°F (–1.1°C)
10	30°F (–1.1°C) to 40°F (4.4°C)
11	40°F (4.4°C) to 50°F (10°C)
12	50°F (10°C) to 60°F (15.6°C)

spring

1

Crocus tommasinianus

I don't know of a more cheering sight at the start of the season than a sunny lawn naturalized with these beautiful little crocus. They seem to come out of nowhere, so slender are the flowers in bud, then suddenly one sunny morning they open wide—silvery mauve and purple stars gleaming against the still-short grass. Among the easiest of all cormous plants to grow, they need virtually no care yet are an important nectar source for early pollinators. Try introducing them below mature trees, where grass can grow more informally. Here, they look lovely with drifts of snowdrops and even the last winter aconites, but I'd probably avoid mixing them with larger, showier selections of crocus. They also go well with the first narcissi, particularly smaller-flowered selections. These crocuses thrive in rock gardens and even in the open border, but it is where they can increase naturally from seed that they are most pleasing. If you grow them in grass, don't mow it too early so that the crocus leaves yellow before the first cut. Plant bulbs in fall and look forward to every spring that follows.

COMMON NAME Early crocus **HEIGHT AND SPREAD** 4in (10cm) tall foliage **FLOWERS** 2in (5cm) tall, in early spring **ASPECT/LIKES** Sun or part shade, undisturbed ground **HARDINESS** Z 4-8

2

Daphne odora 'Aureomarginata'

This is probably the best-known and most reliable daphne, grown for its seductively scented, starry, soft-pink flowers that appear in clusters and reach their peak in early March, just as the blooms of earlier *Daphne bholua* fade. The perfume is even more delicious, carrying well on the air. The flowers appear in profusion and last most of the month, especially if the weather is kind. This is also a rather sturdier, more compact-growing plant, forming in time a stout, wide-spreading mound of fairly dense branches. Its pointed, oval leaves are attractively glossy and, as a bonus, each is margined to a varying degree in yellow. Give it reasonable, well-drained soil and it should thrive. This is not a plant that will do well for long in a container.

COMMON NAME Gold-edged winter daphne **HEIGHT AND SPREAD** 3 x 5ft (1 x 1.5m) **FLOWERS** ⅝in (1.5cm) across, held in 1¼in (3cm) heads in early spring **ASPECT/LIKES** Sun or part shade, open site, well-drained soil, not too dry **HARDINESS** Z 7-9

3. **COMMON NAME** Stonecrop **HEIGHT AND SPREAD** 6 x 39in (15 x 100cm) **FLOWERS** Tiny, held in heads 1¼in (3cm) across in summer **ASPECT/LIKES** Full sun, well-drained soil **HARDINESS** Z 5-9

4. **COMMON NAME** Box-leaf azara **HEIGHT AND SPREAD** 26 x 11½ft (8 x 3.5m) **FLOWERS** ½in (1cm) long, produced in multitudes in early spring **ASPECT/LIKES** Sun, shelter from cold winds, well-drained soil, not too dry **HARDINESS** Z 8-10

5. **COMMON NAME** Giant golden saxifrage **HEIGHT AND SPREAD** 8 x 39in (20 x 100cm) **FLOWERS** Large snowflake-like flower heads 2½in (6cm) across, in early spring **ASPECT/LIKES** Sun or part shade, shelter, moist soil, even mud **HARDINESS** Z 7-9

6. **COMMON NAME** Rosemary **HEIGHT AND SPREAD** 5 x 5ft (1.5 x 1.5m) **FLOWERS** ⅝in (1.5cm) across, from early spring **ASPECT/LIKES** Full sun, warmth, well-drained soil **HARDINESS** Z 8-10

3

Sedum rupestre 'Angelina'

This almost care-free, low-growing, carpeting evergreen is one of the most useful and effective of all plants for a dry position, ideally in full sun, although it will tolerate part shade. It forms a really eye-popping, dense, creeping mat of prostrate stems with bright golden-yellow, succulent, cylindrical leaves. From a distance, plants resemble a pool of sunlight and, being evergreen, the effect lasts year-round but is most impressive early in the year when the color is brightest. By summer, it becomes more lime green in tone. This is when heads of yellow flowers form. Drought-tolerant and hardy, it will grow in really thin soil and makes a good choice for planting in a green roof. It can also look superb in a gravel garden as a foil to taller plants. Alternatively, cascade it down a bank or over a wall. Propagation couldn't be easier—simply detach a stem and plant it. It will soon root.

4

Azara microphylla

If you are after a small, slender, easygoing evergreen tree, this excellent Chilean species should be toward the top of your list. It is of particular interest in winter and early spring, when it produces masses of tiny, yellow-orange flowers that are strongly scented of vanilla. They appear in clusters from the leaf axils and are most easily seen from below the branches. The leaves are small, glossy dark green, and held in pairs, one leaf rather larger than the other. The whole plant has a refined appearance and is naturally upright growing, with quite open growth. In time, it forms a handsome, feathery tree with a slender, gray, often multistemmed trunk. It is easy to keep and reasonably quick to develop. Removing lower branches as the tree develops may enhance its upright appearance. Worth looking out for is a wonderful variegated selection with dainty, silver-edged foliage.

5

Chrysosplenium macrophyllum

For gardens with a consistently moist area, perhaps beside a stream or pond, this lovely, unusual perennial makes an impact early in the year, as long as it has not been too cold. It has bold, rounded, apple-green leaves that are slightly hairy and held in rosettes. During the colder months, the foliage may also be bronze-tinted, and it is at this time that the plant sends up short red stems bearing pinkish-white, true flowers flanked by silvery, petal-like bracts. These are usually at their best in early March. The plant makes good ground cover and, shortly after flowering, sends out stout runners that form new rosettes. Prolonged freezing weather will damage the foliage. Never let it dry out.

6

Salvia rosmarinus 'Miss Jessopp's Upright'

With its gray-green, aromatic, evergreen foliage and displays of normally blue flowers early in the year, rosemary is an easy way to inject a touch of the Mediterranean into our gardens. I enjoy this particular selection for its unusual form. The branches grow in a distinctly upright fashion, forming feathery plumes of growth that contrast well with more rounded plants or with clipped-box and yew shapes. Although small, the blue flowers stud the stems and put on a great display early in spring, attracting pollinators. A trim after flowering, cutting back some of the tallest branches, will keep the plant in good order. Once established, it stands considerable spells of drought.

7

Camellia 'Cornish Snow'

With its simple, single, pure-white flowers enlivened by a central boss of golden anthers, this camellia makes a cool, refined choice. The small but profuse blooms begin to open in late winter, sooner in a mild season, and usually peak in early March. The flowers are slightly cup-shaped and nod gently among the slender branches. In full bloom, the plant looks almost as if a flight of butterflies has come to rest on it, and it is especially lovely with snowdrops planted at its feet. Compact growing, with a naturally almost weeping habit, this selection can be grown as a wall shrub, with its branches trained along wires. It will also be happy in a container for some years. It needs a cool shaded spot, perhaps below deciduous shrubs and trees or on a north-facing wall or fence. It must have acid soil that does not dry out—moisture is important in late summer, when flower buds form for the following spring.

8

Coronilla valentina subsp. *glauca* 'Citrina'

This might just be the longest-flowering plant I know. It seems to bloom nonstop from late fall, pausing to catch its breath over summer. It's a pretty thing, with delicate, sea-green foliage making a dense, sprawling, low, rounded shrub. In flower, it is studded with masses of small, pea-shaped, two-tone, pale- and bright-yellow flowers that are held in rounded heads of about 10 individual blooms. As buds, these look like clover flowers about to open. They have a pleasant scent, too, which can be detected from some distance when the plant is in full bloom—normally at the start of March. The plant can suffer in cold winters, so give it a sheltered corner. It tones beautifully with honeyed stone or pale brickwork, so a position against a wall can make an aesthetically smart move.

9

Vinca difformis Greystone form

This pure-white-flowered periwinkle blooms reliably early in the year. In a mild season, the first large, starry flowers will stud the arching, green stems not long after Christmas, but usually it reaches its peak just as winter's bite is weakening, making an arresting show. It needs some shelter, as it is more tender than many periwinkles. It is not, however, any less vigorous—its arching stems root and grow new plants as they go, forming thick, knee-high ground cover, so it is not a plant for a manicured border. But if you have space—perhaps in dryish shade below trees—this evergreen perennial is a useful and lovely thing. Just shear it back when it oversteps the mark.

10

Edgeworthia chrysantha 'Red Dragon'

An unusual deciduous shrub, this daphne relative is a plant of exceptional beauty in flower. Rounded, slightly domed, silvery heads crowded with buds form at the tips of slender bare stems. When these open during late winter and early spring, the rather tubular individual blooms are flared at the mouth, cream on the outside and orange-red within. It creates a remarkable display, unlike anything else in the garden for a month or so. The blooms are slightly scented too. The plant itself is an open, rounded shrub, bearing oval leaves through summer. It is quite delicate and needs care, but in a sheltered spot in part shade or sun, it will become a highlight of your garden.

7. HEIGHT AND SPREAD 8 x 5ft (2.5 x 1.5m) **FLOWERS** 1½in (4cm) across, from late winter until early spring **ASPECT/LIKES** Shade, shelter from cold winds, well-drained moist acid soil **HARDINESS** Z 7-8

8. COMMON NAME Bastard senna **HEIGHT AND SPREAD** 3 x 5ft (1 x 1.5m) **FLOWERS** ⅝in (1.5cm) long, held in 1in (2.5cm) wide clusters from fall until early summer **ASPECT/LIKES** Sun, shelter, well-drained soil **HARDINESS** Z 3-6

9. COMMON NAME Intermediate periwinkle **HEIGHT AND SPREAD** 1¾ x 6½ft (50 x 200cm) **FLOWERS** 1¼in (3cm) across, from midwinter until late spring **ASPECT/LIKES** Sun or shade, shelter, space to spread **HARDINESS** Z 9-10

10. HEIGHT AND SPREAD 3 x 5ft (1 x 1.5m) **FLOWERS** ⅝in (1.5cm) long, held in 1¼in (3cm) wide heads in late winter and early spring **ASPECT/LIKES** Part shade or sun, shelter from cold winds, moist rich, ideally acidic, well-drained soil **HARDINESS** Z 7-10

11

Hepatica × *maxima* 'Millstream Merlin'

HEIGHT AND SPREAD 6 x 8in (15 x 20cm) **FLOWERS** 1in (3cm) across, in early to midspring **ASPECT/LIKES** Part shade with spring sun, cool, moist well-drained soil, not too dry **HARDINESS** Z 8-9

Hepaticas are more or less evergreen herbaceous perennials and plants of great beauty, with anemone-like, spring flowers in a dazzling range of jewel-like colors. This exceptional cultivar was given to me by nurseryman and renowned hepatica expert John Massey and it's now one of the stars of spring in my garden. It reliably bears beautiful, rich-blue, upward-facing flowers amid lobed, apple-green leaves. The plant has slowly formed a compact clump and thrives undisturbed in a lightly shaded border, where it gets a little spring sunshine at flowering time. I mulch the border annually each winter with well-rotted manure and make sure the plant does not get too dry in summer or encroached upon by other plants. Apart from that, it receives little specific care.

12

Clematis armandi

There are two draws to this attractive plant that make it deserving of attention. First are the early-spring flowers: single, four- or five-petaled, rather open blooms, usually white, but in some selections cream or pink-flushed like apple blossom, held above the foliage. They are deliciously almond scented and last several weeks. Then there is the evergreen foliage, which is the finest in the genus. Mature leaves are sturdy, leathery, rich green, and divided into three fingerlike leaflets that twine around supports. Lush new growth in spring is beautiful—bronze flushed and shining like patent leather. It is vigorous, forming dense cover with its overlapping leaves, and is most lovely cascading down a fence or wall. The plant is not that hardy—young growth can be damaged by frost—so choose a sheltered site, shaded at the root, sunny above. It can be trimmed after flowering to keep it in bounds.

HEIGHT AND SPREAD Climbs to 26ft (8m) **FLOWERS** 2in (5cm) across, in early spring **ASPECT/LIKES** Sun, with shade at root, shelter, somewhere to climb **HARDINESS** Z 6-9

13

Ribes sanguineum 'Tydeman's White'

Traditionally, flowering currants have dangling clusters of distinctive, raspberry-red flowers. Far more choice and, I think, arresting in flower is this splendid selection. In truth, its delicate blooms are not really white at all but pale pink. When hit by the rays of early spring sunshine, the flowers seem to glow to glorious effect—an absolutely lovely sight. Grow it in sun in the open, perhaps as a specimen plant on its own. It forms a large, leafy, rounded shrub that is fairly nondescript in summer but tolerates well being used as a host for an *Eccremocarpus* or scrambling clematis. Keep the plant in bounds once mature by pruning after flowering in late spring, cutting shoots back to a pair of healthy buds. If you prefer pure-white flowers, try WHITE ICICLE, also known as 'Ubric,' which is another beauty.

HEIGHT AND SPREAD 8 x 5ft (2.5 x 1.5m) **FLOWERS** ½in (1cm) wide, held in 2½in (6cm) clusters in early spring
ASPECT/LIKES Sun, open site, well-drained soil
HARDINESS Z 6-8

"When hit by the rays of early spring sunshine, the flowers seem to glow to glorious effect."

14

Kerria japonica 'Golden Guinea'

Many gardeners will know popular *Kerria japonica* 'Pleniflora,' a tough, suckering, deciduous shrub, sometimes known as bachelor's buttons. Far less frequently seen, however, and with considerably more charm, is this fine selection. Similar in appearance, its flowers are single, larger, and almost buttercup-like. They have real delicacy and grace, fluttering in profusion amid bamboo-like stems in early spring, giving the plant a distinctly oriental appearance. It is almost as tough but perhaps slightly less vigorous than bachelor's buttons, and, while it will grow in poor soil in a lacklustre site, it deserves more. Clumps should be thinned after flowering to reduce congestion and old dead branches removed. This greatly improves the plant's appearance, even in winter, when the glossy green stems have surprising appeal.

15

Pulsatilla vulgaris

Within half an hour's drive of where I live is a site renowned locally for the richness of its flora. This native species—one of the most beautiful of our wildflowers—thrives there. Traditionally blooming at Easter, its rich, velvety, royal-purple flowers, each with a central, contrasting crown of golden stamens, can be found on the grassy banks. This beautiful perennial is also widely grown in gardens, where, if anything, it makes more of an impact. Cultivated plants arise in early spring, with flowers that are larger than in the wild soon shining atop rather taller stems. They are followed by attractive, long-lasting, clematis-like seed heads. The soft, downy, finely divided foliage is also attractive, and plants form a small, multiflowered clump. Choose a sunny, open site that does not get too dry in summer; perhaps a pocket in a rock garden or raised alpine bed. Cultivars also come in a range of colors, from white to rich ruby-red.

16

Pulmonaria 'Blue Ensign'

This extraordinary herbaceous perennial is the best pulmonaria I have grown or seen. Forming low, ground-covering clumps of quite large, bristly, rich-green, oval leaves, the plant can be semievergreen in a very mild year, although the foliage can get shabby. In late winter, bell-shaped flowers arise, held in small, outward-facing clusters. They are superb—intense violet-blue, an unusual color at this time, and appear in profusion for a couple of months. They are a perfect contrast to yellow, early-flowering plants, such as daffodils, hellebores, and forsythia. Although good in shade, this selection likes some sun in spring and needs moisture through the year. It can help to cut off old leaves, so the flowers are really shown off.

17

Scoliopus hallii

I'm fond of this unusual little North American woodlander. I grow mine among other special plants in a pot plunged in a raised bed of leaf mold that I keep constantly moist, for it needs cool, shaded, damp conditions. In early spring, star-shaped flowers of unusual beauty appear. Three of the petals are broad and curve downward; they are cream, striped delicately in warm brown. The other three are narrow and point upward. The effect is almost orchid-like, although the plant is actually closely related to trilliums. Once the flowers open, paired leaves arise. These are rich green and broadly oval, but by summer they yellow and wither. The plant gradually forms a little clump and sometimes sets seed.

14. HEIGHT AND SPREAD 5 x 6½ft (1.5 x 2m) **FLOWERS** 1¼in (3cm) across, in early spring **ASPECT/LIKES** Sun or part shade, not too dry **HARDINESS** Z 4-9

15. COMMON NAME Pasque flower **HEIGHT AND SPREAD** 8 x 12in (20 x 30cm) **FLOWERS** 2½in (6cm) across, in early spring **ASPECT/LIKES** Sun, open site, well-drained soil, not too dry **HARDINESS** Z 4-8

16. HEIGHT AND SPREAD 1 x 1¾ft (30 x 50cm) **FLOWERS** ¾in (2cm) across, from late winter to midspring **ASPECT/LIKES** Sun or part shade, well-drained soil, not too dry **HARDINESS** Z 4-9

17. COMMON NAME Oregon foetid adder's tongue **HEIGHT AND SPREAD** 3 x 6in (8 x 15cm) **FLOWERS** ¾in (2cm) across, in early spring **ASPECT/LIKES** Moist shaded woodland conditions **HARDINESS** Z 6-9

18

Camellia × *williamsii* 'Jury's Yellow'

Although there are yellow-flowered camellias in the wild, most are tender and rare, so this selection brings a novel hue to the palette of hardy cultivars. It is an anemone-flowered camellia, with a ruff of small, petal-like structures called petaloids the color of vanilla ice cream in the center. The nine outer true petals are pure-white. In time, the plant forms a rounded evergreen shrub and is easy to grow. Camellias often look best in containers; their flowers can appear rather "blobby" en masse in the garden, whereas close up, the beauty of the blooms is more easily appreciated. If you grow them in containers, keep plants well watered.

HEIGHT AND SPREAD Up to 13 x 13ft (4 x 4m), but usually less **FLOWERS** 2½in (6cm) across, in early to midspring **ASPECT/LIKES** Shade, shelter, moist well-drained acid soil **HARDINESS** Z 6-10

HEIGHT AND SPREAD 2½ x 3ft (75 x 100cm) **FLOWERS** ¾in (2cm), held in 8in (20cm) spikes in succession for much of the year, prolifically in spring **ASPECT/LIKES** Sun, shelter from wind, well-drained soil **HARDINESS** Z 6-9

19

Erysimum 'Bowles's Mauve'

If you are looking for a plant that gives value for money through continuous flowering, you've found it. I can think of few others that bloom for as long as this incredible perennial wallflower. Forming a dense, rounded, shrubby mound of rather brittle stems with gray-green, lance-shaped foliage, it is topped by tall, slender spires of bright purple flowers that appear in succession more or less year-round. It needs an open but not too exposed site and thrives in poor, fairly dry soil. The best plants are often seen sprawling atop walls, in raised beds, or at border edges. In time, either the plant dies of exhaustion or it gets too large and must be replaced. Summer cuttings root easily as long as you can find a shoot that does not have flower buds. Plants look and bloom best if dead-headed regularly.

20

Cupressus sempervirens

Is there a tree more redolent of the Mediterranean than this marvelously distinctive, columnar conifer? Just the sight of it makes you think of Tuscany or Puglia, especially when glimpsed against a cloudless sky. Quick-growing, it forms a slender and dense, arrestingly upright dark-green pillar, providing marvelous contrast to rounded trees and shrubs. It is also a great way to introduce height into small spaces. Italian tradition has it that they should always be planted in pairs, perhaps either side of some steps or framing a focal point, and this certainly adds a sense of structure and formality to a space. It needs sun, shelter, and a warm garden. Winter winds, rain, and particularly snow can damage its shape, pulling down branches. These can usually be tucked or tied back in. Trimming them off is another option, but this temporarily leaves a dent in your column.

COMMON NAME Italian cypress **HEIGHT AND SPREAD** 39 x 10ft (12 x 3m) or more **ASPECT/LIKES** Full sun, shelter, well-drained soil **HARDINESS** Z 8-10

21

Magnolia 'Susan'

If you are looking for an easy, reliable magnolia that flowers well from an early age, this selection is one of the best. It is naturally quite a shrubby plant, with a fairly compact, bushy habit, although you can remove lower branches for a more treelike shape, if you wish. For many weeks from quite early in spring in mild gardens and lasting until early summer, it is resplendent with dark-purple, cylindrical buds that open to elegant, tulip-shaped flowers with slender petals. These are rich reddish-purple on the outside and paler pink within. They also have an appealing fruity scent. Sometimes you even get the odd flower a bit later in the year. Give it a fairly sunny place, although it will also flourish below taller deciduous trees. It is a pretty undemanding plant; just don't let it get too dry while establishing. It will stand some pruning if it becomes too large.

HEIGHT AND SPREAD 13 x 13ft (4 x 4m) **FLOWERS** 6in (15cm) across, from early spring until early summer **ASPECT/LIKES** Sun or part shade, fertile well-drained soil, not too dry or open **HARDINESS** Z 3-8

"If you are looking for an easy, reliable magnolia that flowers well from an early age, this selection is one of the best."

22

Acanthus mollis 'Hollard's Gold'

Plants grown for foliage don't get much more dramatic than this superb, architectural perennial, particularly during a mild spring. Its large, jagged-edged, super-glossy, lush, young foliage arises bright buttercup-yellow, contrasting in color and form with so much other spring growth. Then in late spring, impressive flower spikes of white blooms appear. This is a plant that demands space: when mature, it forms a large, glowing mound of leaves that gradually turn chartreuse-green. It fits well with exotic-style planting, particularly as ground cover under tree ferns. Frosts easily damage the foliage, as do slugs and snails, so protect against both. By the end of summer, the plant can look shabby and may be cropped to the ground. It responds well to a decent annual mulch of garden compost.

HEIGHT AND SPREAD 4 x 3ft (1.2 x 1m) **FLOWERS** 1in (2.5cm) long, held in 4ft (1.2m) tall spires in late spring **ASPECT/LIKES** Sun, shelter from cold winds, well-drained soil, not too dry **HARDINESS** Z 7-10

23

Primula 'Dawn Ansell'

I've grown this charming, old-fashioned primrose for years, as it's among my favorite spring flowers. If well cared for, it is surprisingly enduring. Its attraction is the mass of beautiful, double, pure-white, almost roselike flowers of perfect form that nestle within a ruff of apple-green, leaflike bracts. These make it a so-called double Jack-in-the-Green primrose. It grows best in sun during spring, but with overhead shade in the hotter summer months, and it needs a place that does not get too dry. Plants look particularly fine in a group at the front of a border or at the foot of freshly emerged fern fronds. Single rosettes soon bulk up into small clumps. These slowly lose vigor after a while and ideally need dividing every three years or so. Lift clumps and carefully pull them apart by hand, replanting individual rosettes into soil improved with garden compost or well-rotted manure; they will quickly recover.

HEIGHT AND SPREAD 4 x 6in (10 x 15cm) **FLOWERS** 1in (2.5cm) across, produced freely from early spring **ASPECT/LIKES** Sun or part shade, not too hot or too dry **HARDINESS** Z 4-9

24

Fritillaria meleagris

Given the right conditions, this lovely bulb is a charming garden plant. Slender leaves and stems arise in early spring, the nodding buds usually held singly, opening to bowl-shaped flowers composed of six pointed petals. These are checkered in rich maroon and pink, although the odd plant produces gorgeous white flowers. Despite often being sold as an alpine, rock gardens can be too hot and dry for it. What this plant likes is plenty of moisture: it grows best when naturalized in wet grass and spreads freely when happy if you allow seed to disperse from the rounded pod that forms after flowering. It also thrives if left undisturbed in moist, open borders or grass beside water. Watch out for early red lily beetles. Pick them off if they appear.

COMMON NAME Snake's head fritillary **HEIGHT AND SPREAD** 12in (30cm) tall **FLOWERS** 1¼in (3cm) long, from early spring **ASPECT/LIKES** Sun or a little shade, moist conditions **HARDINESS** Z 4-8

25

Rosa 'Follette'

HEIGHT AND SPREAD Scrambles to 26ft (8m) **FLOWERS** 4in (10cm) across, in early spring **ASPECT/LIKES** Warm very sheltered site, ideal in a large conservatory **HARDINESS** Z 7-9

I've seen this extraordinary climbing rose tumbling out of cypress trees in the Mediterranean. Sadly, it is fairly tender, which makes it only suited to growing under glass in mild climates. It thrives in my perspex-roofed plant house—which I keep just frost-free in winter—and would be a good candidate for a conservatory. But why grow a rose indoors? Well, this one is special: the early flowers are produced from the middle of March and are blooms of great beauty, opening from elegant, pointed buds held singly on new growth. Each flower is large, usually semi-double, and strident pink. When young, the blooms have a classic rose form and are perfect as a buttonhole or in a bud vase. As they age and expand, they become open and loose, nodding from the plant's climbing stems, and they have a powerful, tealike fragrance. Lots of flowers form and the display lasts a couple of weeks. It's just a shame that this rose does not repeat, but for those few weeks it has no equal in beauty, indoors or out.

26

Dryopteris wallichiana

Among the most impressive of truly hardy ferns, this beautiful Asian species is at its captivating best as its fresh foliage arises in early spring. The fronds at this stage have bright chartreuse-green leaflets that contrast dramatically with the stalk and midrib; in the finest plants these are covered in black, hairy scales. The fronds develop into a handsome shuttlecock of growth. In time, the plant may form a small clump, but offsets are usually few, with the main plant simply increasing in size each year. The fronds are more or less evergreen but can get shabby after a rough winter. I usually cut mine off when I can see fresh fronds about to unfurl in spring. Give the plant pride of place—t needs a bit of space to make an impression. It looks good with epimediums, hellebores, and Solomon's seal.

COMMON NAME Alpine wood fern **HEIGHT AND SPREAD** 3 x 2ft (100 x 60cm) **FLOWERS** None **ASPECT/LIKES** Cool shaded spot, shelter, moist fertile well-drained soil **HARDINESS** Z 6-9

27

Exochorda × *macrantha* 'The Bride'

One of the first really free-flowering shrubs of the year, this is an easy-to-grow, deciduous plant. At its best, it can be incredibly profuse, its arching stems bedecked with sprays of pure-white, five-petaled, propeller-shaped flowers that open from almost spherical buds. The display can be impressive and lasts for several weeks. The plant itself is a slightly ungainly thing—naturally quite sprawling and mound-forming, with cascading branches. It needs a bit of space to spread out. It suits growing over a low wall or atop a bank, where it can tumble dramatically. Occasionally you see it grown as a more upright plant trained on a single stem, which gives it better structure but perhaps less grace. It can be informally trained against a wall or fence, too, but again loses a certain amount of charm. Trim right after flowering, as blooms appear on wood made the previous year.

COMMON NAME Pearl bush **HEIGHT AND SPREAD** 6½ x 6½ft (2 x 2m) **FLOWERS** 1in (2.5cm) across, from early to midspring **ASPECT/LIKES** Sun or part shade, fertile well-drained soil **HARDINESS** Z 5-9

28. **COMMON NAME** Downy clematis **HEIGHT AND SPREAD** Climbs to 8ft (2.5m) **FLOWERS** Nodding, 1½in (4cm) long, from early spring **ASPECT/ LIKES** Roots in cool moist well-drained shade, shoots in sun **HARDINESS** Z 4-9

29. **COMMON NAME** Natal lily **HEIGHT AND SPREAD** 2 x 2ft (60 x 60cm) **FLOWERS** 2in (5cm) long, held in a cluster from early to midspring **ASPECT/ LIKES** Part shade, not too wet, above 45°F (7°C) **HARDINESS** Z 7-9

30. **HEIGHT AND SPREAD** 26 x 16ft (8 x 5m) **FLOWERS** Huge, to 12in (30cm) across, in early to midspring **ASPECT/LIKES** Sun, shelter from frost and cold winds, moist fertile well-drained soil **HARDINESS** Z 5-9

31. **COMMON NAME** Primrose **HEIGHT AND SPREAD** 4 x 6in (10 x 15cm) **FLOWERS** 1in (2.5cm) across, produced freely from late winter until early summer **ASPECT/LIKES** Sun or part shade, ideally not too hot or too dry **HARDINESS** Z 4-8

28

Clematis macropetala

This dainty, spring-flowering clematis is a lovely thing in bloom. Its little, nodding, violet-blue flowers appear early in the season, each composed of four broad, outer petals and a multitude of fluttering, petal-like stamens within. Its deciduous foliage is nice, too: serrated, ferny leaflets of bright green make a great foil for the flowers, which appear in profusion.
After flowering, the attractive, long-lasting seed heads are a bonus. Although delicate-looking, this is quite a robust, tough climber and not too choosy about where it grows. Plant it somewhere that its roots can enjoy cool, moist shade, while its twining stems are able to climb up and revel in the sun; over a stone wall is perfect. It won't mind the cold or a fairly open site so long as the roots do not get too dry or waterlogged—it does need good drainage.

29

Clivia miniata

There are not many easy, long-term houseplants that can be relied on to flower year to year. One of the best is *Clivia*. Most of the time, this South African native is a handsome clump of dark-green, strap-shaped leaves. Then in spring, and at other times during the growing season, stout stems arise holding a cluster of long-lasting, shining, trumpet-shaped flowers that are usually orange with a green throat. The plant thrives on a surprising amount of neglect, surviving in quite dark places in the home, although it does better in brighter spots. It doesn't mind being pot-bound and is best allowed to dry out a little between waterings—never let the plant stand in water. It also tolerates quite low temperatures, as long as it doesn't freeze. From midfall until after Christmas, the plant is best kept cool and hardly watered, as this helps initiate flower buds.

30

Magnolia Felix Jury

No garden is complete without a magnolia, and this splendid hybrid selection, also known as 'Jurmag2,' was raised in New Zealand, where some of the finest recent magnolias have been developed. It forms a fairly small, compact, upright-growing, deciduous tree with large, bright-green, oval leaves. After just five or so years, it begins producing displays of astonishing, rich red-pink, goblet-shaped flowers that open quite early in spring. On older trees, they are produced in some profusion over several weeks. The tree runs the risk of frost damage, which in a bad year can ruin the display, and it needs shelter from cold winds. But when the stars align, it is a most remarkable sight in full flower. Avoid root disturbance, and keep an eye on watering as it establishes.

31

Primula vulgaris

Our native primrose has a long flowering season. The first, pale-yellow, scented blooms often open in winter, with the display usually peaking toward the end of March and lasting into early summer. It is a useful garden plant, good for various places—the front of borders, beneath deciduous shrubs, or naturalized in rough grass amid spring bulbs under trees. It spreads freely from seed as long as you don't weed out young plants, which can vary in flower color. Among the yellow blooms can be seedlings with white, pink, or peach-colored flowers. All are remarkably tolerant, surviving in shade, but doing better in sun, especially on a bank. They stand wet ground or bone-dry, seeing it through the driest seasons even if the leaves look bedraggled by end of summer.

32

Gladiolus tristis

I first encountered this lovely bulb in that plant paradise that is Great Dixter. Owner Christopher Lloyd grew it brilliantly and I remember well him showing me his plant in a sunny corner of the Sunk Garden there. He teamed it simply and so effectively with a pale-blue skirt of forget-me-nots, the tall slender stems of the gladiolus bearing distinctive, one-sided spikes of soft-yellow-green flowers that shone above. In all honesty, I've never risked my precious plant in the open garden; instead, I keep it in a tall pot so that I can bring it indoors if a really cold spell is forecast. The flowers last a couple of weeks and have a sweet scent in the evening. Once the flowers finish, the foliage dies down and bulbs go dormant for summer. The plant needs a sheltered, sunny position, as new leaves start to come up in fall and the tall, slender, rushlike foliage then grows through winter, when it can be easily flattened in bad weather. A support will help it stay upright. It needs to be kept fairly dry during summer, something easily achieved in a container.

HEIGHT AND SPREAD 3 x 1ft (90 x 30cm) **FLOWERS** 1½in (4cm) across, in midspring **ASPECT/ LIKES** Sun, shelter, sharply drained soil, dry in summer **HARDINESS** Z 8-10

33

Epimedium stellulatum 'Wudang Star'

Evergreen, ground-covering, clump-forming, and appealingly easy to grow, this lovely perennial makes a great choice for a shady position. In midspring, it produces loose sprays of pendant, star-shaped little flowers, each with four pointed petals and showy yellow stamens. They are held in clouds above the glossy, slightly prickly foliage, which when young—coinciding with flowering time—is attractively bronze-tinted. In time, plants form a decent clump and look superb growing in the shade below trees and shrubs in woodland-like conditions. They are not picky about soil as long as it is not too dry or rooty and reasonably well drained, but benefit from a yearly mulch of garden compost. Cutting away last year's foliage before the flowers and new growth arise shows off the blooms and keeps plants tidy, but it needs to be done early, as the fresh shoots are easily damaged.

HEIGHT AND SPREAD 1¼ x 1¾ft (40 x 50cm) **FLOWERS** ⅝in (1.5cm) across, held in open sprays in midspring **ASPECT/LIKES** Cool shaded position, fertile well-drained soil **HARDINESS** Z 3-7

34

Papaver cambricum

COMMON NAME Welsh poppy
HEIGHT AND SPREAD 1¾ x 1ft (50 x 30cm)
FLOWERS 2in (5cm) across, from midspring to summer **ASPECT/LIKES** Sun or shade, sharp drainage, not too hot or too dry
HARDINESS Z 6-8

This poppy has recently changed genus, from *Meconopsis*, which includes blue Himalayan poppies, to *Papaver*, in which our native field poppy is placed. It certainly seems to flourish in spots where blue poppies would quickly expire. A short-lived perennial, it survives for about three years but seeds around with abandon. The delicate, nodding flowers with petals like crepe paper last only a day but appear in multitudes and are generally bright orange or yellow and held above attractive, toothed, fresh-green leaves. The best examples are always found sprouting between pavers or cracks in concrete by the house, while those transplanted into borders are seldom as good, so it pays not to be too neat and tidy if you grow them. The first blooms open in spring; flowering then continues well on into summer. As a bonus, a few sometimes appear again in early fall.

35

Cerinthe major 'Purpurascens'

This beautiful member of the borage family catches the eye of many a visitor to my garden in midspring. Its oval, silver-blue leaves are held on green, branched stems that arch over at the ends. Purple, bell-shaped flowers nod from the tips, nestling in lush, overlapping, leaflike structures called bracts. These have a rich-purple sheen that gives the plant a shimmering oil-on-water look. Plants set copious seed, which often germinates around the garden in fall. The seedlings survive a mild winter to mature early the following spring. If you collect the seeds, sow them in spring for planting in early summer, or sow in fall and overwinter in a cold frame for spring displays.

COMMON NAME Honeywort **HEIGHT AND SPREAD** 2¾ x 1¼ft (80 x 40cm) **FLOWERS** ½in (1cm) long, in midspring **ASPECT/LIKES** Sun, shelter, open site, well-drained soil **HARDINESS** Z 7-10

36

Daphne × *transatlantica* Pink Fragrance

HEIGHT AND SPREAD 2¾ x 2¾ft (80 x 80cm) **FLOWERS** ⅝in (1.5cm) across, held in clusters from midspring through most of summer **ASPECT/LIKES** Sun or part shade, well-drained soil, not too dry **HARDINESS** Z 6-8

This easy-to-grow, semievergreen shrub, also known as 'Blapink,' is a really useful plant for a small garden, as it is slow growing and stays compact. As a bonus, it flowers throughout spring and summer. The showy clusters of bright-pink, star-shaped flowers appear sporadically amid the green, narrow, oval leaves of the new growth at the tips of branches. The small, tubular, four-petaled blooms are powerfully and sweetly scented and last several weeks. The plant needs little attention once established. It is not too picky about soil, but avoid anywhere that can get waterlogged or too hot and dry. It looks nice filling in the edge of a mixed border, spilling over a path, or beside a doorway, where its lovely scent can be easily enjoyed.

37

Bergenia 'Eroica'

Elephant's ears are underrated as garden perennials: many are tough and easy to grow, tolerant of a range of situations and drought resistant. They have bold, ground-covering, evergreen foliage and heads of showy flowers in spring. Plants form low-spreading rafts of growth, developing from thick, fleshy stems. Some of the best also have foliage that develops dramatic tints over winter, the intense colors brought on by the coldest weather, usually in February. This fine selection has leaves that remain an attractive plummy purple during spring and are then topped by rather tall, red stems bearing heads of rich-magenta flowers. To keep the plants looking good, cut off spent flowers and through the year remove old brown leaves the plants hang on to, which can make them appear shabby. For the best colors, grow the plants in an open, sunny position—try them in a gravel garden or cascade down a bank—but they will survive in part shade too.

COMMON NAME Elephant's ears **HEIGHT AND SPREAD** 1¾ x 3ft (50 x 100cm) **FLOWERS** ¾in (2cm) across, in midspring **ASPECT/LIKES** Sun, open site, well-drained soil, not too dry in summer **HARDINESS** Z 3-8

38

Polygonatum × *hybridum* 'Betberg'

I was astounded by this herbaceous perennial the first time I saw it. Like ordinary Solomon's seal, the stems begin to arise in early spring, but the coloring of this plant's foliage is extraordinary. Instead of fresh, spring green, it shimmers metallic purple-brown, the effect lasting several weeks and quite jaw-dropping when you see a well-grown example. The lush, oval-shaped leaves are carried on elegant, arching stems. Then, dangling beneath, little, white, green-tipped bells appear in pairs. As spring wears on, the color fades. The plant spreads via creeping rhizomes, which in the right conditions eventually form a handsome clump. Give it a spot below deciduous trees or shrubs or perhaps beside a north-facing wall. Sawfly larvae can shred the leaves unless promptly removed; this is easily done.

39

Arum creticum

This is one of the stars of spring in my garden, a plant I wait for with bated breath. A Mediterranean native, it grows from tubers, which early each spring send up bold, glossy, heart-shaped leaves in the manner of lords-and-ladies. However, the large, upright flowers are the chief attraction here: of classic arum-lily form, they are yellow, the leaflike outer petal pale primrose-yellow, the pointed flower spike golden. As the flower ages, the outer petal opens out elegantly. The blooms are sweetly fragrant and last in beauty for a week or so before the plant begins to die down by early summer. Over time, this perennial slowly builds into a multiflowered clump that looks great in a gravel garden. If the site becomes shaded by summer, this won't matter while the plant is dormant. Mark its position with a label so you don't accidentally dig it up.

40

Epimedium 'Amber Queen'

Of all epimediums, this fine hybrid is one of the most upstanding and impactful and is of considerable beauty in flower. A more or less evergreen, clump-forming herbaceous perennial, it has toothy, dark-green foliage that in part shade forms good ground cover for most of the year. In midspring, it really shines as the new leaves arise; these are pale green and wonderfully mottled with purple. Above them, tall, arching stems carry constellations of warm orange-yellow, rather spidery flowers. These appear in great quantity and are held to superb effect above the foliage. The display lasts several weeks. For best results, trim away old foliage before the new arises. Tough and vigorous, the plant is easy to grow as long as the ground is not waterlogged or bone-dry.

41

Camellia × *williamsii* 'Saint Ewe'

Named after the Cornish village where an old plant of this cultivar grows in the local churchyard, this early-flowering, unfussy-looking camellia is a favorite of mine. The first flowers can open in late winter if the weather is mild but are usually best in midspring. The lovely, single, bright-pink flowers with a central boss of golden anthers are nodding and bell-shaped and appear in great abundance for three or even four months. It is a vigorous, upright-growing, and fairly hardy camellia. The evergreen leaves are dark-green and glossy and the perfect foil for the flowers. It will grow well in a large container if kept watered through the year.

38. COMMON NAME Solomon's seal **HEIGHT AND SPREAD** 2¾ x 1¼ft (80 x 40cm) **FLOWERS** ⅝in (1.5cm) long bells, in midspring **ASPECT/LIKES** Shade, cool, shelter, fertile moist well-drained soil **HARDINESS** Z 6-9

39. COMMON NAME Cretan arum **HEIGHT AND SPREAD** 1¼ x 1ft (40 x 30cm) **FLOWERS** 4in (10cm) tall, in midspring **ASPECT/LIKES** Full sun in spring, warm open site, well-drained soil **HARDINESS** Z 8-10

40. HEIGHT AND SPREAD 1¾ x 2ft (50 x 60cm) **FLOWERS** ¾in (2cm) across, in midspring **ASPECT/LIKES** Part shade, cool, fertile well-drained soil **HARDINESS** Z 5-8

41. HEIGHT AND SPREAD 16 x 10ft (5 x 3m) eventually **FLOWERS** 2in (5cm) across, from late winter until late spring **ASPECT/LIKES** Shade or part shade, cool, shelter, moist fertile well-drained acid soil **HARDINESS** Z 6-10

42

Hippocrepis emerus

Spring-flowering shrubs with yellow blooms are not particularly unusual, but this excellent, quick-growing, easy, and drought-tolerant, Mediterranean native should be more widely grown for its terrific displays of golden-yellow flowers in spring. It forms a vigorous, deciduous, rather bushy shrub with dainty, soft-green, pinnate foliage emerging at much the same time as the clusters of little, sweetly scented, pealike blooms. These open in multitudes and attract many pollinating insects well into early summer. Give this plant a sunny position—it thrives against a warm wall or fence, where branches can be tied to wires to keep it tidy—but it will also take part shade. It likes well-drained, quite dry soil. Plants may get too large after a while, with tall, quite leggy stems, but these can be pruned back after flowering to promote a more compact habit.

COMMON NAME Scorpion senna **HEIGHT AND SPREAD** 8 x 8ft (2.5 x 2.5m) **FLOWERS** ⅝in (1.5cm) long, from mid- to late spring **ASPECT/LIKES** Full sun, well-drained soil **HARDINESS** Z 7-8

43

Tulipa 'La Belle Époque'

Midspring is the time for tulips, and so rich is the diversity of flower color, size, and form found among the bulbs that gardeners are spoiled for choice. Each year I give different selections a go, but one I can never resist is this blowsy bloom—a real garden diva, if ever there were one. A double or so-called "peony-flowered" tulip, it has large flowers of an almost indescribable color—a sort of soft, peachy buff-orange, flushed with pink and tinted yellow at the tips—remarkably beautiful, especially en masse. It looks terrific with purple or cream tulips, wallflowers, spires of honesty, or perhaps against acid-green euphorbia. It is also superb as a cut flower—that's if you can bear to part with any (I seldom can). Grow it in the ground or in pots in a sunny position in well-drained soil. It will come up again the following year if left in situ, but after that gradually peters out, so it's worth topping up numbers each fall.

HEIGHT AND SPREAD 18in (45cm) tall **FLOWERS** 3in (8cm) across, in midspring **ASPECT/LIKES** Sun, shelter, fertile well-drained soil **HARDINESS** Z 3-7

44. **HEIGHT AND SPREAD** 18in (45cm) tall **FLOWERS** 3in (8cm) across, in midspring **ASPECT/LIKES** Sun, shelter, fertile well-drained soil **HARDINESS** Z 3-8

45. **HEIGHT AND SPREAD** 13 x 8ft (4 x 2.5m) **FLOWERS** 2½in (6cm) across, in midspring **ASPECT/ LIKES** Shade or part shade, shelter, moist well-drained acid soil **HARDINESS** Z 7-9

46. **HEIGHT AND SPREAD** 6½ x 5ft (2 x 1.5m) **FLOWERS** 2½in (6cm) across, from mid-/late spring until the first hard frosts **ASPECT/LIKES** Sun, sheltered but airy site, well-drained soil **HARDINESS** Z 6-9

47. **COMMON NAME** Mourning widow **HEIGHT AND SPREAD** 3 x 3ft (1 x 1m) **FLOWERS** ¾in (2cm) across, held in a spray from mid- to late spring **ASPECT/LIKES** Shade or part shade, well-drained soil, not too dry **HARDINESS** Z 4-9

44

Tulipa 'Spring Green'

I think this is my favorite tulip of all. It is one I come back to whenever I'm buying bulbs and it always seems to be available. It is quite late in flower and has ivory-white petals marked boldly, like other viridiflora tulips, with contrasting bright green. The elegant blooms have pointed petals and glow atop tall stems. They seem to encapsulate the cool freshness of the season, floating effortlessly above emerging perennials and suiting woodland plantings best. The display lasts at least two weeks, often longer. I also like similar but rather more strident 'Spring Yellow,' where the white is replaced by bright sulfur-yellow. For best results with tulips, buy early (so you have a good range to choose from), but plant late—in late fall or early winter. Perennials will have died back by this time, so planting is easier. It also helps avoid tulip fire, one of few problems these bulbs suffer from.

45

Camellia japonica 'Nuccio's Jewel'

Even if you prefer plants with simple flowers, there is a certain satisfaction to be had in growing the odd one with unashamedly glamorous blooms. In spring, a showy camellia such as this fits the bill perfectly. Its flowers are fully double, with petals in shades of pink and ruffled like the layers of a chiffon party dress. The outer petals are generally richer pink than those in the center, which tend toward cream. As the flowers open fully, golden stamens peak through at the heart. The blooms show up well against the dark, oval, evergreen foliage and fall off cleanly when faded. The plant looks best brightening a shaded corner in a large container; the beauty of the individual flowers is easily lost in the garden. Grow it in acidic potting mix, never letting it get too dry. Keep it cool and out of drying winds.

46

Rosa × *odorata* 'Bengal Crimson'

This extraordinary rose is one of my top garden plants. It bears its large, single, bright crimson flowers in remarkable profusion more or less year-round. In my garden, it is usually still in flower at Christmas and carries on until the frosts bite. The display gets going again in mid- to late spring. The individual blooms are short-lived, but they open from a succession of shapely buds. The plant is vigorous and very disease-free and can be trained on a wall or trellis or grown as a free-standing bush. I have plantswoman Helen Dillon to thank for mine. She propagates from hardwood cuttings taken in winter, popped in the ground, and left to root until spring.

47

Geranium phaeum

I find this spring-flowering perennial fascinating, chiefly because of the variable seedlings plants produce—new variations on a theme turning up each year. The plants are quick-growing and undemanding and form ground-covering clumps. In early spring, attractive, fresh, rather hairy foliage appears, sometimes boldly blotched in chocolate-brown. The five-petaled flowers are small for a geranium and open almost flat on tall, slender stems. They vary greatly in color: some can be close to black, but they are often purple or dusky mauve, sometimes pale gray-pink or even white. They last a month or so. The plants look neater if you trim the stems back sharpish after flowering, but you won't get the excitement of the seedlings, which come up in profusion.

48

Beesia calthifolia

You won't find this semievergreen perennial in older plant books, as it has only become widely grown in the past 20 years, but it makes a highly appealing addition to the garden. Its chief attraction is its handsome, heart-shaped, serrated leaves. These are held on slender stems and are superbly glossy, slightly puckered and, when young, beautifully bronze-tinted with a network of veins contrasting in apple-green. It forms a tidy clump of overlapping foliage. Then in midspring, wands of little, white, starry flowers sparkle above. It is a plant of refined beauty but needs a cool, sheltered, and shaded location in soil that does not get too dry, so be prepared to water it in a dry summer. When happy, it will seed around. It looks superb grown in a drift with small ferns, epimediums, and other woodland plants.

HEIGHT AND SPREAD 1¾ x 1¼ft (50 x 40cm)
FLOWERS ½in (1cm) across, held in a spire in midspring
ASPECT/LIKES Shade, shelter, moist fertile well-drained soil
HARDINESS Z 5-9

49

Magnolia laevifolia

This evergreen magnolia has not been in widespread cultivation for long but has found many gardening friends, owing to its ease of cultivation, versatile nature, and impressive floral displays. It is a compact-growing shrub with leathery, matte, rounded, dark-green foliage. The undersides of the leaves are attractively cinnamon-colored. In midspring, the felted brown flower buds start to open in profusion. The blooms are pure-white and usually composed of six rounded petals, opening to around 2in (5cm) across. The other great thing about them is the creamy lemon scent, which is delicious and carries on the air. Individual flowers fall cleanly from the plant and, shortly afterward, you will notice the buds of next year's blooms appearing in leaf axils. Plants can be grown free-standing or wall-trained, which gives them extra protection in cold areas, and the added warmth may promote greater flowering. It is not picky about soil and, when established, seems to stand dry spells well, but it does best in a sunny place. In my garden, the plant has never been damaged by frost.

COMMON NAME Polished-leaved magnolia **HEIGHT AND SPREAD** 10 x 10ft (3 x 3m) **FLOWERS** 2in (5cm) across, in midspring **ASPECT/LIKES** Sun or part shade, shelter, fertile well-drained soil **HARDINESS** Z 8-11

50

Paris quadrifolia

Most woodland plants are at their most sumptuous in spring, and this unusual perennial is no exception, although it is a plant of perhaps unconventional beauty. It emerges by midspring, its short, stout shoots usually bearing four equal, oval leaves held radiating around the stem. Then, the starry flower arises on a short stalk from the tip of the stem. Looking a bit like a crown atop the leaves, it is composed of slender, pointed, green true petals, broader petal-like sepals, and eight gold stamens. Later in the season, a single blue-black fruit appears. The plant grows from a rhizome and forms a handsome clump in time if left mostly undisturbed. It likes moist but well-drained soil and benefits from an annual mulch of garden compost. Grow it with ferns, primulas, and trilliums below deciduous trees.

COMMON NAME Herb Paris **HEIGHT AND SPREAD** 1 x 1¼ft (30 x 40cm) **FLOWERS** 1½in (4cm) across, in late spring **ASPECT/LIKES** Shade, shelter, moist fertile well-drained soil **HARDINESS** Z 5-8

"The blooms show up really well at this time of year and also have a nice scent."

51

Tulipa 'Brown Sugar'

This impressive new tulip is one I have fallen for in recent years. It is usually in flower in midspring and bears its large, classically shaped blooms atop tall, stout, dark stems. This makes it handy for interplanting among perennials, such as heucheras, mounds of geraniums, and developing lupins in borders, where the blooms will float well above the young growth below. The flowers themselves are gorgeously colored: each overlapping petal is two-toned, coppery orange at the edges with a central area that blushes pinkish apricot. When the flowers open wide toward the end of their life, a yellow heart is revealed. The blooms show up really well at this time of year and also have a nice scent if you pop your nose near. The display lasts a couple of weeks. Bulbs do not endure long in the garden (2–3 years at best), so top up numbers when you can.

HEIGHT AND SPREAD 1¾ft (55cm) tall **FLOWERS** 4in (10cm) across, in midspring **ASPECT/LIKES** Sun, shelter, fertile well-drained soil **HARDINESS** Z 3-8

52

Paeonia ludlowii

COMMON NAME Ludlow's tree peony **HEIGHT AND SPREAD** 8 x 8ft (2.5 x 2.5m) **FLOWERS** 4in (10cm) across, from mid- to late spring **ASPECT/LIKES** Sun or part shade, shelter, fertile moist well-drained soil **HARDINESS** Z 5-8

With their flamboyant flowers, tree peonies add a touch of glamour to midspring gardens. The really large-flowered hybrids are certainly showstoppers, but rather more in keeping with most gardens are some of the species, among which are first-rate, easy-to-grow plants such as this handsome Tibetan native. It forms an upright-growing, vase-shaped, open shrub with a cluster of gray, unbranched stems. In spring, large, apple-green, attractively divided leaves burst open from sizable buds. These are topped off by numerous golden-yellow, bowl-shaped flowers that nod from the tips of the stems. They last in beauty for several weeks. The plant's shape means it is easily underplanted with shorter perennials, so it fits either a herbaceous border or more informal planting. This is the sort of plant you see in Edwardian gardens, where it fits the feel and traditional style of the place perfectly.

53

Euphorbia × *pasteurii* 'John Phillips'

One of the most imposing of all reasonably hardy euphorbias, this large, handsome plant is easy to grow. It luxuriates in warm shelter, where it will form a wide-spreading, dome-shaped shrub of sturdy branches. Its bold, lance-shaped foliage is distinctly exotic. Each leaf emerges pointing upward, with its silvery underside showing, and the upper surface rich-green with a contrasting lime-green midrib. At flowering time in mid- to late spring, the plant sparkles: rounded heads of honey-scented, rust-orange flowers appear atop most of the branches. The display lasts several weeks. In fall and winter, older, lower leaves assume impressive red and orange tints. Ideally, this plant should not be pruned except for removing the odd dead branch. Cut them off with care, avoiding contact with the toxic sap.

HEIGHT AND SPREAD 6½ x 10ft (2 x 3m) **FLOWERS** ½in (1cm) across, held in dome-shaped heads 4in (10cm) across in mid- to late spring **ASPECT/LIKES** Sun, warm shelter, well-drained soil **HARDINESS** Z 9-10

54

Rosa JACQUELINE DU PRÉ

This graceful rose, also known as 'Harwanna,' was one of the first things I planted in my current garden, so eager was I to grow it. Quite an early flowering selection, it has buds that often open by mid- to late spring, which makes it a particularly useful thing, providing a hint of high-summer glamour in borders when all around spring is in full swing. The semidouble flowers are open and carried in clusters and are white with a faint touch of pink. Most distinctive is the beautiful, central crown of long red and gold stamens, quite unlike any other rose I know. The blooms have a subtle perfume. Once the first flowers finish, this rose has a little rest and then repeats its display later in the year. The plant itself is fairly disease-free, upright, and tidy. This is a selection that seems to tolerate growing closely with other plants; many don't, I've found.

HEIGHT AND SPREAD 5 x 3ft (1.5 x 1m) **FLOWERS** 2¾in (7cm) across, in mid- to late spring and summer **ASPECT/LIKES** Sun, any well-drained soil **HARDINESS** Z 5-9

55

Paeonia 'Late Windflower'

If there is a plant I look forward to most in that glorious time between midspring and early summer, I think this elegant peony might be it. Shoots arise in late winter and develop through spring into a great, bronze-tinted dome of handsome, divided foliage. The first blooms open atop tall stems well clear of the leaves. They are beautiful—single, outward-facing, slightly nodding, pure-white, and not quite round. I enjoy them most at dusk, when they almost glow and produce a sweet scent that carries on the air. The display lasts several weeks. This peony is the work of Canadian-born hybridizer Arthur Saunders. Similar *Paeonia* 'Early Windflower' blooms a week earlier.

56

Rosa xanthina 'Canary Bird'

Early flowering and with great appeal thanks to its splendid spring displays, this is a rose I wouldn't want to be without. It needs space, for it makes a large, thorny, wide-spreading shrub with arching branches that bear attractive, delicate green foliage. The plant can be kept more compact, but the elegant, natural shape is then lost. From midspring, it is studded with masses of upright-facing, pointed buds that line the tops of branches. These soon open into beautiful, five-petaled, single, bright primrose-yellow flowers, with the fresh, still-developing leaves making an ideal foil. The display lasts several weeks and the flowers' light, fruity perfume attracts bees and other pollinators. Grow it in a shrub border, at the edge of woodland, or even as a specimen plant in a lawn. It is easy to grow and suffers little disease.

57

Lamprocapnos spectabilis VALENTINE

Also known as 'Hordival,' this cultivar of the familiar garden plant bleeding heart makes a welcome change to the usual pink- or white-flowered selections. Its dusky-red blooms with a contrasting white center tone beautifully with the smoky foliage. The fleshy, rather brittle shoots begin to arise in early spring. The stems are purple-flushed, with attractive, divided foliage that is topped in mid- to late spring by arching sprays of the distinctive, dangling flowers. Turned upside down, they look like a lady in a bath, which is one common name for the plant. The foliage starts to die down in midsummer but will emerge again in spring.

58

Iris albicans

This beautiful plant is associated in some cultures with cemeteries, but we need not let that put us off, as it is an enchanting, easy-to-grow perennial. It grows from a fleshy rhizome that spreads across the top of the soil, producing broad, gray-green, lance-shaped leaves. In spring, it sends up stout flowering stems, each bearing up to three flowers. Tall and narrow with a pointed lower petal, they are pure-white with a pale lemon-yellow beard and have a sweet scent. Give the plants as sunny a place in dry gravelly soil as you can find: the front of a border would do, at the foot of a wall, or in a gravel garden. Cut off old flower stems, and every few years divide rhizomes when they get congested.

55. HEIGHT AND SPREAD 1¾ x 2ft (80 x 60cm) **FLOWERS** 2in (5cm) across, in midspring **ASPECT/ LIKES** Part sun, moist fertile well-drained soil **HARDINESS** Z 3-8

56. HEIGHT AND SPREAD 8 x 13ft (2.5 x 4m) **FLOWERS** 1½in (4cm) across, from mid- to late spring **ASPECT/LIKES** Full sun, open site, any well-drained soil **HARDINESS** Z 5-9

57. HEIGHT AND SPREAD 2 x 1¼ft (60 x 40cm) **FLOWERS** ¾in (2cm) long, held in a spray in mid- to late spring **ASPECT/LIKES** Cool part shade, shelter, moist well-drained soil, not too dry **HARDINESS** Z 3-9

58. COMMON NAME Cemetery iris **HEIGHT AND SPREAD** 3 x 2ft (100 x 60cm) in flower **FLOWERS** 3in (8cm) tall, carried in a spike in midspring **ASPECT/ LIKES** Full sun, good drainage, poor dry soil **HARDINESS** Z 4-9

59

Acer shirasawanum 'Aureum'

Among the most beautiful of trees and small shrubs grown for their deciduous foliage, Japanese maples need no introduction to most gardeners, and this wonderful example is justly popular, for there is nothing else quite like it. Naturally small, compact, and slow-growing, it forms an upright, usually single-stemmed, tree-shaped shrub, at its best in spring after its impressive foliage has emerged. The individual leaves look a little like green-gold fans—rounded with 10 or more pointed lobes. The color dulls slightly during summer, then turns to orange-red in fall just before the leaves fall. In early summer, little bunches of red-tinged seeds follow insignificant reddish flowers. The plant will grow well for a while in a container.

COMMON NAME Golden full moon maple **HEIGHT AND SPREAD** Up to 26 x 26ft (8 x 8m), but usually far less **FLOWERS** Tiny reddish green, in spring **ASPECT/LIKES** Cool part shade, shelter from drying winds, moist well-drained soil, not too dry **HARDINESS** Z 5-7

60

Clematis montana var. *rubens* 'Tetrarose'

HEIGHT AND SPREAD Climbs to 26ft (8m) **FLOWERS** 2¾in (7cm) across, in midspring **ASPECT/LIKES** Sun or part shade, somewhere to climb, cool at the roots, moist well-drained alkaline soil **HARDINESS** Z 6-9

An improved cultivar of the pink-flowered classic, this tough climber is a highlight of midspring. It bears masses of four-petaled, rose-pink flowers, each with a central boss of golden stamens. They are sweetly scented and said to be the largest of any *Clematis montana*. At the height of flowering, blooms can completely cover the plant. It needs plenty of space, as it is vigorous, with mature plants putting on masses of growth each year. It will quickly cover a large fence or unsightly building, so ensure there is sturdy support. But keep an eye on it—it can swamp smaller structures and slower-growing trees and shrubs; cascading from a large, mature tree, however, it is spectacular. Ideally, its roots will be in cool shade, with top growth in the sun. Plants are fine for a north-facing aspect.

61

Rosa banksiae 'Lutea'

I remember the first time I saw this enchanting climbing rose: it was cascading down the facade of a three-story building. Its thornless, arching, green stems were covered in clusters of small, double, yellow flowers that showered the ground below with golden petals. It seemed somehow magical, and from that moment I had to grow it. This is a commitment, however, for it makes a bulky, vigorous plant. It needs a plum position with space—ideally a high sunny wall, but it can also be kept on a large pergola. It is deciduous, although it holds on to some foliage in a mild winter. I have it growing up the front of my terraced house. Prune it hard every 3–4 years right after flowering, thinning the plant's stems by about half to prevent it from becoming congested and shy to bloom. This may sound drastic, but the plant soon recovers. The old, retained stems develop peeling copper bark in time. It is a classic partner for purple wisteria—if you have the space.

COMMON NAME Lady Banks' rose **HEIGHT AND SPREAD** Climbs to 39ft (12m) **FLOWERS** ¾in (2cm) across, held in clusters in midspring **ASPECT/LIKES** Sunny sheltered wall **HARDINESS** Z 6-11

62. COMMON NAME Molly the Witch **HEIGHT AND SPREAD** 2¾ x 3ft (80 x 100cm) **FLOWERS** 3in (8cm) across, in late spring **ASPECT/LIKES** Sun or part shade, open site, fertile well-drained soil, not too dry **HARDINESS** Z 4-9

63. HEIGHT AND SPREAD 16 x 13ft (5 x 4m) **FLOWERS** ½in (1cm) across, held in a cluster in summer **ASPECT/LIKES** Sun, shelter from cold winds, well-drained soil, not too dry **HARDINESS** Z 8-10

64. COMMON NAME Bronze fennel **HEIGHT AND SPREAD** 6½ x 2¾ft (200 x 80cm) **FLOWERS** Tiny, held in a 2in (5cm) head in summer **ASPECT/LIKES** Full sun, open site, well-drained soil **HARDINESS** Z 4-9

65. HEIGHT AND SPREAD 2¼ x 1ft (70 x 30cm) **FLOWERS** ¾in (2cm) across, in late spring **ASPECT/LIKES** Part shade, fertile moist well-drained soil, not too dry **HARDINESS** Z 5-9

62

Paeonia daurica subsp. *mlokosewitschii*

Nicknamed "Molly the Witch", this herbaceous perennial has sumptuous flowers that seem to capture the mood of the moment in late spring. They are delicate, bowl-shaped, pale-lemon beauties that often appear all too fleetingly, although the plant's display actually starts in late winter, when red shoots push through the ground. After flowering, the foliage is nothing exciting, but brightly colored seed heads add something more in fall. The seeds germinate easily and I find the odd seedling popping up in the lawn near my plant. This garden dignitary needs a spot with shade from the hottest summer sun.

63

Eriobotrya deflexa

Trying out plants that are generally thought of as tender can become addictive, especially given the odd success. This evergreen tree or shrub, a relative of the more commonly seen loquat tree, is well worth a go, principally for the beauty of its emerging spring foliage, which from a distance looks almost like the buds of an exotic magnolia. The new growth glows soft raspberry-pink and stands upright like candles from the tips of branches. As the leaves mature, they become bronze-green, glossy, and oblong with a serrated edge. In summer, heads of attractive, white flowers can appear. The plant needs the most sheltered position you have—a sunny south-facing corner is ideal. When established, it will stand some drought. Young plants take well to being grown in pots, which means you can bring them under cover if need be, most important if a sharp spring frost is forecast.

64

Foeniculum vulgare 'Purpureum'

With its aromatic, billowing, smokelike clumps of delicate foliage, bronze fennel creates a remarkable effect in late spring, yet it is such an easy plant to grow in well-drained, gravelly soil. Its leaves make a wonderful foil for wallflowers, late orange tulips, and purple alliums. As the season progresses, tall, slender, rather statuesque stems arise, bearing umbels of acid-yellow flowers in summer. These stems can be left to stand into winter to catch the frost. Plants seed around freely. Some will be plain green-leaved, but I like having both in the garden—just take care that the green do not dominate. Plants tolerate quite a bit of drought, but the foliage will yellow early.

65

Geranium sylvaticum 'Mayflower'

Here is a super herbaceous perennial for shade, perfect for underplanting deciduous shrubs and trees and brightening otherwise dull areas, where its flowers seem almost to sparkle in late spring. The clusters of dainty, five-petaled, white-centered blooms are produced on low stems and open light blue, aging to glowing violet. The plant's foliage also arises in spring, forming low mounds of growth, with the rounded leaves held atop quite slender stems. The flowers last in beauty for about three weeks, but the foliage continues to form reasonable ground cover. This is not a plant for deep, dry shade. For best results, give it somewhere fairly bright but cool. Water if the summer is warm.

Rosa 'Belle Portugaise'

Most books say this rose is far too tender to perform well in mild climate, preferring the Mediterranean or even California, where it grows huge. So, as an experiment, I planted one through an apple tree in my garden and have found it to be a vigorous climber and something of a triumph most years. It produces buds during spring and, while these certainly run the risk of being frozen and killed, the odd light frost does not seem to bother them much, although a long chilly spell with cold winds definitely does. In a good year, the stems are weighed down by huge, double, pale-pink flowers of great beauty. They open from shapely buds—a wonderful sight—and have a distinctive tealike perfume. Even in years with cold springs, it produces reasonable numbers of flowers, albeit several weeks later. The display usually lasts about a month, but, alas, this rose does not repeat-flower. The foliage is glossy and healthy. Give the plant a sunny, sheltered place away from cold winds; on a warm wall it would excel.

HEIGHT AND SPREAD Climbs to 16–30ft (5–9m)
FLOWERS 4¾in (12cm) across, in late spring
ASPECT/LIKES Full sun, warm shelter, somewhere to climb **HARDINESS** Z 7-10

"The stems are weighed down by huge, double, pale-pink flowers of great beauty."

67

Iris 'Tingle'

With their bright, showy, delicate flowers in a vast range of color combinations and patterns, miniature dwarf bearded irises are irresistible in late spring. This one has two lovely tones—the upright petals (known to iris enthusiasts as "standards") are white, while the rounded lower ones (the "falls"), which include the fuzzy "beard," are flushed with neon yellow. These are held on short stems above gray-green leaves that emerge from the creeping rhizome. The plants would look superb in a white border or garden, the yellow adding a touch of warmth to proceedings. However, knowing exactly where to plant these little bearded irises to be safe from slugs can be a problem—in gravel at the front of a border perhaps, or lift them off the ground in an alpine trough or, better still, in a large, shallow, terracotta bowl. Wherever you grow them, provide full sun and sharp drainage.

COMMON NAME Dwarf bearded iris **HEIGHT AND SPREAD** 6 x 6in (15 x 15cm) **FLOWERS** 2¾in (7cm) across, in late spring **ASPECT/LIKES** Full sun, open site, well-drained soil **HARDINESS** Z 3-10

68

Rosa × *odorata* 'Pseudindica'

A gorgeous, vigorous, early flowering rose, this now-rare antique climber is an important historic selection introduced in the 19th century from China, where it has probably been grown for centuries. It is a prickly devil, one that you will not want to spend too much time pruning. The beautiful flowers are not large but appear in quantity. They are semidouble and of rather loose form. From a distance, they appear copper-colored but actually vary in hue from pale to warm orange-yellow, with some flowers shot with pink to a greater or lesser extent. I planted this rose on a south-facing wall, where it grew with a fig tree on one side and an olive on the other, and its branches now cascade from both at flowering time. The blooms last no more than two weeks, but the effect of the fluttery flowers is sublime.

69

Valeriana pyrenaica

This useful herbaceous perennial has not been widely seen in gardens until fairly recently but has proved to be a most worthwhile plant. In spring, a low clump of fresh apple-green, heart-shaped leaves appears, and by late spring, tall, slender stems arise. These also carry leaves and are branched toward the top, where dome-shaped heads of little, pale-mauve flowers open, making an impressive show in the middle of a border or woodland bed. The blooms last in beauty for a couple of weeks, gradually fading to off-white. They are popular with pollinating insects. When happy, the plant seeds around a bit. It suits a fairly naturalistic planting scheme, working well with grasses and daintier-looking perennials. It is quite adaptable and easy to grow: ideally, it wants a moist, semishaded position but will also survive in sunnier, drier places too.

70

Disporum megalanthum

Native to Chinese woodlands, this choice herbaceous perennial is a handsome thing. Almost evergreen, it forms a strong-growing clump of stems, which in moist, cool shade can get surprisingly tall, to around 5ft (1.5m). In spring, it is a particular delight—its glossy, pointed oval leaves are bronze-tinted and carried on chocolate-colored, arching stems that drip with creamy-green, bell-shaped flowers with protruding stamens. Blue-black berries can follow in summer, by which time the rather bamboo-like stems will have elongated and the leaves turned rich-green. The plant looks good into winter, although cold winds can damage it. In drier sites, its vigor and stature are reduced. Give it a mulch of garden compost each year and cut out shabby-looking stems at the base.

71

Saruma henryi

A plant of unusual beauty, this rather curious, clump-forming herbaceous perennial is seldom seen. Native to wooded parts of China, it is grown for its considerable appeal in spring. Densely hairy shoots, rather silvery at first, arise early in the season from rhizomatous roots. As these develop, heart-shaped foliage is revealed. The pale yellow-green leaves are bronze-tinged initially and softly hairy below. During early May, attractive, three-petaled, bright-yellow flowers open toward the tips of the shoots in a display that lasts a couple of weeks. Give it a decent place with some room to spread out—a well-grown plant is a satisfying thing to have and quite a talking point with visitors. It looks good beside ferns. When happy, it will self-seed.

68. **COMMON NAME** Fortune's double yellow rose **HEIGHT AND SPREAD** Climbs to 26ft (8m) **FLOWERS** 2½in (6cm) across, in late spring **ASPECT/LIKES** Sunny sheltered wall or fence **HARDINESS** Z 6-9

69. **COMMON NAME** Pyrenean valerian **HEIGHT AND SPREAD** 4 x 2ft (120 x 60cm) **FLOWERS** Tiny, held in 2½in (6cm) heads in late spring **ASPECT/LIKES** Part shade or sun, moist well-drained soil **HARDINESS** Z 4-9

70. **HEIGHT AND SPREAD** 5 x 1¾ft (150 x 50cm) **FLOWERS** ¾in (2cm) long, in late spring **ASPECT/LIKES** Dappled shade, fertile rich well-drained soil that remains moist year-round **HARDINESS** Z 5-9

71. **COMMON NAME** Upright wild ginger **HEIGHT AND SPREAD** 1¾ x 2¾ft (50 x 80cm) **FLOWERS** ¾in (2cm) across, in late spring **ASPECT/LIKES** Cool part shade, shelter, fertile moist well-drained soil, not too dry **HARDINESS** Z 5-8

72

Jasminum polyanthum

For seductive perfume, few plants can match jasmine. This well-known species has an especially powerful scent and is sold inexpensively as a pot plant. Its sparse clusters of white, pink-backed flowers last a couple of weeks before most plants are no doubt tossed in the trash. But it will grow for years if transplanted to a larger pot and its twining stems are trained on to trellis in a sunroom, conservatory, or cold greenhouse. In our warming climate, it is also increasingly worth trying the plant outdoors on your sunniest, most sheltered wall, ideally against the house. The scent of a large plant in flower in late spring is remarkable, especially in the evening. Mine scrambles up a wisteria, opening its flowers by my bedroom window and filling the room with perfumed air. The evergreen foliage may be burned back in cold winters, but new shoots usually arise from lower down and quickly replace old growth.

COMMON NAME Many-flowered jasmine **HEIGHT AND SPREAD** Climbs to 13ft (4m) **FLOWERS** ¾in (2cm) across, held in clusters in late spring **ASPECT/LIKES** Sun or part sun, very sheltered wall or glasshouse **HARDINESS** Z 9-10

73

Geranium nodosum 'Julie's Velvet'

This lovely herbaceous perennial was raised by and named after nurserywoman Julie Ritchie, of Hoo House Nursery, who specializes in geraniums. It is a fairly low-growing, easygoing plant with jewel-like flowers that start in late spring and go on for several months. Each shimmering bloom is richly hued. The purple-red petals edged with paler pink open atop slender stems that thread themselves through other shade-loving plants such as ferns and hostas, creating delightful compositions. The foliage is bright apple-green and forms good ground cover. The plant will stand drought but does better with some moisture. It gently self-seeds.

HEIGHT AND SPREAD 1 x 1¼ft (30 x 40cm) **FLOWERS** 1in (2.5cm) across, from late spring and through summer **ASPECT/LIKES** Part sun or dappled shade, any reasonable well-drained soil, not too dry **HARDINESS** Z 5-9

74

Rosa 'Mrs Oakley Fisher'

HEIGHT AND SPREAD 3 x 2¾ft (100 x 80cm) **FLOWERS** 4¾in (12cm) across, from late spring until the first frosts **ASPECT/LIKES** Sun, open site, shelter from wind, fertile well-drained soil **HARDINESS** Z 5-9

Single-flowered roses have been overshadowed for too long by classic, double-flowered selections, but their demure blooms bring a touch of delicacy and simplicity to the garden. Many, such as this fine, healthy selection, are also tough and easily grown and seem less prone to disease and wet-weather damage. From late spring, the plant produces clusters of large, five-petaled, warm apricot-orange blooms with a showy, central crown of stamens. The flowers are wonderfully fragrant and appear above glossy, rich-green foliage atop sturdy, purple-flushed, rather thorny stems. If the plant is kept dead-headed, the display continues in profusion on and off all summer. Give it a good, sunny site in well-drained soil. It needs protection from wind, as this can quickly damage the blooms. After flowering finishes in autumn, prune the shrub back to maintain good structure.

75

Rosa × *odorata* 'Mutabilis'

This lovely rose is one of the best, most hardworking shrubs, with many first-rate attributes. The clusters of flowers are carried in profusion for months on end, from the first impressive flush in spring until the first hard frosts if the plant is dead-headed. The blooms are single and delicate, with fluttering petals like tissue paper. Although they have almost no perfume, they undergo a transformation in color, opening soft yellow-peach and aging over a couple of days to quite strident raspberry-pink. The effect of the two tones together is charming. The plant is dense, disease-free, and vigorous, with small, glossy, apple-green leaves and purple-flushed stems. It can be trained on a wall or left to grow as a free-standing shrub. It's a plant you never regret having and one you can usually rely on to provide a flower or two for indoor arrangements at tricky times of year.

76

Lonicera × *brownii* 'Dropmore Scarlet'

Honeysuckles are largely underappreciated, despite being varied and versatile. In flower, this deciduous climber is one of the most beautiful and intensely colored, producing clusters of 15 or so long, tubular flowers. These nod from the branches and are pinkish coral-red on the outside, bright orange inside. Although not scented, they can appear in great profusion and show up well against the rounded, apple-green foliage. The first blooms normally open at the end of spring, with further flushes through summer. Red berries often follow. It is not vigorous, which makes it ideal for scrambling through a climbing rose. Try it with soft-pink 'New Dawn.' Give it a position in some sun, not too dry or hot, as this can cause mildew. In a warm dry area, it is better in more shade, although flowering may be less profuse.

77

Haberlea rhodopensis

I've grown this undemanding alpine in a low terracotta pot for some time. A hardy relative of African violets, it enjoys some shade and moisture. Over the years, my plant has made a mound of overlapping, green rosettes. In late spring, little sprays of delightful, slipper-shaped flowers appear. They are pale lilac inside, darker purple outside. The plant is ideal in a stone wall or alpine trough, somewhere cool with excellent drainage. I occasionally pull out any brown leaves.

78

Iris 'Broadleigh Rose'

Unsurprisingly, so-called Pacific Coast irises are very popular in the US. Low-growing, clump-forming, evergreen herbaceous perennials, they are spectacular in flower and easy to keep, standing short periods of drought well as long as there is plenty of organic matter in the soil. The lovely blooms appear amid the grassy foliage in profusion for a couple of weeks at the end of spring and are a smoky-rose color, with lower petals marked with yellow. I grow it with *Iris* 'Broadleigh Carolyn' at the base of a sunny hedge, and they never fail to amaze. It would also do well in a raised bed, alpine trough, or at the top of a wall.

75. HEIGHT AND SPREAD 5 x 5ft (1.5 x 1.5m) **FLOWERS** 2½in (6cm) across, from late spring until the first frosts **ASPECT/LIKES** Sun, open site, shelter from wind, any soil except waterlogged **HARDINESS** Z 5-8

76. HEIGHT AND SPREAD Climbs to 10ft (3m) **FLOWERS** 1¼in (3cm) long, held in a cluster in late spring, with more flushes throughout summer **ASPECT/LIKES** Part sun, shelter, not too dry **HARDINESS** Z 3-9

77. HEIGHT AND SPREAD 6 x 16in (15 x 40cm) **FLOWERS** 1in (2.5cm) long, in late spring **ASPECT/LIKES** Cool shade or part sun, moist well-drained soil **HARDINESS** Z 6-9

78. HEIGHT AND SPREAD 6 x 12in (15 x 30cm) **FLOWERS** 2¾in (7cm) across, in late spring **ASPECT/LIKES** Sun or part sun, humus-rich well-drained soil **HARDINESS** Z 8-9

79

Papaver 'Beauty of Livermere'

HEIGHT AND SPREAD 3 x 3ft (1 x 1m) **FLOWERS** 7in (18cm) across, in late spring and early summer **ASPECT/LIKES** Sun, moist well-drained soil **HARDINESS** Z 3-7

I love oriental poppies: at their glorious best, nothing matches their huge yet delicate flowers. This popular and vigorous selection has superb, chalice-shaped, black-blotched, blood-red flowers rising on stout stems. These sun-loving, herbaceous perennials form large mounds and need quite a bit of space. They look lovely after a spring downpour, their hairy leaves all silvered with raindrops. The best moment is as the bud bursts open, freeing crinkled petals within, like a butterfly emerging from its chrysalis. Flowers last several splendid weeks, but then the foliage turns shambolic. A classic solution is to grow perennial sweet peas over them. I prefer to cut them down, mulch, and water well, allowing fresh leaves to rise. I then use pots of summer bedding or lilies to fill the gap, and grow ornamental grasses or *Geranium psilostemon* in front to mask it all. A fiddle, but worth it.

80

Lonicera calcarata

Having seen this remarkable, hardy, giant honeysuckle in plantsman Roy Lancaster's garden, I long dreamed of owning it, but it is rare and recently introduced from China. Eventually, I was given a rooted cutting by my friend David Jewell at the Sir Harold Hillier Gardens. It grew prodigiously up the side of my house and for two weeks in late spring is now the star of my garden. In flower, it is a plant of great beauty. Arching spurs grow from a framework of sturdy, climbing stems. From the tops of the spurs, large, outward-facing, paired flowers open in the axils of each dark-green, oval, leathery leaf. They appear in succession and are creamy white to begin with, turning pinkish orange and finally lipstick-red. In the evening and early morning, the air is heavy with a delicious perfume similar to lilies-of-the-valley. The plant is annoyingly not yet commercially available, but it's bound to be eventually.

HEIGHT AND SPREAD Climbs to 26ft (8m) or more **FLOWERS** 1¼in (3cm) long, held in long sprays in late spring **ASPECT/LIKES** Sun, shelter, summer heat, plenty of space **HARDINESS** Z 2-7

81

Allium hollandicum 'Purple Sensation'

Who would have guessed 30 years ago how popular a flowering onion would now be as an ornamental? Among today's most-loved bulbs, it has become an irreplaceable, even ubiquitous part of late spring and early summer. Obliging and so useful, it suits many sites and planting styles, thriving in sun or part shade. Its spherical heads of starry, purple flowers on slender stems are just tall enough to float above developing perennials, rise through unmown grass, or intermingle with still-to-flower shrub roses. The flowers are also just the right tone, blending with almost everything. In summer and fall, the seed heads provide further interest. The foliage withers as the flowers open, but, at this stage, leaves can be whipped off if unsightly. Left undisturbed, it seeds around, although resulting plants have flowers in varied hues. After a few years, the original plants may begin to peter out, so add new bulbs occasionally in fall.

HEIGHT AND SPREAD 3ft (90cm) tall **FLOWERS** Small, held in heads 2¾in (7cm) across in late spring and early summer **ASPECT/LIKES** Sun or part shade, some shelter, well-drained soil **HARDINESS** Z 4-9

82

Digitalis purpurea

This biennial needs no introduction: gardeners up and down the land know and love foxgloves for their soaring spires of one-sided, purple or white tubular flowers, each usually beautifully freckled within. Few plants are more useful in shady places, gracing the backs of borders below trees or tall shrubs from May into summer. They seed around with abandon, and it pays to take care of a few seedlings, lifting and potting them in fall and keeping them somewhere sheltered over winter. That way, the following spring you will have good, large plants ready for putting in exactly the places you need them—in gaps that need a short-lived filler, for instance. To get the best and tallest plants, improve the soil with garden compost. Some people prefer to keep only white-flowered selections, which are easily identified, as their leaves are paler green than those with purple blooms. Personally, I can't be that ruthless.

COMMON NAME Common foxglove **HEIGHT AND SPREAD** 8 x 1¾ft (250 x 50cm) **FLOWERS** 2½in (6cm) long, held in a spire in late spring and early summer **ASPECT/LIKES** Sun or part shade, fertile moist soil **HARDINESS** Z 4-9

83

Cistus x *purpureus*

I think this is one of the best shrubs of all, ideal for dry, sunny, well-drained gardens. Quick-growing, evergreen, and needing almost no care once established, it explodes into bloom each year in late spring and summer in a display that takes your breath away. The large flowers are impossibly delicate and look as if they are made from tissue paper. Each is composed of five overlapping, lightly creased petals that are pink-purple with a maroon blotch at the base. At the heart of each one lies a boss of golden stamens. The overall effect is not unlike a single rose, but the flowers appear in greater profusion than any rose. They have no scent and do not last long, just a day, but open in succession for several weeks. The small, crinkled leaves are dark-green, rough, and slightly sticky. The shrub becomes broad and dome-shaped after a few years. It can be lightly shaped to no ill effect after flowering but will not stand hard pruning. Eventually, it may outgrow the space, in which case summer cuttings root easily to replace it. It resists drought admirably.

COMMON NAME Purple-flowered rock rose **HEIGHT AND SPREAD** 4 x 4ft (1.2 x 1.2m) **FLOWERS** 3in (8cm) across, in late spring and early summer **ASPECT/LIKES** Full sun, warmth, well-drained soil **HARDINESS** Z 7-10

84. **COMMON NAME** Woodbine **HEIGHT AND SPREAD** Climbs to 26ft (8m) **FLOWERS** 2½in (6cm) long, held in clusters from late spring until well into summer **ASPECT/LIKES** Cool shade or part sun, somewhere to climb, not too dry **HARDINESS** Z 4-9

85. **HEIGHT AND SPREAD** 5 x 5ft (1.5 x 1.5m) **FLOWERS** 2½in (6cm) wide, held in clusters in spring and early summer **ASPECT/LIKES** Sun, open site, any well-drained soil **HARDINESS** Z 5-9

86. **HEIGHT AND SPREAD** 3 x 1¼ft (90 x 40cm) **FLOWERS** 4¾in (12cm) tall, in late spring **ASPECT/LIKES** Full sun, open site, well-drained soil **HARDINESS** Z 3-9

87. **COMMON NAME** Hutton's Cape tulip **HEIGHT AND SPREAD** 3 x 1¾ft (100 x 50cm) **FLOWERS** 2½in (6cm) across, in late spring **ASPECT/LIKES** Full sun, shelter, well-drained soil, moisture in summer **HARDINESS** Z 6-9

84

Lonicera periclymenum 'Graham Thomas'

This refined selection of woodbine was found by and named after a great plantsman and gardening hero of mine. It has a long flowering period, and the display in late spring is perhaps the most impressive, with loads of flower heads produced, but it will bloom on and off all summer if happy. The large, tubular flowers are held in circular heads and are cream-colored in bud but open to yellow, distinctively without the purplish tints usually found in this species. They are highly scented, especially at night. Try growing the plant through an old apple tree or up trellis, perhaps with a climbing rose for company.

85

Rosa 'Buff Beauty'

A lovely, easy-to-grow, old rose, this makes a good garden plant, providing you can give it some space, as in time it can form quite a large shrub. The stems are upright then arching and bear healthy, dark-green foliage, followed in late spring by generous trusses of warm, creamy apricot flowers that also have a nice, so-called "tea" perfume. The flowers are not huge, but the initial display lasts several weeks, and it repeats later in summer. I grow this rose under an apple tree and was delighted to find it has scrambled up into it, so it will also grow as a climber. It never gets much in the way of disease, certainly nothing that looks especially unsightly. The flowers tone well with *Allium* 'Purple Sensation' (see p.61), which blooms at much the same time. Give it some sun and decent soil, and enjoy.

86

Iris 'Benton Susan'

Expert growers will tell you that there are far better irises than this old but vigorous, tall, bearded selection, but, for me, it has great charm. The flowers in late spring are two-toned: the upper petals (the "standards") are a lovely, muted golden-orange, while the lower petals (the "falls") are cream with an orange edge and brown markings; the beard itself is gold. The blooms are carried on little, branchlike side stems and have a nice scent. Bearded irises need as much sun as possible, and the rhizomes they grow from must be kept open to the sky. The best spot is in a dedicated border, perhaps by a sunny wall. They are fine at the front of a border but further back may be too shaded. Divide clumps when they get congested after flowering.

87

Moraea huttonii

Closely related to irises, the genus *Moraea* mostly comprises bulbous plants that need more sun and better drainage than gardeners in mild climates can provide outdoors. This South African species is a bit of an exception: given a sheltered, warm site and moist but sharply drained soil, it is a good garden plant. It is surprisingly large—the tall, arching, grassy, evergreen leaves reach around 3ft (1m) high and form a small clump in time. In late spring, numerous flower stems arise above the foliage, carrying golden, irislike blooms with lower petals marked with brown. The flowers are comparatively small for the height of the stem, which gives the plant an unusual appearance in bloom. They also have a lovely sweet perfume. Give it a plum position away from too much competition, as it is something special and seldom seen.

88

Rosa 'Hugh Dickson'

This old rose has a special place in my heart, as an ancient plant of it once grew up the front of our family home. Popular in Edwardian times, it is now not often grown, partly because it is ungainly kept as a free-standing shrub, producing rather lanky, thorny stems. In times gone by, these would have been arched over and tied to low pegs on the ground to create a curious, spider-shaped plant that produced masses of blooms. Rather easier is to tie them to a wall and train them, then the whole plant becomes perfectly manageable. Its beautiful, powerfully scented flowers first appear in late spring and are large, fully double, and crimson red. They also nod down, which is perfect when they are seen on a high wall. They repeat well all season and into fall. The plant likes a place that does not get too hot and dry, as drought can encourage black spot.

HEIGHT AND SPREAD Climbs to 13ft (4m) on a wall **FLOWERS** 3in (8cm) across, from late spring and through summer **ASPECT/LIKES** Sun or part sun, open site, any well-drained soil **HARDINESS** Z 5-9

“This particularly delightful species of *Philadelphus* is one I wouldn’t want to be without.”

89

Philadelphus purpurascens

I’ve become increasingly interested in mock oranges over the years, and this particularly delightful species of *Philadelphus* is one I wouldn’t want to be without. An easily grown, multistemmed, deciduous shrub with oval leaves, it forms a thicket of arching stems to around 6½ft (2m) tall. In late spring to early summer, these produce numerous clusters of flowers. The individual blooms are four-petaled, bell-shaped, downward-facing, and beautifully perfumed. They are also pure-white. The purple part of the name comes from the showy, red-purple calyces that hold the flowers to the stems. These contrast with the flowers perfectly. The display lasts around two weeks. Plants are best cut back straight after flowering, as blooms appear on wood made the previous season. To promote new growth, I trim out a third of the oldest stems. Give this plant a spot in a shrub or mixed border.

COMMON NAME Mock orange **HEIGHT AND SPREAD** 6½ x 5ft (2 x 1.5m) **FLOWERS** 1¼in (3cm) across, in late spring to early summer **ASPECT/LIKES** Sun or part sun, fertile well-drained soil **HARDINESS** Z 6-10

90

Calycanthus x *raulstonii* 'Hartlage Wine'

A newcomer to the ranks of spring- and summer-flowering plants, this fine, potentially tall, wide, deciduous, multistemmed shrub has much to recommend it. Its large, oval, glossy green leaves appear on upright to gently arching branches, making quite a dense canopy of growth. Then, from the tips of shoots appear rounded buds. These open to unusual-looking, almost magnolia-like flowers. The larger, outer petals are wine-red, while the smaller ones in the center are held almost in the form of a cup around stamens edged with cream. The plant bears many flowers over several weeks and the blooms have a light fruity scent.

HEIGHT AND SPREAD 13 x 13ft (4 x 4m) **FLOWERS** 2½in (6cm) across, in late spring and early summer **ASPECT/LIKES** Part shade or sun, shelter from cold winds, fertile moist well-drained soil **HARDINESS** Z 5-9

91

Allium cristophii

COMMON NAME Star of Persia **HEIGHT AND SPREAD** 20 x 8in (50 x 20cm) **FLOWERS** 1¼in (3cm) across, held in a 8in (20cm) wide head in late spring **ASPECT/LIKES** Sun, well-drained soil **HARDINESS** Z 5-8

Native to the Middle East, this ornamental onion makes a remarkable sight in late spring. Its huge, globelike heads are composed of dozens of starry, metallic-purple flowers held on stout stems—a floral firework if ever there was one. The leaves are silvery gray and start to yellow as the flowers peak but are easily hidden or ignored. The stems could almost be considered too short for the huge flower heads—to around knee height. If you want them to rise above other planting, you need to make sure that this is pretty low-growing. Try them, for example, with shorter grasses, such as *Stipa tenuissima* or *Anemanthele lessoniana*. The plant is easy to grow and persistent as long as it gets sun and well-drained soil. The heads last well, both in the garden or dried in a vase.

92

Myrrhis odorata

This edible, herbaceous perennial makes a perfect substitute for cow parsley, a wild flower that, although loved by many, is rather too badly behaved for all but the largest, most relaxed garden. Forming clumps, sweet cicely rises in spring, its delicate, soft apple-green, fernlike foliage soon topped by flat umbels of tiny, white flowers (*pictured, left*). Grown in a drift, it is beautiful, especially seen at twilight, and is lovely edging a path below trees. It flourishes in cool shade but is easy and adaptable to warmer, drier sites. Plants set masses of seed and these germinate freely the following year. By late summer, the plants may begin to look scrappy and can be cut to the ground. The leaves have a sweet, aniseed-like taste and are sometimes used to tone down sharp-tasting, stewed produce such as rhubarb. The foliage lasts well in a vase and is the perfect foil for freesias.

COMMON NAME Sweet cicely **HEIGHT AND SPREAD** 5 x 3ft (1.5x1m) **FLOWERS** Tiny, held in 2½in (6cm) heads in late spring **ASPECT/LIKES** Cool part shade, not too dry **HARDINESS** Z 4-8

summer

93

Cestrum × *cultum* 'Cretan Purple'

I planted this unusual shrub expecting it to be tender, but my free-standing plant has now survived several winters well. In colder years, though, it will be cut to the ground by frost, sending up vigorous new shoots in spring. In some gardens, it might be best planted against a warm wall or even grown under glass. Small, five-petaled flowers are carried in numerous panicles that droop appealingly from the stems and look unusual, especially at this time of year. Further flowers appear later in the summer. It is generally deciduous, unless you live in a really mild area, forming an upright then slightly weeping shrub with rather slender stems and lanceolate leaves. The flowers have some evening scent, but not of the same magnitude as *Cestrum parqui* (see p.126), which it resembles. Give it your warmest place in well-drained soil.

94

Clematis 'Paul Farges'

While many summer-flowering clematis have much showier, more glamorous blooms, this refined but tough cultivar brings a rather different character to the garden. Its lovely flowers are similar to *Clematis vitalba* (old man's beard), only rather larger, each with six back-swept, pure-white petals displaying a central spray of long white stamens, ivory-tinged in the middle. They have a sweet scent. The blooms appear in clusters atop long stalks held clear of the soft-green foliage and open in great multitudes, often covering the plant and lasting in beauty for several weeks to superb effect. The plant itself is easy to grow and vigorous, needing plenty of space, covering fences, outbuilding walls, and scaling high trees. It thrives in any aspect, even doing well on a north-facing fence and, as with other clematis, likes its roots in shade.

95

Chionochloa rubra

One of the loveliest grasses, this is a plant to treasure—its fine, long-flowing blades, tinted coppery red, form an attractive dome-shaped clump that shimmers in the breeze. It is at its best as soft, new growth arises. Later in the summer, flower panicles emerge, but these add little to the overall appearance. As they age, plants improve year on year initially, though after a while, they become full of old thatch and need lifting, splitting, the old material pulling out, and the new growth replanting—a job for late spring. The plant looks elegant in a tall terracotta container, but don't let it get dry in summer—it likes plenty of moisture in the growing season. Move it somewhere sheltered and on the dry side for winter if in a pot.

96

Philadelphus coulteri

Rare and desirable, this Mexican mock orange is one to search out. It makes a handsome, vase-shaped, deciduous plant with rather lax, upright then arching stems, the small, pointed, oval leaves pale green above but distinctively silver backed. Then in early summer, pure-white, four-petaled flowers appear, each with a central mass of stamens. The blooms open almost flat and are held in open clusters along the stems. They are beautifully scented. I give my plant the support of an obelisk, which may not be needed once it gets a little older. It needs your warmest place but seems easy enough to grow, once established.

93. HEIGHT AND SPREAD 6½ x 6½ft (2 x 2m) or more in a frost-free place **FLOWERS** Unusual drooping clusters of tubular, ¾in (2cm) long, violet flowers from early summer onward **ASPECT/LIKES** Sunny warm sheltered site, best against a wall **HARDINESS** Z 9-11

94. COMMON NAME 'Summer Snow' clematis **HEIGHT AND SPREAD** Climbs to 13ft (4m) or more **FLOWERS** 1½in (4cm) across in early to midsummer **ASPECT/LIKES** Happy in any, likes roots in cool shade **HARDINESS** Z 5-9

95. COMMON NAME Red tussock grass **HEIGHT AND SPREAD** 3 x 3ft (1 x 1m) **ASPECT/LIKES** Sun, open site, well-drained moist soil **HARDINESS** Z 7-10

96. HEIGHT AND SPREAD 6½ x 3ft (2 x 1m) **FLOWERS** 1½in (4cm) across in early summer **ASPECT/LIKES** Sheltered hot sunny site, free-draining soil **HARDINESS** Z 8-9

97

Hosta 'Jade Cascade'

A perfect hosta for a large container, this handsome perennial develops slowly into a sizable clump. Tall, quite slender dark shoots arise from the ground in midspring, opening up into wonderful, large, arching oval but highly elegant leaves with an elongated tapering point. They are beautifully ribbed and bright green at first, aging to a richer tone, the edge of each leaf slightly rippled. In a raised container, this aptly named plant forms a perfect cascade of overlapping leaves, topped off in summer by stems of pale-lavender, tubular flowers. Keep plants moist, in shelter and part-shade. If in a pot, feed with liquid fertilizer every couple of weeks. Top-dressing pots with blended farm manure in spring also benefits them. Growing hostas in containers allows easier control of slugs and snails, most important in spring when the new shoots are succulent. Space out plants so they don't touch each other or anything else, as close proximity aids the travel of these pesky mollusks. Mulching pots with gravel helps, but nighttime raids with a flashlight are the best way to deal with them.

HEIGHT AND SPREAD 3 x 2¼ft (90x70cm) **FLOWERS** Lavender tubular flowers in midsummer **ASPECT/LIKES** Moist soil, position in sun or light shade **HARDINESS** Z 3-8

98

Rosa Alissar, Princess of Phoenicia

HEIGHT AND SPREAD 4 x 2¾ft (120 x 80cm) **FLOWERS** Striking multicolored semi-double flowers with a dark-red center in early to midsummer **ASPECT/LIKES** Sun, open site, well-drained moist soil **HARDINESS** Z 7-10

This exquisite rose, also known as 'Harsidon,' is the result of breeding with *Rosa persica*, a distinctive Asian species with flowers blotched dark red at their heart. That coloration has passed to this selection, which bears masses of semi-double, red-centered flowers that open warm ivory and age to peach then pink. To see an established plant in full flower is impressive, such is the variation in the blooms. The display is repeated later in the summer. Flowers have a faint scent. This is a typical shrub rose, with glossy bronze-tinged foliage, usually disease-free. Plants are best pruned after flowering to keep them compact and healthy. Thorny, single-flowered *Rosa* For Your Eyes Only, also known as 'Cheweyesup,' has similarly blotched pink blooms. It, too, is excellent and flowers all summer.

99

Chamaenerion angustifolium 'Album'

Rosebay willowherb is a beautiful pink-flowered plant notorious for colonizing waste ground, spreading by seed and underground runners. This white selection is identical in some respects. It, too, bears tall slender spires of attractive flowers (in this case, white) in early summer, above lance-shaped, soft-green leaves. It also spreads by runners, although these are quite easily controlled with a trowel. A key difference is that its seeds are sterile, so any wider colonizing ambition is curtailed. It is a plant of great beauty at dusk, when its flowers seem to glow, and a perfect occupant for a relaxed white border, adding height but not great bulk, and forming an open, sparse clump. After flowering, it starts to look shabby, so flower heads are best cut off. Try standing pots of lilies or white cosmos to mask the gap it leaves.

COMMON NAME White rosebay willowherb **HEIGHT AND SPREAD** 5 x 6½–10ft (1.5 x 2–3m) **FLOWERS** ¾in (2cm) across, produced in profusion in early summer **ASPECT/LIKES** Sunny open site, fine in poor soil **HARDINESS** Z 4-9

100

Calycanthus chinensis

Here is an unusual but lovely Chinese shrub. It forms an upright but quite wide-spreading deciduous bush, with impressive large oval papery leaves paired on either side of the stems; they turn butter yellow in fall before falling. The main event, however, is in early summer, when superb magnolia-like flowers open from nodding globular buds at the end of the stems. The white petals are tinged palest pink, with central flower parts held in a soft-yellow cup shape around the stamens. I grew it for years in sun, where it did not do well, suffering from a black spotting of leaves and flowers. Moving it to a cooler, semishaded position with more moisture solved the spot problem, and the plant is at last happy.

COMMON NAME Chinese sweetshrub **HEIGHT AND SPREAD** $6\frac{1}{2}$ x 10ft (2 x 3m) **FLOWERS** Showy magnolia-like flowers, $2\frac{3}{4}$in (7cm) across in early summer **ASPECT/LIKES** Semishade, moist fertile soil **HARDINESS** Z 3-8

COMMON NAME Striped cobra lily HEIGHT AND SPREAD 16 x 10in (40 x 25cm) FLOWERS Arumlike flowers, 4in (10cm) tall in early summer ASPECT/LIKES Cool moist well-drained shade HARDINESS Z 6-9

101

Arisaema costatum

Tuberous perennial aroids native to Asia and the US, *Arisaema* can produce remarkable flowers and spectacular foliage. This Himalayan species is among the easiest and most dramatic. Its trilobed leaves (or, rather, leaf—plants produce only one) can be huge. In early summer, leaflets join at the tip of green or purple stems and are glossy, ribbed, and rich green. The flower arises at the same time and develops quickly. It looks like a cobra's head. The plant will grow outside with shelter, moisture, and shade. Always mark the position of the tubers with a label, as they are easily damaged by digging. You can also grow plants in a pot in a cool greenhouse or plunged in a frame of sharp sand or leaf mold.

102

Hosta 'June'

This hosta is surely one of the most reliable and beautiful of all, at its best in early summer, when the leaves are lush and unblemished. The foliage arises early—little pointed, lilac-blue, clawlike buds emerging in a tight clump. As the season passes, these elongate, leaves unrolling and forming a low mound of overlapping foliage. Each leaf is oval and pointed, the center irregularly marked in yellow-green, margins blue-green. In sun, leaves end up with a more yellow-green center, while in shade the blue-green predominates. Later in the summer, spires of short-lived flowers arise. Grow in fertile soil that is well-drained yet moisture-retentive. When established, plants stand heat and dry spells well. This selection does not seem to attract slugs and snails too much, but keep your eyes open for these pests if you want leaves to stay pristine. This is easier done when plants are grown in a pot.

HEIGHT AND SPREAD 16 x 32in (40 x 80cm) FLOWERS Lavender tubular flowers in midsummer ASPECT/LIKES Moist soil, position in sun or light shade HARDINESS Z 3-8

103. COMMON NAME Mexican rose syringa **HEIGHT AND SPREAD** 6½ x 6½ft (2 x 2m) **FLOWERS** 1½in (4cm) wide, slightly nodding with a violet heart, in early summer **ASPECT/LIKES** Sun, warmth, and shelter **HARDINESS** Z 9-10

104. HEIGHT AND SPREAD 2¾ft (80cm) tall, clump 1¼ft (40cm) across **FLOWERS** 4in (10cm) tall and across in early summer **ASPECT/LIKES** Full sun and sharp drainage **HARDINESS** Z 3-10

105. HEIGHT AND SPREAD 6½ x 6½ft (2 x 2m) **FLOWERS** Tiny but long-lasting flowers held in umbels 2½in (6cm) across in early to midsummer **ASPECT/LIKES** Sun, open site, good drainage **HARDINESS** Z 6-10

106. HEIGHT AND SPREAD Climbs to 13ft (4m) or more **FLOWERS** Nodding, double, 3in (8cm) across, profuse first flush in early summer, then lasting into early winter **ASPECT/LIKES** Sun or shade, decent drainage, and sturdy support **HARDINESS** Z 5-9

103

Philadelphus mexicanus

In full flower, this mock orange is one of the loveliest things in my garden. The large, individual, downward-facing, four-petaled blooms are bowl-shaped and, from the outside, ivory white. But lift up a flower and you will see a charming soft-violet flush to the base of each petal and, at the heart, a golden crown of anthers. Blooms crowd the plant's slender arching stems in an elegant fashion for 2–3 weeks. Better still is the seductive scent, the best of any *Philadelphus* I know, most powerful at twilight. I leave my back door open and let the perfume drift through the house. The plant itself is almost a climber and, in mild gardens, vigorous—I have seen it scale the front of a house. Stems are not self-supporting, yet training the plant on a fence or wall can look ungainly. I prefer to grow mine up a free-standing obelisk, from which it cascades out. In anything but a mild winter, cold weather will defoliate the plant and damage stems, but in a sunny sheltered place, it usually recovers the following spring.

105

Bupleurum fruticosum

This is a useful evergreen shrub if you have an open, sunny place in rather poor, dry, well-drained soil. It quickly makes a dense vigorous rounded bush with upright stems, the oval- to oblong-shaped foliage glossy rich green above, with a contrasting paler midrib, silver green below. In late spring, numerous rounded umbels of flowers form at the tips of stems, green in bud, but opening acid-yellow. The blooms last for weeks. This is the perfect plant for a gravel garden or somewhere with a Mediterranean feel. It can be pruned after flowering to keep it tidy—foliage has a rather pungent odor when cut. The plant will gently self-seed.

104

Iris 'Mer du Sud'

Blue flowers are not easily come by, even in summer, but this sumptuous tall bearded iris is one of the best I know, even if there is sometimes a slight hint of violet to the huge blooms, which shimmer like silk in the sun. Lower and upper petals are beautifully ruffled, the blooms opening in succession atop sturdy stems above the usual gray-green lance-shaped leaves. It is a vigorous and reliable selection, developed in the late 1990s and easy to grow. Like others of its kind, it needs full sun and sharp drainage so is great on a sunny bank or in front of a wall, where its thick rhizomes can bake. If you like irises, I recommend a visit to a specialty grower at flowering time in early summer, when you can pick out the ones you like best, such is the dazzling variety now available.

106

Rosa 'Madame Alfred Carrière'

This venerable climber is known to some gardeners by the nickname "Mad Alf," a term of endearment, as this is one of the most reliable and easygoing of all old roses. It is particularly vigorous—suitable for a large expanse of wall or fencing, an outbuilding, or even for scaling a tree; grow it on an arch or trellis and it will soon smother the lot. This vigor also means it is remarkably disease- and problem-free. It thrives on north-facing walls and grows in almost any soil. Stems, while not entirely thorn-free, are easy to handle, the foliage glossy, dark green, and healthy. Individual blooms open palest pink and age to white. They nod gracefully and have a lovely scent.

COMMON NAME Color-changing tobacco plant **HEIGHT AND SPREAD** 4 x 1¾ft (120 x 50cm) **FLOWERS** Profuse displays of multihued flowers ¾in (2cm) across from early summer onward **ASPECT/LIKES** Sun, shelter, fertile moist soil **HARDINESS** Z 8-10

107

Nicotiana mutabilis

The word "mutabilis" in a Latin name quite often means the plant's flowers change color as they age. A lovely example is this ornamental tobacco—a desirable, short-lived perennial often grown as an annual. Its soft, sticky leaves form a clump before wiry, branched stems arise bearing clouds of dangling trumpets. These open white and change color through shades of pink before turning magenta and falling—a transformation that takes a week. Each plant includes flowers at every stage to superb effect. The display lasts weeks—as stems fade, more arise, with the plant developing a stout stem. Frost usually finishes plants, but they can survive mild winters; in a cool conservatory, they flower on and off most of the time. Outside, seedlings turn up the following spring in paving cracks; best to save seed and sow in spring for planting out in sunny spots or containers.

108

Hosta 'Sum and Substance'

For bold foliage, few perennials can touch hostas, and this large, popular selection is one of the most impressive, for the size of its beautiful leaves. Pointed, toothlike purple-tinged shoots emerge in spring. These develop, leaves dramatically unraveling one after another, to form a huge mound of overlapping foliage. Each rounded leaf glows yellow-green, slightly cup-shaped at first, then convex, the surface handsomely veined and puckered, the edges slightly wavy. Held on stout stalks, they can be 20in (50cm) across and the whole plant has a luminous beauty, particularly in early summer, when the leaves are most succulent. Although not slug- or snail-proof, they are quite tough and slightly less prone to damage than other hostas, but it is easiest to keep a plant perfect if grown in a big pot. An annual mulch of blended manure helps it produce big leaves.

HEIGHT AND SPREAD 3 x 4ft (90 x 120cm) **FLOWERS** Lavender tubular flowers in midsummer **ASPECT/LIKES** Moist soil, position in sun or light shade **HARDINESS** Z 3-8

109

Erigeron karvinskianus

I once heard this perennial called "dancing daisies," a name that stuck in my mind, as it captures the flowers' joyful nature. This is a low-growing plant you'll see spilling over bricks and stonework in all the famous old gardens. You will probably plant it in a border initially, but it is always best as a self-set plant. The next generation that pops up, often in paving cracks from seeds your plant readily sets, will be the one that impresses. Little white daisies form in multitudes from late spring; held on wiry stems, they become increasingly pink-tinged as they age. Plants make a mat of growth, merging to form a billowing blanket of flowers that spans summer and fall. With cold weather, flowers peter out. Trim plants back to a few centimeters from the base and give the area a sweep and tidy in late winter—shoots will readily form for next year. Remove old plants in favor of new ones. When self-set, plants grow anywhere—best in sun, they are also happy at the base of a north wall and perfectly hardy. Drainage is key—it must be sharp.

COMMON NAME Mexican fleabane **HEIGHT AND SPREAD** 8 x 20in (20 x 50cm) **FLOWERS** Daisies ¾in (2cm) across produced in masses from late spring until fall **ASPECT/LIKES** Sun and cracks in paving **HARDINESS** Z 6-9

"This is a low-growing plant you'll see spilling over bricks and stonework."

110

Fuchsia magellanica 'Lady Bacon'

Hardy fuchsias are one of the joys of the summer garden, with displays that can last until the first frosts, and this selection is one of the most striking. Although fairly small, its flowers appear at the ends of slender stems that carry little oval green leaves. Blooms are red at the base, the four outer petals opening to near-white, in contrast with a purple bell at the flower's heart. It is a delight all summer, the show starting early if the plant hasn't been cut back by frost, something that now seldom happens in many sheltered gardens. This one is a pretty hardy deciduous shrub, even shooting from ground level after long freezing spells. Plants can get quite large and may be trimmed in spring after the coldest weather has passed.

HEIGHT AND SPREAD $6\frac{1}{2}$ x $6\frac{1}{2}$ft (2 x 2m) **FLOWERS** Slender, dangling, 1in (2.5cm) long, tricolored flowers from summer to late fall **ASPECT/LIKES** Sun, well-drained soil, and shelter from winter cold—near a wall is ideal **HARDINESS** Z 8-9

111

Campanula persicifolia

If there were an award for most obliging perennial, this bellflower might win it, for it could not be easier to grow. I don't remember planting it, but in my garden it springs up everywhere, usually in light shade, but also in other spots. Its glowing blue or white flowers (*pictured, left*) look lovely in the evening. Plants form mats of growth with long, slender, green leaves. From these arise 2ft (60cm) stems, which carry buds that open over weeks in a first flush of showy flowers. After blooms fade, another flush opens from the same stems, so don't rush to cut them down. If you get a good seedling, keep it going by dividing clumps in spring.

COMMON NAME Peach-leaved bellflower **HEIGHT AND SPREAD** 3 x 1ft (100 x 30cm) **FLOWERS** White or blue bell-shaped flowers, 1¼in (3cm) across, held on a spike, from early to midsummer **ASPECT/LIKES** Sun or part-shade, not fussy **HARDINESS** Z 3-8

112

Geranium nodosum 'Silverwood'

HEIGHT AND SPREAD 1 x 1¾ft (30x50cm) **FLOWERS** ¾in (2cm) across, produced for weeks from early summer until fall **ASPECT/LIKES** Sun or shade, not fussy **HARDINESS** Z 7-10

People are always after plants that grow well in shade, particularly dry shade, and this little perennial is probably one of the best. In spring, it forms a tidy, low-spreading clump of attractive, soft-apple-green, lobed leaves. Shortly afterward, shining, pure-white, delicate, five-petaled flowers begin to stud the plant, and these are produced in succession for months on end, lasting into fall. This geranium looks well growing next to ferns or epimediums or threading through hellebore foliage, the white flowers adding cool highlights. It tolerates almost complete neglect and survives in the sort of conditions other plants completely fail in, even standing shade under shallow-rooted shrubs, which is notoriously hard to deal with. That said, it does better if you take a bit of care of it—an annual mulch of garden compost and some water in times of drought are worth lavishing on this hardworking and dependable garden friend.

113

Buddleja 'Pink Delight'

For ease of cultivation and butterfly-attracting abilities, few shrubs can match buddleias, and there are many fine cultivars. I like clean, distinct colors and, as far as pink-flowered selections go, this Dutch plant from the mid-1980s is probably the best. The scented blooms are open early in the season—reliably in mid- to late June—initially in profusions of wide, long primary panicles that arch out from the plant, the blooms of a clear hue with little trace of purple. The key is to deadhead after primary panicles fade, as this promotes secondary ones that, while smaller, prolong displays; it also removes faded flowers. This can be a chore, but this buddleia is reasonably compact if pruned each spring, although plants are best reduced by half in fall first. As well as being one of the most popular plants with butterflies, in my garden it attracts hummingbird hawkmoths too.

COMMON NAME Butterfly bush **HEIGHT AND SPREAD** 8 x 6½ft (2.5 x 2m) **FLOWERS** Tiny but held in panicles to 1ft (30cm) long from early to late summer if dead-headed **ASPECT/LIKES** Sunny open site **HARDINESS** Z 5-9

114

Hosta 'El Niño'

This is a great selection, well worth growing for its eye-popping foliage. The broadly heart-shaped, fairly thick leaves are an intense glaucous-blue, edged with a feathered narrow margin of white. As summer progresses, the color contrast seems to get stronger, the white leaf edges growing progressively broader to really dramatic effect. As a bonus, spires of funnel-shaped flowers arise. Keep the plant somewhere in cool shade, as the blue leaf color fades with sunshine; it looks terrific beside ferns or other hostas, especially the dark-green *Hosta* 'Devon Green.' It is also perfect for growing in a low pot, where it can be more easily cared for—top-dress each year with garden compost and finish with a layer of gravel to keep your plant happy and to deter leaf-munching pests, although this selection happily seems less appetizing to slugs and snails than many.

HEIGHT AND SPREAD 2 x 2¾ft (60 x 80cm) **FLOWERS** Lavender tubular flowers in midsummer **ASPECT/LIKES** Moist soil, position in sun or light shade **HARDINESS** Z 3-8

115

Geranium maderense

Many gardeners refer to true geraniums as "hardy geraniums" to distinguish them from pelargoniums, but there are also a few true geraniums that are quite tender; this superb perennial is the best known. For a couple of years, it builds a handsome rosette of long-stalked, purple-flushed, almost fernlike foliage about 4ft (1.2m) across. A short trunk gradually develops that retains leaf stems that reflex and help support the plant; don't cut them off. Flowering is dazzling—a dome of shimmering purple blooms starts in early summer and lasts weeks. Plants die afterward. They do not make side shoots but set seed generously. If you have a sheltered spot in semishade that does not get too wet, it is worth risking outdoors; otherwise, grow in large pots under glass and stand out for summer.

HEIGHT AND SPREAD 5 x 4ft (1.5 x 1.2m) **FLOWERS** 1in (2.5cm) across, held in a flower head, from early summer and lasting several weeks **ASPECT/ LIKES** Semishade and shelter, ideally frost-free **HARDINESS** Z 9-11

"A dome of shimmering purple blooms starts in early summer and lasts weeks."

116

Hypericum 'Rowallane'

This is possibly the finest of all the sadly underrated hypericums and was named after the garden in Northern Ireland where it is said to have been found as a seedling in the 1940s. It is a graceful shrub, at its best arching with flowers. It is fairly tender so needs to be given a plum spot in a sheltered, sunny place—ideally by a warm wall—if it is to perform. Believe me, the outlay of such a choice position is worth it for the impressively large, open, outward-facing, cupped flowers that appear in succession through summer and well into fall on upright then arching stems. Blooms are a delectable shade of golden yellow—almost the color of the yolk from a fresh, free-range hen egg. The leaves are oval and semideciduous. In a mild winter, they may be retained, but often most of them fall. The plant likes sun but will do well in part-shade during the hottest hours of the day. Moisture at the root is also important—this is not a plant for really dry soil.

HEIGHT AND SPREAD 5 x 2¾ft (150 x 80cm) **FLOWERS** Gorgeous golden flowers 1½in (4cm) across, from early summer to fall **ASPECT/LIKES** Sun, shelter, and moisture, ideally near a wall **HARDINESS** Z 7-9

117

Clematis 'Perle d'Azur'

An old but incredibly desirable selection, this is my favorite summer-flowering clematis by some margin. Said to be hard to propagate, it has never been common but is certainly well worth tracking down. The flowers are produced in profusion, opening from pointed buds. Initially, the blooms are tinged with pinkish purple, particularly along the midrib of each petal, but as they open wide and flat, they gradually age to a perfect sky-blue hue. The plant looks superb cascading from roses and other shrubs. I enjoy it with the yellow flowers of *Cestrum parqui*, but it also suits silvery and purple planting combinations well. While it seems to do best teamed with a partner climber or wall shrub, it can also be grown on trellis on a fence or wall or over an arch. Give it some consideration when planting, aiming to position the roots in cool shade and the top growth in sun. Prune the deciduous stems down to about 1ft (30cm) in winter, cutting just above a decent pair of buds.

118

Lilium regale

Plants that are popular are usually so for good reason; this majestic lily is a fine example, for it is probably the most often grown of all lilies and irresistible at bulb-planting time in fall. Willowy stems rise up in spring to around 6ft (1.8m), with slender lanceolate foliage radiating out, the tip crowned by flower buds—sometimes 10 or more. The buds, which are purple-flushed along the midrib of each petal, swell gradually until, one long-awaited day, the first burst open to sumptuous white trumpet-shaped flowers with a yellow heart. They have a heavenly perfume, at its best in the evening. I like to grow several lily bulbs together in a container—I find the plants live longer that way and are more versatile in the garden. I stand the pots in borders, moving them away after the flowers fade. Use a deep pot and include canes at planting, as stems need support. For earlier, taller plants, start under glass. Check for scarlet lily beetle regularly and pick off as they appear.

119

Persicaria alpina

A misleading name if ever there was one. You might imagine this perennial to be a diminutive alpine species. In fact, it is a garden giant, albeit a gentle well-behaved one, ideal for the back of a border, where its stout, well-branched stems can soar, forming a domed clump of growth to around 8ft (2.5m) or more. The shoots first appear in April and develop quickly. In early summer, plumes of flowers, held above healthy pointed lance-shaped foliage, collectively form a vast billowing cloud. The hollow stems can be cut to the ground in winter. It is related to knotweed, but rest assured: this is a well-behaved, easily managed, and first-rate garden plant.

120

Geranium 'Nimbus'

Summer-flowering herbaceous perennials do not come much more useful or easygoing than this excellent geranium, which teams attractive filigree foliage with masses of rather open starry flowers. It forms a low-spreading mound but is a fairly neat plant and can usually be accommodated toward the front of a border. It also looks good used in gravel gardens, where its foliage may be better appreciated. At the end of the year, crop all growth off at ground level and the plant will arise again the following spring, at which time a mulch of garden compost is appreciated. Clumps are easily divided, again in spring. It will grow in any soil except waterlogged.

117. HEIGHT AND SPREAD Climbs to 8ft (2.5m) **FLOWERS** Four- to six-petaled, 4in (10cm) across, produced in profusion from early to late summer **ASPECT/LIKES** Sunny, with roots in cool moist shade **HARDINESS** Z 4-11

118. COMMON NAME Regal lily **HEIGHT AND SPREAD** 6 x 3/4ft (180 x 20cm) **FLOWERS** Spectacular scented trumpets 8in (20cm) long in early summer **ASPECT/LIKES** Fertile moist soil with shelter and sun **HARDINESS** Z 3-10

119. HEIGHT AND SPREAD 8 x 6 1/2ft (2.5 x 2m) **FLOWERS** Tiny white flowers held in panicles 6in (15cm) long in early summer and lasting for a month or more **ASPECT/LIKES** Sun, shelter, and fertile moist soil **HARDINESS** Z 4-9

120. HEIGHT AND SPREAD 1 3/4 x 2ft (50 x 60cm) **FLOWERS** Five-petaled, violet-blue starry flowers, 1 1/4in (3cm) across in early summer, lasting for a month or so, with more throughout the summer **ASPECT/LIKES** Sun or part-shade **HARDINESS** Z 5-8

121

Aloe striatula

A remarkable hardy species native to mountainous parts of South Africa, from a genus of mostly tender, exotic-looking succulents, this terrific plant is essential for any tropical- or desert-style planting. The fleshy, dark-green leaves are long and pointed, with slightly serrated edges, and are held on initially upright then sprawling, rather woody, spreading stems, which arise from a clump. In high summer, from the tips of these stems emerge dramatic spikes of downward-pointing, waxy, yellow-and-green tubular flowers, which look a bit like those of red hot pokers and drip with nectar, attracting pollinating insects. Sharp drainage and full sun is key to success and, when happy, plants can get large. The best plants I know of grow on a sunny dry bank protected above by branches of a yew tree. A sheltered gravel garden or a spot by a sunny wall would suit them well. Once established, they never need watering, even in droughts. Stems root when they make contact with the ground, forming new plants, so propagation by detaching stem cuttings is easy. In a cold winter, top growth may be burned back, but shoots usually arise from the base.

COMMON NAME Striped-stemmed aloe **HEIGHT AND SPREAD** 3 x 3ft (1 x 1m) **FLOWERS** Tubular, 1in (2.5cm) long held on 8in (20cm) spikes atop tall stems in midsummer **ASPECT/LIKES** Full sun; dry, well-drained soil **HARDINESS** Z 8-12

122

Nemesia 'Wisley Vanilla'

This is a charming, low-growing perennial sold as an annual bedding plant, but in mild gardens, it often happily survives winter. It is a first-rate selection, plants bearing flowers on multitudes of stems that are initially upright and later become slightly sprawling. The pretty little blooms are white, sometimes tinged pink, with yellow eyes, and produce a delicious and quite distinctive sweet vanilla-like scent that carries really well on the air. Plants grow rapidly once bedded out and are also great in containers—perhaps in mixed compositions or in half pots on their own. Try growing them in the soil below potted standard bay or olive trees and keep well watered to prevent plants from going over early. Feed with a general-purpose liquid feed to keep flowers coming all summer. If you protect plants from winter cold and shear back in spring, they perform again the following year.

HEIGHT AND SPREAD 1 x 1ft (30 x 30cm) **FLOWERS** $^{5}/_{8}$in (1.5cm) across, produced in great profusion for months from early summer **ASPECT/LIKES** Sunny warm place, best kept frost-free in winter **HARDINESS** Z 9-11

123

Olea europaea

It's not difficult to understand why olives are now regularly planted in milder gardens—easy to grow, drought-resistant when established, and with wonderful silver leaves that at their best shine in the sun against a blue midsummer sky, they are so redolent of warmer climes. Your tree will even crop, although fruit need to be cured to make them edible. Small plants can be pot grown until large enough to plant, but bear in mind that they are not reliably hardy, so choose a warm, sunny, open yet sheltered place. They are quick growing, so there is no need to buy a mature specimen. A treelike shape can be encouraged by removing lower branches from canopies (a process known as "legging up"), but trees take a while to develop the characterful trunks so desired by garden designers. I love my tree but thought hard before recommending this plant. Most are imported, risking introducing the bacterial plant disease Xylella, which has devastated groves in parts of Italy. Before you buy, ensure that phytosanitary regulations have been strictly observed.

COMMON NAME Olive **HEIGHT AND SPREAD** 16–26ft (5–8m) tall and across **FLOWERS** Tiny white flowers held in clusters in late spring **ASPECT/LIKES** Full sun, shelter from cold, good drainage **HARDINESS** Z 8-10

124

Jasminum officinale 'Inverleith'

If a climber with perfumed flowers is required, jasmine is usually a default choice, but, sadly, seldom is this particular selection recommended. The strongly scented flowers appear in clusters at the end of stems in midsummer, as usual, but this plant differs from others most obviously in that its bud are cherry red. On opening, the little blooms, although the usual white inside, remain conspicuously red outside. This is enhanced further by the deciduous pinnate foliage, which is tinged bronze red when young, aging to rich dark green, the leaflets smaller and better defined than usual, giving the plant a most refined look. And then, in the fall, the final surprise: before falling, these leaves reliably go on to develop impressive rich-red tints. The plant makes a great specimen climber for a wall, fence, or pergola, as long as support is provided for its twining stems.

COMMON NAME Jasmine **HEIGHT AND SPREAD** Climbs to 13ft (4m) **FLOWERS** Trumpet-shaped flowers, 3/4in (2cm) long, in midsummer **ASPECT/LIKES** Sun or part-shade, needs support, but easy **HARDINESS** Z 7-10

125

Hemerocallis 'Fried Green Tomatoes'

COMMON NAME Daylily **HEIGHT AND SPREAD** 2 3/4 x 2ft (80 x 60cm) **FLOWERS** Funnel-shaped, 4 3/4in (12cm) across, each lasting just a day in midsummer **ASPECT/LIKES** Sun and fertile well-drained moist soil **HARDINESS** Z 3-9

I wasn't a big fan of *Hemerocallis* until I visited Strictly Daylilies, a wonderful nursery near Cambridge run by Paula Dyason, who introduced me to this superb plant with its eye-popping flowers. An American hybrid (the US is where many of the best new daylily selections come from), it has vibrant two-tone flowers around 4 3/4in (12cm) across. They are rich red with a bright green throat, although the green color extends well into the centers of the petals. As the flower opens, these petals sweep back, emphasizing the green even more. The many flowers open atop slender stems to around 32in (80cm) tall. They last just a day, but, this being a modern hybrid, more stems are thrown up during the summer for a long flowering season. It even does well in a large container.

126

Himalayacalamus falconeri

The upright, green canes of this bamboo are tinged burgundy as they emerge and reach around 13ft (4m) before arching gracefully outward. Plants form a large, tight clump and resemble feathery fountains of emerald green that shift and sway in the breeze. Canes become ever narrower toward the tips and carry slender, lanceolate papery leaves, at their best in midsummer. Winter takes its toll on this tender species and, in a cold year, plants can be defoliated. New leaves will arise from canes in spring, but it can be midsummer before the plant fully recovers. Before new leaves develop, remove old dead canes, to keep the plant looking its best. Bamboos have a reputation for being invasive, but this never misbehaves.

COMMON NAME Bamboo **HEIGHT AND SPREAD** 13 x 13ft (4 x 4m) **ASPECT/LIKES** Sheltered, lightly shaded site, moist well-drained soil **HARDINESS** Z 9-10

127

Melianthus major

This perennial is a shrubby plant but is normally herbaceous in colder areas, top growth and hollow stems cut to the ground by winter cold. The large pinnate, deeply toothed leaves reach around 16in (40cm) and have a striking, jagged look, at their best from midsummer onward. They are held on sturdy upright stems that spread out from the base. Leaf color varies, so it is best to pick your plants carefully before buying. I have two in the same position—one with sea-green leaves, the other a remarkable duck-egg blue. If your *Melianthus* retains top growth, you might get to enjoy its honey-scented flowers. But I feel that foliage is the main event here, and cropping old stems to the ground in spring for the freshest, largest leaves later in the year is a better bet. Give the plant a protective winter mulch.

COMMON NAME Honey flower **HEIGHT AND SPREAD** $6\frac{1}{2}$ x $6\frac{1}{2}$ft (2 x 2m) with shelter **FLOWERS** Dark red held in a spike to 1ft (30cm) long in late spring **ASPECT/LIKES** Sun, warmth, fertile soil **HARDINESS** Z 9-10

128

Bergenia ciliata

This unusual bergenia is unlike the usual evergreen elephant's ears that often divide gardeners' opinions. To begin with, its foliage is not shiny; instead, the fresh green rounded leaves are coated in fine pale hairs, particularly at the slightly crimped edges, making them tempting to touch and beautiful to look at throughout summer, especially after rain or heavy dew. They are also larger and lusher than most other species', and deciduous, fading with the first frosts. What is familiar are the trunk-like rhizomes the plant gradually develops, in time forming a sizable clump. The flowers come in early spring, just before the foliage starts to appear. It's a time to hope for mild weather, as they are easily spoiled by frost. They are carried on reddish stems in rounded clusters, opening white, aging pink. *Bergenia ciliata* suits exotic planting well but also adds a lush touch to traditional schemes.

HEIGHT AND SPREAD 1¼ x 2¾ft (40 x 80cm)
FLOWERS Pale pink, held in clusters in early spring
ASPECT/LIKES Sheltered warm position in part-shade or sun, moist fertile soil **HARDINESS** Z 5-8

129. COMMON NAME Oak-leaved hydrangea **HEIGHT AND SPREAD** 5 x 6½ft (1.5 x 2m) **FLOWERS** ¾in (2cm) across in 8–12in (20–30cm) long panicles from midsummer to fall **ASPECT/LIKES** Part-shade, fertile well-drained soil **HARDINESS** Z 5-9

130. COMMON NAME Daylily 'Mini Pearl' **HEIGHT AND SPREAD** 12 x 16in (30x40cm) **FLOWERS** Funnel-shaped, 2¾in (7cm) across, each lasting just a day in midsummer **ASPECT/LIKES** Sun and fertile well-drained moist soil **HARDINESS** Z 3-9

131. COMMON NAME Artichoke agave **HEIGHT AND SPREAD** 16 x 20in (40 x 50cm) rosette **FLOWERS** Yellow, tubular, to 2¾in (7cm) long on 13ft (4m) spikes in summer **ASPECT/LIKES** Full sun, shelter, drainage, protection from winter wet **HARDINESS** Z 9-11

132. COMMON NAME Cape leadwort **HEIGHT AND SPREAD** Climbs to 13ft (4m) **FLOWERS** ¾in (2cm) long, five-petaled flowers carried in clusters from midsummer to fall **ASPECT/LIKES** Sunny frost-free conditions **HARDINESS** Z 8-11

129

Hydrangea quercifolia Snowflake

I have only recently been converted to the charms of hydrangeas and it was this plant, also known as 'Brido,' that helped me see the light, for it is a great shrub—easily grown, vigorous, but fairly compact, doing well in some shade and providing interest for months. The show starts in early spring with the handsome emerging large oak-leaf-shaped gray-green foliage. By the time this matures, numerous flower heads appear from tips of shoots—to around 1ft (30cm) long, arching outward. Individual flowers have a touch of green and appear to be double, owing to the extra bracts, resulting in impressive flower power that endures all summer. By fall, the heads begin to turn parchment brown and foliage develops fiery hues. The plant will also stand some sun and, once established, seems to tolerate drought surprisingly well.

130

Hemerocallis 'Mini Pearl'

July is the peak month for daylilies, and this rather dainty selection is worth growing for its lovely soft-peach-pink blooms, the throats of which are a gently contrasting warm yellow. These trumpet-shaped flowers are not particularly large, to around 2¾in (7cm) across, but are beautifully formed, with backswept, slightly ruffled petals. While each flower lasts just a day, each 1ft (30cm) slender stem carries plenty of buds, and more stems may arise through summer in good conditions, held above rather grassy, arching green foliage. It is an easy plant for sun and fertile soil that does not get too dry, although established plants shrug off drought well. It needs little care, other than snipping off faded flower stems and cropping off yellowed foliage to the ground in late fall. The flowers are good for adding an unexpected touch of warmth to cool planting schemes of silver, pink, and white.

131

Agave parryi var. *truncata*

This succulent is a typical agave, but the fleshy leaves are rather short and rounded, although still edged in fearsome spines. It creates a handsome rosette, like a huge houseleek. The leaves are beautiful silver-blue, with contrasting black spines. I've never risked my original plant outdoors all winter. It does freely produce offsets, and one of these I've had outdoors in a pot by a house wall through mild winters with little damage. One day my plant may flower and die, a spectacular if sad event. If planted outside, protect from winter wet with a sheet of polycarbonate over the top.

132

Plumbago auriculata

An indispensable conservatory or greenhouse climber, this tough, reliable plant delights in summer with nonstop heads of soft-blue flowers. It is vigorous and will scale a 10–13ft (3–4m) wall, the climbing stems needing support by wires or trellis. Grow in as large a pot as you can, or plant in the ground. If temperatures drop close to freezing, the plant will defoliate, but new shoots will appear in spring. Grow in full sun or light shade for part of the day; in summer it likes plenty of air if under glass. Young plants may be bedded out for summer, grown up an obelisk. In very mild gardens, it is worth trying out all year in a very sheltered position. There are selections with blooms of richer blue or white.

133
Nicotiana alata 'Grandiflora'

I like to have white-flowered tobacco plants in the garden for their evening presence; both the elegance of their flowers and their powerful fragrance. This selection is great for pot cultivation or bedding out and is easily raised from seed sown under cover in midspring. The resulting plants will be ready to put out after the last frosts.
At first, plants consist of a clump of soft, slightly sticky foliage, but by midsummer this is topped by 2ft (60cm) tall branched stems bearing masses of flowers that are sweetly scented, especially after dark. Flowers are apt to be rather floppy and do best in light shade, perhaps with morning sun. If too dry, plants can suffer from mildew. I like to grow three plants in a 1-gallon pot of commercial potting mix. That way, you can sink pots in borders or place among other containers for evening interest.

134
Francoa sonchifolia

This useful herbaceous perennial makes an appealing sight in summer, when it produces numerous airy wands of five-petaled flowers. The lovely blooms are usually white or pale pink with pink streaks, but there are also more richly colored selections. Flowers can appear over 2–3 months on successive flower spikes. Helpfully, this Chilean native is also evergreen and ground covering so is a good choice for a sunny or lightly shaded place, as long as the soil is not too dry. It's also ideal for underplanting a taller plant—I once saw it flowering below the tree fern *Dicksonia antarctica*, its foliage forming a lush skirt. The basal leaves are glossy green with wavy margins. They may develop red tints in fall and, as long as conditions are not too cold, look good well into winter. Any leaves that are a little shabby can be removed.

135
Tulbaghia violacea

Whether in a container or in the ground, this bulbous perennial is easily grown and flowers all summer. Plants arise in spring after winter—fine, grassy gray-green leaves forming a clump smelling distinctly of garlic. Then, from early summer, slender flower stems carrying dainty blooms develop. The flowers have a sweet scent and appear in succession into fall. In winter, the plant retreats below ground; it is not entirely hardy. If in the ground, it is best with a mulch of garden compost over the top; if in a pot, place in a cold frame or somewhere sheltered, just in case. The plant wants as much sun as possible in a freely drained place—a rock garden, the foot of a sunny wall, or gravel garden would suit.

136
Plectranthus argentatus 'Hill House'

The large velvety, silver leaves of this sprawling, shrubby, tender perennial are edged handsomely with cream. It is ideal for summer pots in sun, perfect with white geraniums, pink *Diascia*, or in front of *Melianthus major*. It flowers in fall, but the leaves are the main event. Move plants indoors in winter, or root cuttings in a jar of water at the end of the summer.

133. COMMON NAME Tobacco plant **HEIGHT AND SPREAD** 2 x 1ft (60 x 30cm) **FLOWERS** Five petaled, green-tinged ivory-white, tubular with flared opening, 2in (5cm) long in midsummer **ASPECT/LIKES** Sun, fertile moist soil **HARDINESS** Z 10-11

134. COMMON NAME Bridal wreath **HEIGHT AND SPREAD** 2¾ft (80cm) in flower, 6½ft (2m) spread **FLOWERS** ½in (1cm) across, held in 2¾in (7cm) spires atop tall stems in mid- to late summer **ASPECT/LIKES** Sunny, sheltered site, not too dry **HARDINESS** Z 4-9

135. COMMON NAME Society garlic **HEIGHT AND SPREAD** 16 x 8in (40 x 20cm) **FLOWERS** Violet-mauve starry blooms, ½in (1cm) across, carried in clusters all summer **ASPECT/LIKES** Sun and sharp drainage **HARDINESS** Z 7-10

136. HEIGHT AND SPREAD 2½ x 2ft (75 x 60cm) **FLOWERS** Tiny, off-white, held in a 1¼in (3cm) long spire in fall **ASPECT/LIKES** Sun and shelter, frost-free over winter **HARDINESS** Z 7-10

137

Sedum takesimense ATLANTIS

This plant is perfectly suited to the conditions many gardeners have today. Drought resistant and completely hardy, it will grow in really shallow soil so could thrive as a plant for a green roof but is equally versatile in full sun in a rock garden, gravel garden, planted sink, or alpine pot. A compact carpeting perennial, it has brightly variegated foliage held in whorls around spreading stems. The little serrated oval leaves are typically edged broadly with cream, the centers green. Some stems are all cream, others more green. As the shoots emerge in spring, they can be pink tinted, then through summer they are capped with heads of yellow flowers, which readily attract pollinators. Watch for vine weevil. Treat plants in containers with Nemasys biological control.

HEIGHT AND SPREAD 6 x 16in (15x40cm) **FLOWERS** Tiny, bright yellow, held in heads 3/4in (2cm) across in summer **ASPECT/LIKES** Full sun and sharp drainage **HARDINESS** Z 4-9

138

Hebe 'Midsummer Beauty'

Extraordinary in its flowering performance, this evergreen shrub is probably the most valuable hebe of those cultivated mostly for their blooms. Easy and quick to grow, it forms a large rounded bush, its relatively large, long, rich-green leaves glossy and tinged purple when young. Then, from early to midsummer, the flowers begin. They are tiny, held in long slender flower heads (racemes) to around 6in (15cm) long, the blooms opening purple but fading to white as they age. Flowering can be impressively profuse: at their peak, plants are covered in racemes at varying stages of maturity, displaying different tones of purple and regularly attracting bees and butterflies. And the flowers just keep on coming, the plants remaining impressive well into fall, and even flowering in winter if the weather is mild—I've had cut flowers decorating the table at Christmas. Despite its appearance, it is pretty hardy, best with some shelter from cold in a sunny spot, but it tolerates part-shade and likes somewhere not too dry. Plants can be pruned in spring if they've grown too big.

HEIGHT AND SPREAD 10 x 6½ft (3 x 2m) **FLOWERS** Tiny, held in flower heads up to 6in (15cm) long almost year-round **ASPECT/LIKES** Sunny site, not too cold **HARDINESS** Z 9-10

139

Bidens ferulifolia 'Bee Alive'

Mexican *Bidens ferulifolia* has kept breeders busy in recent years, much to the advantage of gardeners, for many selections make excellent summer bedding and every year more seem to arrive. With season-long flower power, this selection, a low-growing tender perennial, is a knockout, blooming for months. It has spreading stems that lie on the soil surface, bearing rich-green dainty fernlike foliage, ideal for cascading from hanging baskets or over the edge of containers but equally at home at the front of sunny borders. The flowers have five to seven pointed petals and are dramatically two-tone, each with a wide circular central eye, the petal tips contrasting in red-orange. Flowers smother the plant for weeks on end and attract pollinating insects. This is a plant for a sunny open place. Dead-head occasionally until the first frost.

140

Dierama pulcherrimum

Among the plants I wish I were able to grow well, angel's fishing rods come near the top. A cormous, evergreen perennial native to southern Africa, the plant forms clumps with tough, upright lance-shaped, grassy foliage to around 3ft (1m) tall. In summer, upright then arching wiry stems arise. These stand clear of the foliage and bear showy blooms in pink or mauve but occasionally in white or dark-purple. The effect is enchanting, bells swaying in the breeze for several weeks. The downside is finding a place where they flourish. Summer moisture and good drainage are key, although I've seen great plants in heavy clay, and the best ones I've admired sprouted from paving cracks on a sunny terrace. Plants are easy from seed and it's the best way to propagate, as they hate being moved or divided. It is tempting to tug at browning foliage, but this often results in breaking off entire tufts of growth.

141

Itea ilicifolia

Wall shrubs are such useful plants for masking fences, walls, and garden buildings, and many are so exciting, they make these situations desirable rather than a problem. This special evergreen looks, at first glance, like a holly with glossy, broadly oval leaves that have spiny tips, but the spines are barely prickly at all, and the stems slender. You can grow it as a free-standing plant to form a wide, dome-shaped shrub, but, trained against something, it presents its dangling tassels of flowers in a more impressive manner. The surprise comes at dusk, when they give off a distinctive and delicious honeyed scent that carries well on the air. It is easy to grow in any well-drained soil and needs little care when established.

142

Phlox paniculata 'Blue Paradise'

Perennial phlox may seem a bit old-fashioned, but there are some arresting selections that deserve a closer look, as they fit well into modern gardens, with their upright habit and long-lasting flowers that are fresh at a time after midsummer when early perennials are petering out and late ones have yet to get going. This is a stunner. It bears showy panicles of large, red-eyed flowers, with each of the five petals paler toward the center. They seem to glow in the evening and are sweetly perfumed, attracting pollinating insects. They are carried on reddish stems, which may need staking in windy sites, the display lasting a month. Mildew is generally not a problem.

139. COMMON NAME Fern-leaved beggar tick **HEIGHT AND SPREAD** 8 x 12in (20 x 30cm) **FLOWERS** Rounded, flat, and daisy-like, 1¼in (3cm) across, from midsummer to late fall **ASPECT/LIKES** Full sun and fertile soil, not too dry **HARDINESS** Z 10-11

140. COMMON NAME Angel's fishing rod **HEIGHT AND SPREAD** 5 x 3ft (1.5 x 1m) **FLOWERS** Bell-shaped, up to 1¼in (3cm) long, through midsummer **ASPECT/LIKES** Sun, open site, free-draining moist soil **HARDINESS** Z 7-10

141. COMMON NAME Holly-leaved sweet spire **HEIGHT AND SPREAD** 10 x 6½ft (3 x 2m) **FLOWERS** Tiny, in 8in (20cm) long clusters from midsummer until fall **ASPECT/LIKES** Sun or part-shade, shelter, position by a wall or fence **HARDINESS** Z 7-10

142. HEIGHT AND SPREAD 3 x 1¾ft (100 x 50cm) **FLOWERS** ¾–1¼in (2–3cm) across, held in 4in (10cm) wide heads through midsummer **ASPECT/LIKES** Sun or light shade, fairly moist fertile soil **HARDINESS** Z 4-8

143

Phlox paniculata 'Grey Lady'

When I first encountered this bewitching phlox, I was so impressed, I bought a plant for a herbaceous border and so far it has done well. Its 3ft (1m) stems hold large heads of what initially seem to be lavender-gray flowers, but on closer inspection, the individual blooms are actually pale mauve with a large white central eye. They are also scented. Lower leaves fade a little by flowering time, so position it in the middle of a border in sun; mine is behind shrubby silver *Artemisia* 'Powis Castle.'
Be prepared to water in summer during dry spells. This phlox would be great in a garden planted for evening effect, the flowers providing a ghostly touch at dusk.

HEIGHT AND SPREAD 3 x 2ft (100x60cm) **FLOWERS** ¾in (2cm) wide, held in 4in (10cm) wide heads in midsummer **ASPECT/LIKES** Sun, fertile well-drained soil **HARDINESS** Z 4-8

HEIGHT AND SPREAD 16 x 20in (40x50cm) FLOWERS Five-petaled, dark-veined magenta blooms produced in profusion all summer and into fall ASPECT/LIKES Sun, open site, poor well-drained soil HARDINESS Z 5-9

144

Erodium manescavii

Most erodiums are small herbaceous perennials well suited to rock gardens or alpine beds, but this outstanding species is larger, showier, and more adaptable and fits easily into the open garden. It is also simple to grow. Plants form low neat clumps of rather attractive soft, featherlike foliage. Then in summer, 8in (20cm) tall stems arise, bearing a succession of flowers. As individual blooms fade, more arise. *Erodium* seeds around freely, but young plants are easily removed if unwanted. It suits the fronts of borders well and thrives in gravel gardens, standing up to prolonged dry spells. As flower stems fade, they can be gently tugged off to keep plants tidy. Leaves mostly die down over winter, when they can also be trimmed off.

145

Lantana camara

Although it is a ubiquitous weed in tropical countries, I find this exotic-looking tender shrubby perennial irresistible. Sold as bedding in garden centers, it bears round heads of flowers in jewel-like colors, from red, yellow, and orange, to purple, pink, and even white. The individual flowers change color as they age and are held above rough rich-green pungent-smelling foliage. Grow it in a container in sun or enjoy it in a frost-free greenhouse or conservatory, where it will overwinter. Sometimes plants are available grafted atop a tall stem, like a standard fuchsia. I'm not the only one drawn to this plant; I first noticed it as a child in a glasshouse at a zoo, where plants were smothered with tropical butterflies. In Puglia, in southern Italy, where it is common, I've seen swallowtail butterflies drink its nectar.

HEIGHT AND SPREAD 1¼ x 2ft (40x60cm), much larger if kept frost free FLOWERS Small, held in heads 1¼in (3cm) across all summer long ASPECT/LIKES Sun, heat, frost-free in winter HARDINESS Z 10-11

146

Lotus berthelotii

A wondrous thing, this tender perennial is, in fact, a member of the pea family and originally native to the Canary Islands, where it is thought now to be extinct. Happily, it is widespread in cultivation, a great example of the conservational value of gardening. Plants produce cascading stems of fine, silver-green, soft, needle-shaped foliage, then in summer dramatic rich-red pealike flowers are held in twos or threes, just above the foliage. Commonly, this plant is grown in hanging baskets, a spectacular sight, but it is also attractive spilling from raised pots and urns. Alternatively, allow it to carpet a sunny bank or gravel garden as a change from traditional bedding. Frost will finish it, but if you bring it into a heated conservatory, it can survive winter. *Lotus maculatus* is similar, with slightly wider leaflets and yellow-orange flowers, and there are hybrids between the two.

COMMON NAMES Parrot's beak, coral gem **HEIGHT AND SPREAD** Cascading to 2ft (60cm) or more **FLOWERS** ¾–1¼in (2–3cm) long, held in small clusters in mid- to late summer **ASPECT/LIKES** Sun, warmth, well-drained soil **HARDINESS** Z 10-11

147

Impatiens tinctoria

From the African rainforests comes this incredible, surprisingly hardy relative of the humble busy lizzie. Plants grow as herbaceous perennials, developing an open shrubby shape and forming fleshy underground tubers rather like those of a dahlia. Shoots arise from the ground in late spring and grow quickly, the large lush oval leaves carried on thick succulent, almost translucent branching stems that can reach 6½ft (2m) in a sheltered position. From mid- to late summer, flowers appear on slender stems from upper shoots. They are quite remarkable, looking rather like moths—white with red-purple markings, two large winglike rounded lobes, and a long spur at the back. They have a sweet scent, strongest in the evening and morning. The display can last into fall; the first hard frost will cut plants to the ground and end the fun for the year, but they survive winter well, especially given a mulch of garden compost. Choose a sheltered corner with a little sun during the day in a fertile, well-drained, moist soil. Capsid bug can trouble plants—pick them off if you see them.

COMMON NAME Dyers busy lizzie **HEIGHT AND SPREAD** 6½ x 5ft (2 x 1.5m) **FLOWERS** 2½in (6cm) including spur, from midsummer until fall **ASPECT/LIKES** Sun, shelter, moist fertile soil **HARDINESS** Z 7-10

148. COMMON NAME Lilac-flowered honeysuckle **HEIGHT AND SPREAD** 6½ft (2m) **FLOWERS** Small, tubular, held in clusters in midsummer **ASPECT/LIKES** Sun, well-drained open site **HARDINESS** Z 4-7

149. HEIGHT AND SPREAD 13–20 x 10ft (4–6 x 3m) **FLOWERS** 6in (15cm) across, scented, in midsummer **ASPECT/LIKES** Sun, warmth, well-drained site **HARDINESS** Z 6-9

150. COMMON NAME Salsilla **HEIGHT AND SPREAD** Climbs to 6½ft (2m) or more **FLOWERS** Tubular, ¾in (2cm) long, held in heads 4in (10cm) across in mid- to late summer **ASPECT/LIKES** Sun, shelter, fertile moist soil **HARDINESS** Z 7-10

151. COMMON NAME Marvel of Peru **HEIGHT AND SPREAD** 1¾ x 1ft (50 x 30cm) **FLOWERS** Tubular, ¾–1¼in (2–3cm) across, from midsummer until the first frosts **ASPECT/LIKES** Sun, open site, well-drained soil **HARDINESS** Z 7-10

148

Lonicera syringantha

When I first encountered this easy-to-grow deciduous shrub, I was stumped: is it a curious lilac or possibly some daphne? In fact, it is a rather super honeysuckle, native to China. It forms a well-branched, bushy plant around 6½ft (2m) or more high and across. The small oval blue-green leaves are held on slender purple stems. In summer, pale-mauve flowers appear in multitudes from leaf axils. They are tubular, starry seen end-on, each with four petals, and are sweetly perfumed, the scent carrying on the air when the plant is in full bloom. For good displays of flowers, plants are best in sun, although they will take a little shade. The plant I first encountered was growing on clay, while my own is on sand, so it is not picky about soil. Keep the plant trim by removing the oldest flowered stems after the display has finished.

149

Magnolia grandiflora 'Kay Parris'

Noble evergreen *Magnolia grandiflora* is a spectacular but large tree that needs a pretty big garden for its handsome foliage and impressive flowers to be appreciated fully. However, this fine, fairly recent and, importantly, compact arrival is one that can be accommodated more readily. Easily grown, hardy, and upright rather than spreading, it forms a broadly column-shaped tree to 13–20ft (4–6m) high. The elliptical leaves are dark green above with soft-coppery-brown undersides and are handsome all year round. One of the great characteristics of this superb selection is that the flowers appear even on young plants in summer; these are large and ivory-white, with the delicious creamy lemon fragrance common to the species. Plants are best in full sun, although they will stand some shade. For a few years, it will even grow in a container.

150

Bomarea edulis

Few climbing herbaceous perennials are widely grown in gardens, yet many are great garden plants. This one, native to Mexico, is among the more exotic-looking, and it's worth spending time making it feel at home. In late spring, shoots emerge from the ground and when they find vertical support—a cane perhaps—they twine their way upward, stems carrying pointed oval leaves. By mid- to late summer, flower heads appear. The outer petals are pink, inner ones greenish-yellow with dark speckles. On young plants, heads carry around 10 flowers; established specimens have 20–30; once multiple stems arise, numerous flower heads can be enjoyed for weeks. Plants are not particularly hardy, so it is wise to mulch over the tubers with garden compost in winter.

151

Mirabilis jalapa

If you fancy something different for your summer borders, marvel of Peru might be for you. Growing from a carrot-shaped tuber, this perennial has a neat, helpfully bushy habit with lush pointed leaves and, from midsummer, lots of funnel-shaped flowers in neon colors, including purple, pink, yellow, and orange, as well as white. Some blooms are marbled in two tones. Flowers do not open until late afternoon and give off a sweet scent. The display lasts until the frosts, when you can dig up the tubers and store like dahlias or leave them in the ground and let them take their chances—in a mild winter they survive. I save some of the seeds to sow in spring; they are easy to germinate.

152

Punica granatum var. *nana*

If not grown only for their edible fruit, pomegranates are also grown for their showy orange flowers and drought-tolerant nature. However, to make displays worthwhile, the small trees or large deciduous shrubs need the sunniest site against a south-facing wall, a luxury few gardeners will have in quantity. The solution is to grow this superb dwarf selection, ideal for a container, which you can move to the hottest, sunniest spots. Plants are late coming into leaf in spring, reddish shoots emerging from slender but densely twiggy growth. The little leaves are glossy and yellow-green and, in time, plants make a miniature treelike shape. In summer, the little orange flowers begin to form, far more freely than in full-size selections, and these may go on to form tiny inedible fruit. Leaves briefly turn yellow before falling. I pop my plant into a cold greenhouse for winter to keep off excess wet, but against a house wall is fine too.

COMMON NAME Dwarf pomegranate **HEIGHT AND SPREAD** 1 x 1ft (30 x 30cm) **FLOWERS** 1¼in (3cm) long in mid- to late summer **ASPECT/LIKES** Full sun, warmth, and well-drained soil **HARDINESS** Z 7-10

153

Fascicularia bicolor subsp. *canaliculata*

Bromeliads (members of the pineapple family) are common house plants, but this is one that will grow outdoors in some areas. Native to Chile, it has slender dark-green serrated foliage that forms a circular rosette. Mature plants can reach 3ft (1m) across, while older plants make mounded clumps of rosettes. In mid- to late summer, inner leaves turn lipstick-red, and at the center of rosettes appear heads of white buds that open to blue flowers with orange stamens, in a display that lasts weeks. In the wild, plants are pollinated by hummingbirds and usually grow in the ground, although sometimes on tree branches—something adventurous gardeners might like to try. Plants need sun to flower and hate waterlogging, so sharp drainage is vital. Choose a spot sheltered from rain and frost at the base of a tree or in a rock garden. Alternatively, grow in a pot and move to shelter for winter. If you can keep plants frost-free, *Fascicularia bicolor* subsp. *bicolor* is more dramatic, but tender.

HEIGHT AND SPREAD 1¼ x 3ft (40 x 100cm) **FLOWERS** Tubular, ¾in (2cm) long, from mid-/late summer to early fall **ASPECT/LIKES** Sun or part-shade, warmth, shelter, and sharp drainage **HARDINESS** Z 8-10

154
Eucomis bicolor

For a hit of the exotic, this easy-to-grow bulb has much to recommend it. Broad, lush, bright-green strap-shaped foliage forms a rosette during summer, but, as the season reaches its peak, this is overtopped by a stout green stem speckled with dark purple, bearing a cylindrical head composed of dozens of pale-green and purple bell-shaped flowers, all sheltering below a distinctive leafy topknot. The floral display is long-lived and, even after flowers set seed, the pineapple-like appearance continues, often until frost finally melts everything away. Plants will bulk up in mild areas and eventually form a handsome clump. They look best in groups of 3–5 bulbs initially and also do really well in containers. They are not fully hardy, so mulch bulbs in the ground with garden compost, and move pots into a cold frame for the winter. *Eucomis* like well-drained rich soil, sun, and moisture.

155
Bergenia pacumbis

This species is the most exotic-looking of bergenias. I remember vividly seeing a clump in the Cornish garden of plantsman Charlie Pridham—the mound of superbly glossy leaves 1ft (30cm) or more across took my breath away. A deciduous species, it grows like other bergenias from a trunklike rhizome that creeps across the soil surface. Foliage gets going in early spring and can be damaged by frost, but flowers arise before it develops—clusters of pink-tinged white blooms held on slender pink stems—pretty enough, but secondary to the leaves. These reach peak size in late summer—the young growth bronze tinged, the vast mature leaves with a slightly puckered surface. If any species has foliage remotely like an elephant's ear, this is it. Plant it somewhere sunny and open but sheltered in well-drained, moist soil. Frost will kill off the foliage swiftly, so it's worth protecting the clump over winter with mulch.

156
Passiflora 'Betty Myles Young'

Among all the plants we can grow outdoors, perhaps the most distinctive are passion flowers. Few survive winter outside in mild climates, so this wonderful, vigorous and, importantly, hardy cultivar with astonishing flowers was a revelation when I first saw it at the home of passion-flower breeder Myles Irvine, who named the plant after his late mother. Since then, it has become quite widely grown—and with good reason, for this evergreen climber bears masses of purple flowers that stand out well from the rich-green, five-lobed foliage. It is hardy to 18°F (–8°C), although young plants may need protection from both the cold and the attentions of slugs and snails.

157
Woodwardia radicans

I simply love this fern. I have admired it in so many of my favorite exotic gardens, all of which provide the plant with what it needs to survive—namely, moisture, shade, and protection from almost all frost. In return, the plant will form a clump, producing its extraordinary arching apple-green fronds, which are at their best by late summer, reaching 3ft (1m) in length. When the fronds touch the ground, they form plantlets at the tips, which then root. Except in the mildest districts, it is, at least in winter, a plant for the conservatory or greenhouse, where, in a large pot or border, it makes an elegant choice for a cool shaded corner, since, when growing happily, it is a plant of great beauty.

154. COMMON NAME Pineapple lily **HEIGHT AND SPREAD** 2¾ x 2ft (80 x 60cm) **FLOWERS** ¾in (2cm) across, bell-shaped, in 12–20in (30–50cm) spikes, from midsummer until midfall **ASPECT/LIKES** Sun, fertile well-drained soil **HARDINESS** Z 7-10

155. COMMON NAME Chinese elephant's ears **HEIGHT AND SPREAD** 1¾ x 2¾ft (50 x 80cm) **FLOWERS** Small, held in 4in (10cm) heads in spring **ASPECT/LIKES** Sheltered warm site, well-drained moist soil **HARDINESS** Z 6-7

156. HEIGHT AND SPREAD Climbs to 10ft (3m) or more **FLOWERS** 4¾in (12cm) across, from spring until midfall **ASPECT/LIKES** Sun, shelter, support, well-drained soil **HARDINESS** Z 8-10

157. COMMON NAME European chain fern **HEIGHT AND SPREAD** 3 x 6½ft (1 x 2m) **ASPECT/LIKES** Very sheltered, shaded, and moist, with protection from frost **HARDINESS** Z 8-9

158

Salvia 'Hot Lips'

Perhaps now the most widely grown of all flowering salvias—thanks in part to its memorable name but also because it's so dependable—this plant is an easy and attractive performer with an admirably long flowering season. A shrubby evergreen perennial, it forms a broad dome-shaped plant of brittle stems to around 2ft (60cm) high and across. From the tips of shoots appear sprays of small but striking flowers—usually two-tone in white with bold red lower petals, although in the heat of summer all-red and all-white flowers also emerge, which further add to the plant's appeal. The flowers don't stop coming until it gets really chilly. The display is not dazzling, but there is always something to enjoy, and it is a good plant for mixing with other sun lovers, such as *Artemisia*, sedum, lavender, and *Cistus*, and even for growing between roses. The foliage is nicely scented (it reminds me rather of black currants) and, best of all, the plant is really tolerant of heat and drought once established. Salvias can get a bit scrawny after a few years; to keep them looking good, give them a regular trim each spring.

HEIGHT AND SPREAD 2 x 3ft (60 x 100cm) **FLOWERS** ¾in (2cm) long, variably bicolored, nonstop from late summer until winter **ASPECT/LIKES** Sunny well-drained open site **HARDINESS** Z 7-10

159

Dianthus barbatus Festival Series

If put together well and looked after, summer containers brimming with seasonal plants usually last in beauty well into fall, but there are times when things do not go as planned and you need something to fill a pot or two late in the season. I have found these terrific dianthus a superb solution, far better than I ever expected after I had to plant some containers for an August wedding—my own, in fact. These plants are compact, and in a sunny, fairly open place, they thicken out well and are great around a feature plant, such as a variegated *Plectranthus* or pelargonium. The green foliage is slender and topped by short stems bearing clusters of sparkling confetti-like flowers, the edges of the petals beautifully zigzagged. Blooms open to shades of pink, exquisitely patterned and marked in red and white, and they just keep on coming, with the plants staying fresh into fall, when cool weather seems to invigorate them. Leave in situ over winter—they are hardy and will flower again the following spring, which can be a dilemma: to keep something from last year or try something new and exciting? Why not hedge you bets and hold on to the best plants, replanting and feeding well.

HEIGHT AND SPREAD 6 x 4in (15 x 10cm) **FLOWERS** ¾–1¼in (2–3cm) across, held in clusters in late summer and fall **ASPECT/LIKES** Sun, open well-drained site **HARDINESS** Z 3-9

160. COMMON NAME Blue daisy **HEIGHT AND SPREAD** 8 x 12in (20 x 30cm) **FLOWERS** ¾in (2cm) across, produced in multitudes in late summer **ASPECT/LIKES** Sun, sheltered open site, frost free in winter **HARDINESS** Z 8-11

161. HEIGHT AND SPREAD Climbs to 13ft (4m) **FLOWERS** ¾in (2cm) across, held in 3–4in (8–10cm) bunches, from late spring to late fall **ASPECT/LIKES** Sun, shelter, somewhere to climb **HARDINESS** Z 9-10

162. HEIGHT AND SPREAD 8 x 16in (20 x 40cm) **FLOWERS** ½–¾in (1–2cm) across, appearing in masses through summer and fall **ASPECT/LIKES** Sun or part-sun, frost free in winter **HARDINESS** Z 10-11

163. HEIGHT AND SPREAD 10 x 5ft (3 x 1.5m) **FLOWERS** 2½in (6cm) across, in late summer and early fall **ASPECT/LIKES** Full sun, well-drained soil **HARDINESS** Z 5-8

160

Felicia amelloides 'Variegata'

With its rather unusual, cheery blue daisy flowers, this tender South African evergreen perennial or sub-shrub is a lovely plant to have outdoors. It usually has dark-green foliage, but this variegated selection is particularly striking, with its tiny, slightly sticky oval leaves edged in cream, an effect that complements the flower color really well. The plant is compact, growing to around 8in (20cm) high, and does well planted in a half-pot, forming a mound of growth topped by dozens of daisies on short stalks. Flowers are best trimmed as they fade, to ensure plenty of replacements follow, but, other than that, it is an easy plant for a sunny open patio and won't mind the odd missed watering. In a mild winter, plants often make it through to spring, something you can ensure if they are taken under glass and kept just frost free.

162

Begonia 'Glowing Embers'

With a season of interest from early summer until the first frosts, this wonderful begonia's beautiful foliage sets it apart from lesser bedding plants. Each roughly triangular leaf is burgundy underneath and dark-reddish-bronze with contrasting silvery veins above. The plant is spangled at all times with glowing tangerine-orange flowers that stand out perfectly from the leaves. It is neat and dense, making a dome of slightly cascading growth perfect for containers seen from below, such as hanging baskets and pots on stands. It's best on its own, rather than in mixed plantings. Plants may survive winter if kept frost free and allowed to become dormant. New shoots appear in spring.

161

Solanum laxum 'Coldham'

One of the best climbers for clusters of white starry flowers from late spring to late fall is *Solanum laxum* 'Album.' 'Coldham' is even better. Its blooms are tinged with blue, before fading to white, the color strongest in bud. Flowers seem also to be held in rather larger bunches, the foliage slightly darker in tone, with plants reaching their zenith at the end of summer and into fall. It will climb vigorously, but a cold winter will cut it back. This happened with my plant, but a strong sucker then rose from the root and the plant swiftly regrew. There are other similar-looking named selections available that may be the same clone.

163

Hibiscus syriacus 'Oiseau Bleu'

Many garden plants are popular for the simple reason that they are terrific performers, and this hardy deciduous shrub is a case in point. It is one of those plants that, every time it begins to flower, you feel glad you invested in it, and the display reaches its best as so many other plants are looking tired. The beautiful flowers are large for a selection of this species and produced generously from the ends of branches. But what makes them really stand out is their glorious color—a sort of shimmering lavender-blue, each overlapping petal with red striations that bleed into a maroon heart at the base, and a prominent central white cone of stamens. It is quite late coming into leaf in spring, which helps it avoid frost damage. Foliage is dark green, the growth upright and fairly dense. Plants seem to stand drought well once established.

Agapanthus Poppin' Purple

With their dramatic rounded heads of usually blue or white flowers, agapanthus have seen an explosion in popularity in the past 20 or so years, with a wide range of selections of these perennials available for hot, dry, sunny sites. A few have distinctly purple-tinged blooms. This one, also known as 'Mp003,' is among the best. Arising above strappy leaves on stout upright stems to around 2ft (60cm), flower heads are crowded with dark-purple buds that open to long-lasting violet flowers. Impressively, more stems arise after the initial flush, keeping interest going. It is strong-growing and, as long as it gets sun, bulks up into a decent clump quickly. Too much shade will reduce flowering. Plants are almost as good in containers as in a border. Foliage is more or less evergreen, which indicates it needs winter shelter in a cold season: mulch heavily, if in a border; put into a cold frame, if in a container.

HEIGHT AND SPREAD 2 x 1ft (60x30cm) **FLOWERS** ¾in (2cm) long heads, 4¾in (12cm) across, in late summer and early fall **ASPECT/LIKES** Sun, heat, well-drained soil **HARDINESS** Z 8-11

"Agapanthus have seen an explosion in popularity in the past 20 or so years."

165

Geranium Rozanne

This superlative herbaceous perennial, also known as *Geranium* 'Gerwat,' deserves the many accolades it has received. It is perhaps the most reliable, long-flowering plant of its kind and has eclipsed many blue-flowered geraniums that were once popular, particularly one of its parents, *Geranium wallichianum* 'Buxton's Variety' (still nice but with smaller flowers and a shorter season). One thing it shares with this parent is its growth habit of sprouting from a central crown—it is not a clump former. The trailing stems radiate out, climbing or weaving through neighboring plants, and bear large bright violet-blue flowers, each with a paler eye. It also looks great in containers—I remember seeing one cascading down a terracotta urn to splendid effect. It is sterile so will not set seed. Propagation is tricky—try careful division of mature crowns in spring.

HEIGHT AND SPREAD Scrambles to around 2ft (60cm) **FLOWERS** 1¼–1½in (3–4cm) across, from early summer to midfall **ASPECT/LIKES** Sun or part shade, fertile well-drained soil **HARDINESS** Z 5-8

166

Fuchsia 'Gartenmeister Bonstedt'

HEIGHT AND SPREAD 2 x 1¼ft (60 x 40cm) **FLOWERS** Tubular, 1½–2in (4–5cm) long in late summer **ASPECT/LIKES** Sun or part shade, shelter, fertile well-drained soil, frost-free in winter **HARDINESS** Z 10-11

I'd not be without this lovely tender fuchsia in my summer pots for its splendid flowers and foliage. It is a selection of *Fuchsia triphylla*, which feature long, slender tubular flowers that are supremely ornamental, making them ideal plants for tall containers or pots that are raised up, where flowers are at or above eye level. This selection is an old favorite, cultivated in Germany at the start of the 20th century. It teams clusters of pendent fiery-red flowers with broad oval purple-bronze foliage. It is almost identical to *Fuchsia* 'Thalia,' which has slightly more slender, orange-tinged flowers. Both are plants to treasure and worth overwintering under glass before frosts strike. Leaves may fall, but the plant will grow again in spring. Water and feed generously in summer.

167

Buddleja agathosma

Most buddleias are grown for flowers, but this is primarily a foliage plant. A deciduous shrub, it can be freestanding or wall trained but needs space, as it can reach 13ft (4m) high and across. Interest starts in late winter, when last year's naked stems bear clusters of gray-mauve flowers—moderately attractive, given the paucity of the season, but they open against the sky, which is often the same color. Better to sacrifice these flowers and cut back hard at this time. New shoots appear alarmingly late in spring but grow vigorously, bearing the long-awaited foliage—broad oval leaves reaching 8in (20cm), with undulating margins. But the appeal is in their color, for leaves are dramatically silver above, with almost white undersides, remarkable in contrast with purple *Cotinus* or behind a dark-leaved canna in late summer. It needs a sunny and sheltered site and good drainage but is otherwise easy.

168

Buddleja fallowiana var. *alba*

If you are looking to grow a white-flowered buddleia, this is probably the best. Superficially similar to numerous white selections of *Buddleja davidii*, this large deciduous shrub has a more refined character. Young stems and undersides of the broadly oval foliage are coated with white feltlike hair, the upper sides of foliage silvery green. In late summer, sweetly scented flowers open on long, rather slender arching panicles held at the tips of branches, each white flower with a conspicuous central orange eye. Grown well, it is a lovely sight, the silvery foliage and white flowers shimmering in the sun—ideal for a white- or silver-themed border and as popular with butterflies as its better-known cousin. But it's more delicate, so grow it in a sunny, open position with space for it to make a nicely shaped plant. Prune in spring.

169

Solenostemon scutellarioides

Few plants match the beauty of coleus's spectacular foliage, marked in red, orange, purple-pink, and yellow. Shrubby tender perennials, they can be grown as house plants or used outdoors in summer. Named selections with the best coloration are available as cuttings from specialists, but plants are also easy from seed sown indoors in spring. Prick out and grow on a sunny windowsill. Pinch out when young to make plants bushy. By summer, they will be big enough for outdoors or keep inside by a bright window. Feed and water freely in summer. Keeping older plants frost-free through winter indoors or under glass is tricky. It's easier to take cuttings of plants in late summer—they root easily in water.

170

Begonia emeiensis

This super plant is one of the best winter-hardy begonias if you have a cool sheltered shaded corner where it can luxuriate. A herbaceous perennial, it has bold exotic bronze-green leaves atop fleshy reddish stems (petioles). Foliage forms a dome of growth, then, late in summer, flowers appear. They are quite large—pale pink, each petal with darker tips, and carried on short stems held below the foliage, so they need a bit of searching for. Curiously, in fall, the part of the leaf that joins the petiole becomes a little tuber, falling to the ground when the leaves die down and sprouting in spring. Plants have fleshy rhizomes that spread across the soil; cover these with a thick mulch over winter to protect them.

167. HEIGHT AND SPREAD 13 x 10ft (4 x 3m) **FLOWERS** Tiny, held in 6in (15cm) long clusters in late winter **ASPECT/LIKES** Sun, shelter, support from a wall **HARDINESS** Z 8-10

168. HEIGHT AND SPREAD 8 x 6½ft (2.5 x 2m) **FLOWERS** Tiny, held in 8in (20cm) long clusters in late summer **ASPECT/LIKES** Sun, shelter, well-drained soil **HARDINESS** Z 8-9

169. COMMON NAME Coleus **HEIGHT AND SPREAD** 2½ x 1¾ft (75 x 50cm) **FLOWERS** Minute, best removed to keep foliage tiptop **ASPECT/LIKES** Bright or sunny position, moist well-drained soil **HARDINESS** Z 10-11

170. COMMON NAME Mount Emei begonia **HEIGHT AND SPREAD** 16 x 16in (40 x 40cm) **FLOWERS** 1½in (4cm) long in late summer **ASPECT/LIKES** Shelter, moisture, shade **HARDINESS** Z 7-10

171

Canna × *ehemanii*

I grow several cannas in big tubs that I shift out of my greenhouse into a sunny sheltered place when they are growing happily in summer. If I could have only one, it would be this beauty, with its superb foliage and wonderful flowers. The banana-like leaves are apple-green, to 2ft (60cm) long, and held on sturdy stems. Unlike other cannas, it produces large pink pendulous flowers that sway from an arching flower cluster at the end of the stems. Side branches develop from the cluster, bearing more flowers, with displays continuing through September. Plants do best planted in spring and lifted each winter before the frosts, but it is simpler to grow in a tub, although plants need daily watering and weekly feeding in summer. In mild areas, with a thick mulch and sheltered site, plants may survive outdoors over winter.

COMMON NAME Ehemann's canna **HEIGHT AND SPREAD** 6½ x 3ft (2 x 1m) **FLOWERS** 2½in (6cm) across, held in clusters from late summer until midfall **ASPECT/LIKES** Sun, shelter, fertile moist soil **HARDINESS** Z 8-11

172

Ligustrum quihoui

Privets get a bad press; synonymous with suburbia 50 years ago, they are mocked despite the fact that some make excellent hedges, while others are of considerable ornamental value. This is one of the "others," a large shrub with outstanding flowers. Upright then gently arching branches bear masses of 20in (50cm) panicles of tiny, white flowers that stand out against the small, oval, dark-green leaves, which are more or less deciduous. Flowers are popular with pollinating insects and, as they visit, older blooms float to the ground like a scene from a snow-dome paperweight. The plant needs pruning to a bushy framework in late winter, which will encourage the long-flowering spurs.

COMMON NAME Waxyleaf privet **HEIGHT AND SPREAD** 13 x 13ft (4x4m) **FLOWERS** Tiny, held in large panicles to 20in (50cm) long in late summer and fall **ASPECT/LIKES** Sunny open place **HARDINESS** Z 6-8

173

Epiphyllum oxypetalum

COMMON NAME Queen of the night **HEIGHT AND SPREAD** 6½ x 3ft (2 x 1m) **FLOWERS** 8in (20cm) across in late summer **ASPECT/LIKES** Light shade indoors, above 50°F (10°C), moist but not wet fertile soil **HARDINESS** Z 10-11

Flowers that open at night have real allure and, if they appear only for a single night, the fascination deepens. Many cacti are night-flowerers, and some of the most spectacular blooms of all are produced by forest cacti that grow in jungles, often on branches of trees. This cactus, commonly called "queen of the night," is the best known of these and it's also the most free-flowering. Its branched, spineless, leaflike stems grow surprisingly tall so need support and space—a conservatory or a spot by the patio doors is ideal. Flowers usually appear in late summer; scaly pinkish buds emerge from the stems, swelling and elongating until one night they burst open to reveal a huge, incredibly beautiful funnel-shaped flower with a powerful, heady scent. Sometimes several flowers open at once in a spectacle worth holding a party to celebrate. By morning it's all over, the faded flowers hanging like burst balloons.

174
Selinum wallichianum

By late August, herbaceous perennials can look rather like variations on a theme: there's still a wealth of daisy-flowered plants to enjoy, but the diversity is diminished. Then you encounter this star performer, which looks more like the sort of plant you'd see in spring. An elegant, clump-forming member of the cow-parsley family, it has finely divided, almost fernlike fresh-green foliage that arises rather late in spring and remains dainty all summer. Then, branched, purple-flushed stems begin to arise, bearing numerous umbels of pure-white flowers, to around 4ft (1.2m), sometimes more. It is most arresting when grown well—the key to success is moist, fertile soil, perhaps with a little shade in the hottest part of the day. It hates dry, thin soils; in my sandy garden, it is a disaster, as the soil is often bone-dry by flowering time.

COMMON NAME Wallich milk parsley **HEIGHT AND SPREAD** 4 x 1¼ft (120 x 40cm) **FLOWERS** Tiny, held in heads 8in (20cm) across in late summer to early fall **ASPECT/ LIKES** Sun or part shade, moist soil **HARDINESS** Z 6-10

175
Musa basjoo

Thirty years ago, few gardeners knew you could grow a banana outdoors in a mild climate, so this remarkable plant was seen only in botanic gardens or grown by lovers of exotica. Now that it's popular, it is still an incredible sight when well grown. Despite its treelike size, it is an herbaceous perennial, forming trunklike stems to 16ft (5m) or more and bearing colossal paddle-shaped leaves 5ft (1.5m) long. In summer, these unfurl at a surprising rate—around one a week. After a few years, plants flower and bear inedible fruit, and suckers form a clump of stems. For this plant to meet its potential, trunks must survive winter, which means protecting them by packing straw around them. Youngsters are best kept under glass over winter for a couple of years and grown before planting. The apple-green leaves are easily torn, so shelter is important. The plant needs as much sun as possible, in a moist place with fertile well-drained soil. It also needs space—the clump can spread to 10ft (3m) and you need easy access to provide winter protection, mulches of well-rotted manure, and extra water in summer.

COMMON NAME Japanese banana **HEIGHT AND SPREAD** 16 x 13ft (5 x 4m) **FLOWERS** Tubular, yellow, 1½in (4cm) long, held in a huge hanging bunch to 3ft (1m) long **ASPECT/LIKES** Sun, heat, fertile moist soil, protection from frost in winter **HARDINESS** Z 5-11

176

Cestrum parqui

I love this plant for its long-lasting, powerfully scented flowers. It does best against a wall, where it makes a medium-size deciduous shrub, starting growth late in spring. The elliptic leaves are dark green with a pungent smell when crushed. If the winter was mild, an early flush of flowers appears, and the cone-shaped panicles of acid-yellow, starry, tubular flowers make a long-lasting display. At this time, the flowers' heady scent, a mix of jasmine and vanilla, is not freely produced, but later in summer comes the second, main flush of flowers, the panicles more generous than before. By now, evenings are warm and the perfume hangs in the air, especially on still, sultry nights. Plant it by a window and the house is perfumed, too. Flowers last weeks, certainly into October. Winter shelter aids retention of old wood, allowing early flowering. If plants need pruning, do it in spring, but you will lose the early blooms.

178

Convolvulus sabatius

This pretty plant is often sold as a seasonal, to be tossed away at the end of summer. It is, however, a bona fide herbaceous perennial, ideal for growing from year to year in a gravel or rock garden, where it will spill over stones or tumble from the top of a wall. Its spreading stems arise from a central growing point, bearing gray-green oval leaves, the growth making quite dense ground cover once established. Masses of blooms appear over the summer—azure blue with a white throat. Opening with the sun, they are short lived individually, but plenty appear in succession. With the frost, top growth dies away, but if the ground is well drained and winter not too cold, fresh shoots will appear the following spring.

177

Escallonia bifida

People often ask what plants will attract pollinators. The blooms of this one will draw in multitudes of them. A large evergreen shrub, it can even be a small tree in the right conditions. It is not entirely hardy and is best against a sunny wall or in a sheltered corner away from winter winds. The long oval foliage is attractive—dark-green, shiny, and slightly sticky to touch. The brittle growth is upright at first but then spreading. In late summer, showy terminal panicles of flowers open, the individual five-petaled blooms small and pure-white. The display lasts around a month. This *Escallonia* needs plenty of space. When mature, you can remove the lower branches, which allows underplanting and exposes the coppery bark.

179

Agapanthus inapertus subsp. *hollandii* 'Sky'

With its slender flower stems topped by drooping, quite tubular bells, demure *Agapanthus inapertus* looks less dramatic than other agapanthus but no less ornamental, with an added touch of elegance. This selection has beautiful clear pale-blue flowers with a hint of violet—a really lovely tone. The flowers appear helpfully late in the season, just as other selections are fading. Its strappy deciduous foliage is fairly low growing, to around 1ft (30cm), but the flower stems often exceed 3ft (1m) tall, making this a super plant to combine among grasses such as *Deschampsia* or *Chionochloa* or to mingle with *Verbena bonariensis*. The flowers also seem to attract late butterflies. The plant does really well in containers. Any shade will reduce flowering performance.

176. COMMON NAME Willow-leaved jessamine **HEIGHT AND SPREAD** 10 x 6½ft (3 x 2m) **FLOWERS** Tubular, ¾in (2cm) long, held in 6in (15cm) heads from late summer until midfall **ASPECT/LIKES** Sun, heat, well-drained soil, shelter of a wall **HARDINESS** Z 8-11

177. HEIGHT AND SPREAD 13 x 13ft (4 x 4m) **FLOWERS** ½in (1cm) across, held in 4in (10cm) clusters in late summer **ASPECT/LIKES** Sun, well-drained soil, shelter from a warm wall **HARDINESS** Z 7-10

178. Blue rock bindweed **HEIGHT AND SPREAD** 8 x 20in (20 x 50cm) **FLOWERS** Funnel-shaped, upward-facing, 1¼in (3cm) across through summer and fall **ASPECT/LIKES** Full sun, dry gravelly soil **HARDINESS** Z 7-11

179. HEIGHT AND SPREAD 3 x 1¾ft (100 x 50cm) **FLOWERS** 1¼in (3cm) long in heads 3in (8cm) across in late summer **ASPECT/LIKES** Full sun, well-drained soil, winter shelter **HARDINESS** Z 7-10

180

Cyperus papyrus

I find this tropical plant irresistible—nothing is more redolent of a watery paradise than papyrus. Known as the plant from which the ancient Egyptians derived paper and out of which Moses's floating bassinet was fashioned, it has a remarkable appearance. Its sturdy, curiously three-sided, upright dark-green stems terminate in arrowlike tips that open into glorious verdant pom-poms of threadlike foliage. In summer, papyrus is easy to care for, performing strongly if given sun and water. Grow it in a pond as a marginal or on a sunny patio in a cistern of water. If you have wet soil, you can bed it out. Over winter, plants need a glasshouse above 45°F (7°C). Indoors, they take up too much space and require more light than can generally be provided. There are solutions: split off a section in summer and grow over winter, grow a dwarf selection on a windowsill, or raise yearly from seed.

COMMON NAME Papyrus **HEIGHT AND SPREAD** 6½ x 3ft (2 x 1m) **ASPECT/LIKES** Sun, warmth, feet in water, under heated glass in winter **HARDINESS** Z 10-11

"In summer, papyrus is easy to care for, performing strongly if given sun and water."

181

Tetrapanax papyrifer 'Rex'

Plants don't come more majestic than this one, which produces the largest leaves of any woody plant that survives winter outdoors. This cultivar is a relative newcomer and is, in effect, a deciduous, supersized fatsia. Given a sheltered place in rich moist soil, it forms a branched woody trunk. When you see treelike plants of it in gardens, it is a triumph, soaring to 16ft (5m). In light, dry soils, it is smaller, around 6½ft (2m), but suckering for a multistemmed effect. Foliage is vast and at its most spectacular in late summer. Deeply lobed dark-green leaves 3ft (1m) across are held on upright petioles with a tawny-colored indumentum (powdery coating) that extends to leaf undersides. In fall, frost permitting, spikes of rounded creamy flower clusters arise. Leaves soon collapse in the cold, leaving the trunk over winter; this may need protecting in a wigwam of straw. Leaves emerge early in spring and are vulnerable to frost.

HEIGHT AND SPREAD 16 x 10ft (5 x 3m) **FLOWERS** Small, held in 1ft (30cm) panicles in late fall **ASPECT/LIKES** Sun, shelter, moist fertile soil **HARDINESS** Z 6-10

182

Hedychium densiflorum 'Assam Orange'

Hardy gingers are a group of plants that have found popularity in recent years as gardeners take advantage of climate change and try something a bit different. This perennial has been in widespread cultivation for years and is one of the most reliable and hardiest. It also fits more easily with a range of garden plants than other gingers. Plants grow from fleshy rhizomes that run just under the soil, forming a dense leafy clump. In late spring, reddish shoots arise, which form upright stems reaching around 4ft (1.2m). These bear handsome green foliage, the leaves fairly slender and lance-shaped. In late summer and fall, stems are topped for several weeks by bright-orange candles of ginger-scented flowers. This is an easy-to-grow plant in well-drained soil in a sheltered spot, enjoying sun but standing a little shade. To give it a good start, mulch over the crown with garden compost in spring before growth emerges.

COMMON NAME Ginger lily **HEIGHT AND SPREAD** 4 x 4½ft (1.2 x 1.4m) **FLOWERS** Small, in 4in (10cm) spikes from late summer until fall **ASPECT/ LIKES** Sun, shelter, fertile moist soil **HARDINESS** Z 8-11

183

Hydrangea aspera Villosa Group

HEIGHT AND SPREAD 13 x 10ft (4 x 3m) **FLOWERS** Fertile and sterile, held in 8in (20cm) heads in late summer and fall **ASPECT/ LIKES** Sun or part shade, moist fertile soil **HARDINESS** Z 7-10

This is a gorgeous, late-flowering, deciduous shrub, a noble plant I would always find space for, although it becomes quite large. It has two areas of appeal. First, the foliage, which is bold and hairy, the oval leaves to around 8in (20cm) long when the plant is growing well, covered in purplish hairs that give a velvety appearance. In late summer and fall, this is teamed with beautiful, long-lasting flower heads, to around 8in (20cm) across, which are composed of showy white sterile outer blooms surrounding smaller inner purple-blue fertile ones. The plant is quite easy: give it some shade, ideally below deciduous trees or beside a cool wall. Once established, it is resistant to drought. It is, however, sensitive to frost and often spring shoots will be damaged. But don't worry—it recovers well.

184

Dahlia 'Twyning's After Eight'

This superb dahlia is one for those who enjoy contrasts. A white-flowered selection, it bears masses of lovely single 3in (8cm) wide blooms throughout late summer, each with a central golden crown of stamens, petals occasionally with a tinge of pink toward the center. Blooms are produced generously on compact shrubby well-branched plants to around 4ft (1.2m) tall. What sets this dahlia apart is that the white blooms are held against near-black foliage—in truth, the darkest purple-bronze, with the leaf color most intense when growing in full sun. As with all dahlias, plants are best in the open ground, although they will survive in pots. Start tubers off under glass and plant after the frosts in a sunny well-drained spot in fertile soil. Although easy to grow, this is a selection to lift in fall each year—it is too precious to risk losing over winter. Store tubers somewhere frost-free and dry until the following spring.

HEIGHT AND SPREAD 4 x 2ft (120 x 60cm)
FLOWERS 3in (8cm) across in late summer
ASPECT/LIKES Sun, shelter, fertile moist soil
HARDINESS Z 8-11

fall

185

Cyclamen hederifolium

These tuberous perennials must be among the most reliable, versatile, and easily grown bulbous plants. As well as the little purple, pink, or white flowers in fall, they have the most marvelous marbled foliage, which forms a low, dense carpet through winter before withering away in late spring. Plants thrive in sun or fairly deep shade and are quite untroubled by soil that dries out completely in early to midsummer when they are dormant. They also spread freely through seed, springing up here and there, so often in convenient places. I have a drift of them planted on the sunny side of a yew hedge, where almost nothing else will grow. The flowers appear in late summer from now-substantial, saucer-size tubers just under the soil surface and are followed by the foliage rising again for a new year.

186

Kirengeshoma palmata

This delectable herbaceous perennial is a member of the hydrangea family and among the most desirable of all fall-flowering plants. Grown well, it is a knockout for its unusual primrose-yellow, shuttlecock-like flowers, which appear above the bold, rather refined foliage for weeks. The plant begins growth early in spring. At this stage, watch out for slugs and snails, which find the leafy shoots very tasty. Plants form substantial clumps in time, with toothed leaves similar in size and shape to those of a sycamore, held on dark slender stems to 3ft (1m) or more. The blooms are substantial—they never really open fully and are waxy, weighing sprays down so they arch over elegantly. It is an exacting plant; it hates drying winds and, alas, does not enjoy life in a container.

187

Ficus carica 'Adam'

A remarkable, seldom-seen edible fig, this French selection is grown principally for its impressive foliage—the rounded, three-lobed leaves can be huge, to around 20in (50cm) long, the central lobe rather elongated. There is a fable that this is the fig Adam used to cover his modesty. It is quite hardy outdoors and would look great trained on a wall as a backdrop to exotic subtropical planting. My own plant is under glass and fruits well—the figs, while not huge, ripen in September and October, maturing to an attractive silvery green with violet ridges on the outside, purple flesh within. Although not of outstanding flavor, they are perfectly edible, especially eaten still warm from the tree. I love the smell of fig leaves, something this selection provides me with on hot days. Under glass, it is best in a large pot.

188

Fuchsia 'Delta's Sara'

A few years ago, I was given a couple of plants of this hardy fuchsia. At the time, it was a new introduction and I didn't realize what a great selection it would be. The large dangling flowers are very showy—long white outer petals opening and sweeping back elegantly to reveal a purple-blue skirt. Avoid pruning hardy fuchsias until they regrow in spring; blooms are produced from midsummer if you retain plenty of last year's growth after winter. If not, flowers will appear in multitudes from the end of summer and on into fall, when they are at their best, making a delightful contrast with the hues of falling leaves. The flowers are carried on arching branched stems to around 3ft (1m) tall, less if growth is cut by frost, but fear not—new shoots will arise from the base in spring.

185. COMMON NAME Ivy-leaved cyclamen **HEIGHT AND SPREAD** 4 x 6in (10 x 15cm) **FLOWERS** ¾in (2cm) across, produced in multitudes in fall **ASPECT/LIKES** Sun or shade, well-drained soil **HARDINESS** Z 5-9

186. HEIGHT AND SPREAD 4 x 3ft (1.2 x 1m) **FLOWERS** 1¼–1½in (3–4cm) long, held in an open spray from early to midfall **ASPECT/LIKES** Cool shade, shelter, perhaps by a north-facing wall, consistently moist acidic soil **HARDINESS** Z 4-8

187. HEIGHT AND SPREAD 13 x 13ft (4 x 4m) **FLOWERS** Inside the fruits **ASPECT/LIKES** Full sun, heat, any well-drained soil, needs to be under glass for fruit to ripen **HARDINESS** Z 8-11

188. HEIGHT AND SPREAD 3 x 1¾ft (100 x 50cm) **FLOWERS** 2½in (6cm) long, from midsummer until late fall **ASPECT/LIKES** Sun or part shade, shelter, fertile well-drained soil **HARDINESS** Z 6-7

189

Agave montana

Some years ago, a friend gave me seed of this agave species originally collected from plants growing below pine trees at high altitude in Mexico. A great lover of exotic plants, especially hardier cacti and succulents, he knew it had potential to grow year-round outdoors, since it thrived in damp cool conditions in the wild. I raised several individuals and what handsome if spiny plants they have developed into. The bold rosettes of dark, shiny green serrated foliage are embossed with silver patterns from the imprint of the neighboring leaf. Plants eventually reach 3ft (1m) or more across before sending up a flowering spike several yards high. The plant then glows orange-red before dying. It does not seem to produce offsets. I have left one plant outdoors in a pot by a warm wall for several years and so far it has been unscathed by cold; it also laughs in the face of summer drought.

COMMON NAME Mountain agave **HEIGHT AND SPREAD** 2 x 3ft (60 x 100cm) **FLOWERS** Rare, yellow-green tubular, 2½in (6cm) long on a 10ft (3m) spike **ASPECT/LIKES** Full sun, heat, well-drained soil, shelter from winter wet **HARDINESS** Z 7-10

190

Salvia patens

Flowers don't come much bluer than this terrific Mexican salvia, a clump-forming herbaceous perennial at its best from late summer. Overwintered plants grow from tuberous roots. Shoots emerging in late spring are susceptible to frost so may need fleece dropping over them on cold nights. Foliage is soft and aromatic as it develops. When the flowers appear, it is an event—each shoot terminating with slender spikes of large, hooded, slightly nodding blooms. Some selections are soft-blue or white. All continue until the first frosts. Then, either lift your clump, pot it, and keep frost-free in a greenhouse or mulch thickly with garden compost. Plants are easily grown from seed sown in spring or as summer-raised cuttings.

COMMON NAME Gentian sage **HEIGHT AND SPREAD** 2 x 1½ft (60 x 45cm) **FLOWERS** 1¼in (3cm) long, held in spikes from late summer until the first frosts **ASPECT/LIKES** Sun, well-drained site, frost-free in winter **HARDINESS** Z 8-10

191

Buddleja 'Pride of Hever'

HEIGHT AND SPREAD 6½–10ft (2–3m) **FLOWERS** Tubular, ¾in (2cm) long held in 8in (20cm) long sprays, from late summer until the first frosts **ASPECT/LIKES** Sun, support from a wall **HARDINESS** Z 5-9

This late-summer- and fall-flowering deciduous shrub is rare; I can't understand why it is not widely grown. It is not a new plant, having been raised in 1958, and a hybrid between silvery-leaved, pink-flowered *Buddleja crispa* and *B. lindleyana*, a plant I once had but threw out, after I grew bored of its sparse, rather miserable, gloomy-purple flowers. This, however, proves far more exciting, Although it has similar dark-green oval leaves to *B. lindleyana*, it has much greater vigor and real flower power, producing masses of showy, bright-violet blooms on long slender racemes in late summer and fall until the first frosts. It is excellent as a wall shrub, cut back hard to a framework in late winter. For extra late appeal, I have *Clematis rehderiana* (see p.152) clambering through mine. Give it sun and support somewhere not too dry in well-drained soil.

192

Clerodendrum bungei

COMMON NAME Rose glory flower **HEIGHT AND SPREAD** 6½ x 3ft (2 x 1m) **FLOWERS** ¾in (2cm) across, held in 8in (20cm) wide heads in late summer and early fall **ASPECT/LIKES** Sun, heat, shelter, well-drained soil **HARDINESS** Z 7-10

One of the stars of the end of summer, this terrific and distinctly exotic-looking plant is a suckering deciduous shrub with upright-growing, branching stems that form a thicket of growth in time. In late summer and fall, large showy, dome-shaped heads of starry five-petaled, pink-purple flowers appear, opening from rich-purple-red, jewel-like buds. The blooms are sweetly scented and stand out beautifully from the bold, purple-flushed, broadly heart-shaped leaves in a display that lasts several weeks and attracts masses of pollinators. The foliage has a mildly unpleasant odor if bruised, so plants are best positioned away from paths. Suckers can arise several yards from the main plant; these are easily detached and grown. It is not especially hardy, so choose somewhere sheltered. Plants seem to grow particularly well against a sunny wall, enjoying the warmth.

193

Hedychium gardnerianum

Spectacular is the best way to describe this exotic, vigorous ginger with its lush, tropical foliage and huge spikes of yellow flowers. It grows from thick fleshy rhizomes that spread out at the soil's surface. New shoots arise in late spring, leafy stems rising to around 5ft (1.5m), foliage broad, oval, and glossy. Then, at the tips of each stem, develops a 1ft (30cm) spike of dozens of flowers. The petals are yellow with prominent red stamens, and the blooms produce a delicious spicy scent. The plant is tender, surviving outside only in sheltered borders. If leaving outdoors, mulch rhizomes with a thick layer of garden compost and straw after frost cuts down the stems. But it is easy to keep in a large, broad container overwintered frost-free or, better still, in the border of a glasshouse or conservatory, where it can spread freely. Give it plenty of water and sun, and feed regularly in summer.

COMMON NAME Kahili ginger **HEIGHT AND SPREAD** 5 x 6½ft (1.5 x 2m) **FLOWERS** 1½in (4cm) across, held in a 1ft (30cm) spike in late summer and fall **ASPECT/LIKES** Full sun, shelter, moist fertile soil **HARDINESS** Z 8-11

194

Chlorophytum saundersiae

It surprises people to learn that this dainty but unusual herbaceous perennial is, in fact, related to the spider plants grown so commonly indoors. It starts into growth in late spring, sending up arching, slender, green, lance-shaped foliage and forming a clump. From afar, it looks just like an ornamental grass. Then in summer, wiry stems, rather taller than the foliage but again arching, bear masses of little, starry, five-petaled, white flowers with prominent yellow stamens. While not a plant with great impact, *Chlorophytum saundersiae* is graceful, easy to grow, and flowers well into fall. It's also ideal for a container, where its elegant form can be most easily admired. In recent years, a variegated selection, 'Starlight,' has been available, but I prefer the plain-green-leaved form. It needs a sunny, sheltered site if planted, with well-drained soil and a thick mulch over winter to help protect it. If kept in a pot, it is safest to pop it into a greenhouse or cold frame for the coldest spells in winter.

HEIGHT AND SPREAD 16 x 8in (40 x 20cm) **FLOWERS** ½in (1cm) across, held in sprays above the foliage in early to midfall **ASPECT/LIKES** Sun, shelter, moist well-drained soil **HARDINESS** Z 8-11

"*Chlorophytum saundersiae* is graceful, easy to grow, and flowers well into fall."

195

Epilobium canum 'Olbrich Silver'

This Californian herbaceous perennial is a favorite of mine, and I'm surprised it is not more widely grown, especially given its ease of cultivation in dry conditions and displays of fiery flowers that last into late fall. It forms low-spreading clumps around 1ft (30cm) high and has mildly running roots, especially in light soil. This selection is especially good for its exceptional silvery foliage, which is attractive from its appearance in spring until the first frosts. Flowers are fire-red, long-tubed trumpets produced at the end of stems. They contrast with the silvery foil in a striking way—few hardy, silver-leaved plants have red blooms. In California, it is pollinated by hummingbirds. It looks superb in a gravel garden and clashes wickedly with nerines, which it grows well with. Give it as much sun and heat as you can. Established plants shrug off drought and survive winter easily if the soil is well drained.

COMMON NAME California fuchsia **HEIGHT AND SPREAD** 1 x 2ft (30 x 60cm) **FLOWERS** 1½in (4cm) long, from early to late fall **ASPECT/LIKES** Sun, heat, sharp drainage **HARDINESS** Z 8-11

196

Arundo donax

In the Middle East, it is said that this plant "whispers in the breeze, but is silent in the storm," leaves rustling pleasingly in light wind, while in a gale the long, pointed, lance-shaped foliage is, I suppose, held out from the stems. Regardless of its sound, this grass is essential for any exotic garden, the biggest member of its family (bamboos excluded). Plants form clumps with running rhizomes, the sturdy, hollow stems measuring up to 1¼in (3cm) across and reaching 16–20ft (5–6m) tall in gardens and at their best by fall. The gray-green leaves are held alternately. I've seen plants in southern Italy bear terminal flower plumes, but not everywhere. Clumps may need some controlling, but be aware that rhizomes are exceptionally tough to cut, even with a saw. *Arundo* likes a sunny place and thrives in any soil as long as it is not too dry, although it stands spells of drought well when established. Shelter is not vital, but plants look better with protection and stems are best cut down in winter when they get shabby; new shoots arise in spring. Plants propagate easily in water from stem cuttings with a node. The variegated selection ('Variegata'), with its spectacular white-striped foliage, is among the finest of all grasses, although it is less hardy and in most gardens needs protection. Still, well worth a go.

COMMON NAME Giant reed **HEIGHT AND SPREAD** 16–20 x 13ft (5–6 x 4m) **FLOWERS** Not everywhere **ASPECT/LIKES** Sun, heat, fertile well-drained soil **HARDINESS** Z 6-10

197

Hypericum henryi subsp. *henryi* 'John Hillier'

This fine, late-flowering hypericum is a tidy, fairly compact shrub, eventually reaching around 5ft (1.5m), with at first upright then lightly arching branches. These are furnished with neat oval leaves that are usually deciduous, but in a mild winter may be semievergreen. The slightly cupped, five-petaled, shining golden-yellow flowers open in profusion from rounded buds, the lovely display continuing well into October and looking remarkably fresh, the flowers outward-facing at the end of the current season's growth. In all, it is a rather more refined-looking plant than the better-known *Hypericum* 'Hidcote,' with a really usefully late flowering season at what can be a rather scruffy time in the garden.

HEIGHT AND SPREAD 5 x 3ft (1.5x1m) **FLOWERS** 1½in (4cm) across, produced in profusion from late summer to midfall **ASPECT/LIKES** Sun or part shade, well-drained soil **HARDINESS** Z 6-7

198

Zingiber mioga

Grown widely in Japan for its edible flower buds and new shoots, this ginger is surprisingly hardy and a good choice for sheltered, moist, shaded borders, although it will also stand some sun and drier soils. A clump-forming herbaceous perennial growing from fleshy rhizomes, it sends up lush, exotic-looking leafy stems to around 3ft (1m) tall, the pointed foliage rich green, slender, and lanceolate, perfect for an exotic garden, perhaps as underplanting for *Musa basjoo*. It is rather more graceful than closely related *Hedychium* and its fall flowers are quite different. Curious rather than beautiful, they emerge at soil level and are pale lemon in color. Frost will burn the foliage to the ground, at which point it can be cut off, and the roots mulched with garden compost. Mark the positions of plants well, as they are late to emerge, appearing in late spring or even early summer.

COMMON NAME Japanese ginger **HEIGHT AND SPREAD** 3 x 1¾ft (100 x 50cm) **FLOWERS** ¾in (2cm) across, at ground level, in early fall **ASPECT/LIKES** Part shade or sun, shelter, fertile moist soil **HARDINESS** Z 8-11

199

Cobaea pringlei

A hardy perennial sprouting late in spring from tuberous roots, *Cobaea pringlei* is a super strong-growing species when established. The new shoots climb by tendrils during summer, the first flowers opening with the turn of the season. These are rather more elegant than those of the better-known *Cobaea scandens* (cup and saucer vine), and perhaps a touch smaller, the blooms cream-white and without the leafy saucer. It flowers profusely until the first hard frost, so, on a sheltered sunny wall, it often continues into December. The roots need protection, so a good thick mulch of garden compost applied after the stems have started to die back is sensible. Another perennial species I grow is vigorous *C. paneroi*, with bells of greenish white that change color to a curious biscuit-brown hue before finally becoming purple.

200

Cyrtanthus elatus

A South African bulbous perennial once popular as a houseplant, this now-forgotten indoor plant is spectacular in late summer and fall, when it produces heads of 5–7 usually vivid red flowers, held aloft on 2ft (60cm) stems. Blooms are funnel-shaped and upward facing with six petals. Flowering can be a bit unpredictable, with individual bulbs not flowering each year, but plants quite quickly form a potful, and some years multiple flower stems will arise for a really dramatic show. The foliage is strappy, glossy, and unremarkable—it may not entirely die down, but plants seem to stop growing in winter. Water and feed bulbs through summer, reducing moisture in winter. Plants may need splitting eventually. Individual bulbs can be potted and given away, as these plants are seldom bought; instead, they are passed on between friends.

201

Streptocarpus 'Falling Stars'

Few houseplants are as dependable for their displays of flowers as *Streptocarpus*. New selections of the genus often have large, showy, patterned blooms in a range of colors. This particular cultivar is rather different. Its flowers are fairly small and soft blue with a pale throat. They appear in great profusion, with numerous branched flower stalks arising together, producing clouds of flowers held just above the clumps of fleshy, lance-shaped foliage. Apart from a winter rest, they may be in flower for most of the year but have two distinct high points—spring and early fall, when the plants can have hundreds of blooms and are a wonderful sight. Key is to avoid plants standing in water. I always have a thick layer of expanded clay granules in the tray below the pot to help prevent this.

202

Vitex agnus-castus f. *alba* 'Silver Spire'

One of the finest of all shrubs in fall for its flowers, the chaste tree is a handsome deciduous wall shrub or, eventually, small tree. This selection has lovely long, quite airy, fingerlike racemes of ivory-white, almost buddleia-like flowers. They tone in perfectly with the silvery leaves and open in profusion during September, attracting pollinating insects from all around. It is a wonderful plant for the back of a pale-color-themed border and a great choice for Mediterranean-style plantings, as it stands drought well. All-important is the site—for the plant to flourish, the soil must be well drained and the position as hot as possible. It will not tolerate any shade and ideally needs the shelter and support of a wall.

199. HEIGHT AND SPREAD Climbs to 13ft (4m) **FLOWERS** 3in (8cm) long, produced in profusion from early fall until the first hard frost **ASPECT/LIKES** Sun, shelter, well-drained soil **HARDINESS** Z 9-11

200. COMMON NAME Scarborough lily **HEIGHT AND SPREAD** 2 x 1ft (60x30cm) **FLOWERS** 2½in (6cm) long, held in a cluster for a couple of weeks between late summer and late fall **ASPECT/LIKES** Sunny windowsill **HARDINESS** Z 10-11

201. HEIGHT AND SPREAD 16 x 8in (40 x 20cm) **FLOWERS** 1¼in (3cm) long, held in loose heads for most of the year **ASPECT/LIKES** Bright windowsill with indirect light, kept moist but never wet, drier in winter, away from drafts **HARDINESS** Z 10-11

202. COMMON NAME Chaste tree **HEIGHT AND SPREAD** 10 x 6½ft (3 x 2m) **FLOWERS** Individually small, held in 8in (20cm) long clusters, produced in profusion in early fall **ASPECT/LIKES** Sunny wall, heat, sharp drainage **HARDINESS** Z 6-9

203

Anemone x *hybrida* 'Richard Ahrens'

Japanese anemones come into their own in fall, providing color, freshness, and an impression of delicacy in the garden. Their elegant pink, white, or purple flowers form a display that lasts well into October. This selection is an easy, dependable, and vigorous herbaceous perennial with lovely pale-pink, semidouble flowers, each with a central gold crown of stamens. The blooms often start opening in late summer, swaying on sturdy stems to around 4ft (1.2m) high. Although it is a fairly tall anemone, it never needs staking. It spreads at the root, forming a running, open clump of quite bold, silver-green foliage. In sunny borders with good moisture, it grows strongly, forming great patches of flower. In smaller gardens, it may be a better bet to try it in quite dry, semishade below deciduous trees, where in my garden it performs and behaves well, spreading modestly, its enthusiasm slightly curtailed.

COMMON NAME Japanese anemone **HEIGHT AND SPREAD** 4 x 6½ft (1.2x2m) **FLOWERS** 2½in (6cm) across from late summer to midfall **ASPECT/LIKES** Sun or part shade, any well-drained soil **HARDINESS** Z 4-8

"Their elegant pink, white, or purple flowers form a display that lasts well into October."

204

Solanum betaceum

Tamarillos are delicious fruits. Egg-shaped, red-orange, and not unlike a tomato, they have a sweet tangy flavor. Fruits are borne on small trees, which will grow in a greenhouse or conservatory. Mature plants overwinter in cool temperatures—around 41°F (5°C) as a minimum. They produce downy, oval, rather pungent leaves, which can be large on well-fed plants, to 10in (25cm) long. Grow from summer cuttings or spring-sown seed, overwintering your plant on a sunny windowsill for the first year. Move it under glass in spring, pot, and water well, feeding with tomato fertilizer. The plant will grow strongly, to around 6½ft (2m) in its second year. Keep it cool and drier over winter—leaves will fall, but shoots appear in spring, when the plant will start branching to form a treelike canopy in its third year and reaching full height. Little white flowers then appear, with fruit setting by end of summer and ripening in fall. It is best to replace old plants regularly or to prune them to lower shoots.

COMMON NAME Tree tomato **HEIGHT AND SPREAD** 11½ x 8ft (3.5x2.5m) **FLOWERS** ½in (1cm) across, in mid- to late summer **ASPECT/LIKES** Airy but sunny, frost-free greenhouse **HARDINESS** Z 10-11

205

Streptocarpus saxorum

This easy-to-keep houseplant is seldom flowerless: from the branches, fine wirelike stems bear masses of small soft-blue flowers, the blooms produced for weeks, if not months, on end. Plants grow quickly and will soon cascade over the edges of containers—they look great in hanging pots. Another bonus is that stem cuttings root really well in water. This way, young plants can be brought on once parent plants get too top-heavy, and those that are surplus can be popped into hanging baskets or window boxes, where they make effective summer bedding. With their succulent growth, plants stand being kept on the dry side so will not resent the odd missed watering.

HEIGHT AND SPREAD 8 x 8in (20 x 20cm) **FLOWERS** ¾–1¼in (2–3cm) long, carried in clusters in summer and fall **ASPECT/LIKES** Bright windowsill away from direct sun, soil kept on the dry side **HARDINESS** Z 10-11

206

Sternbergia lutea

COMMON NAME Winter daffodil **HEIGHT AND SPREAD** 4 x 6in (10x15cm) **FLOWERS** 2½in (6cm) tall in early fall **ASPECT/LIKES** Full sun, good drainage but not too dry **HARDINESS** Z 6-9

One of the highlights of fall is seeing this gorgeous bulb burst into flower. The plant goes unnoticed in the garden for most of the year, but at the end of summer, it sends up glossy, rich-green, strap-shaped leaves, followed shortly by the flowers. Held on short stems, these glorious golden-yellow chalices composed of six petal-like tepals look a little like large crocuses from a distance. In time, bulbs multiply, forming a decent multiflowered clump—a wonderful sight amid the falling leaves. The foliage will overwinter, dying down early the following summer. Plants like a dry period in summer if they are to flower well. Bare bulbs can be planted during the dormant period in summer or bought as pot-grown plants.

207

Pennisetum orientale 'Tall Tails'

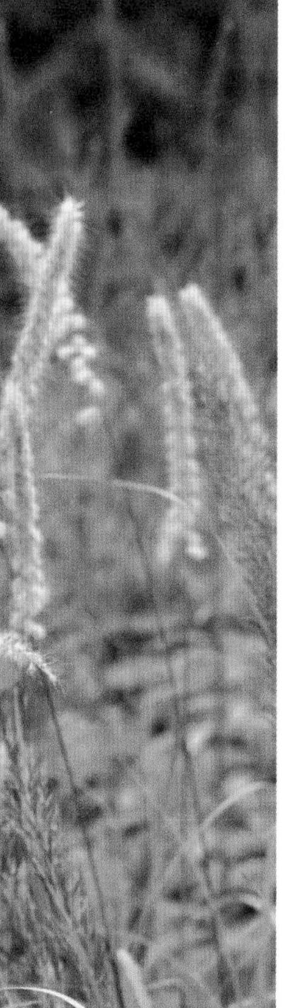

Are any plants more tactile than flowering *Pennisetum* grasses? With their fluffy, bottlebrush-like flower panicles, usually produced at hand height, their soft touch proves irresistible to almost anyone. This selection is an especially vigorous, large-growing grass when happy. The long, slender, bright-green, arching blades form a lush fountain of growth through summer. This is then overtopped by flower stems in fall, so allow it space to develop. The arching, creamy-brown, pink-tinged spikes of flowers usually look good until the first hard frosts after Christmas, by which time the foliage will have turned bright yellow. By the end of winter, the plant may look quite shabby, but wait until March before cutting it to the ground. Give it shelter from winter cold, as it is not that hardy.

HEIGHT AND SPREAD 5 x 5ft (1.5 x 1.5m) **FLOWERS** Held in an arching bottlebrush-like spike to 8in (20cm) from early fall until early/midwinter **ASPECT/LIKES** Sunny, well-drained open site **HARDINESS** Z 5-9

208. **HEIGHT AND SPREAD** 26 x 16ft (8 x 5m) **FLOWERS** ½in (1cm) long, produced in clusters in midspring **ASPECT/LIKES** Sun or part shade, shelter, fertile well-drained soil that is never too dry **HARDINESS** Z 5-9

209. **HEIGHT AND SPREAD** 16 x 8in (40x20cm) **FLOWERS** ¾–1¼in (2–3cm) wide, held in an 3in (8cm) wide head in early fall **ASPECT/LIKES** Full sun, sharp drainage, mild site **HARDINESS** Z 8-10

210. **COMMON NAME** Rooper's red-hot poker **HEIGHT AND SPREAD** 4 x 3ft (1.2 x 1m) **FLOWERS** Tubular, 1¼in (3cm) long, held in dense spikes from early to late fall **ASPECT/LIKES** Sun, fertile well-drained but moist soil **HARDINESS** Z 6-9

211. **COMMON NAME** Bieberstein's crocus **HEIGHT AND SPREAD** Foliage to 8in (20cm) tall **FLOWERS** 6in (15cm) tall in early to midfall **ASPECT/LIKES** Sun or part shade, good drainage, site in rough grass **HARDINESS** Z 4-8

208

Cercis canadensis 'Forest Pansy'

A popular ornamental plant for its fiery-colored tints in fall, this compact deciduous tree is also attractive in spring, when it flowers, and in summer, with its handsome purple, heart-shaped foliage. A good choice for a fairly small garden, it reaches around 26ft (8m). The plant may be single- or multistemmed, with a broad, open canopy, and trunks with rough, dark bark. In midspring, displays of small, bright-pink, pea-shaped flowers appear; they may sprout directly from the branches. Foliage follows late in spring, the purple leaves translucent like stained glass, when young. In summer, the plant is glorious, especially contrasting with gold- or silver-leaved trees and shrubs. Then, quite early in fall, its leaves turn orange and yellow before falling, making a wonderful sight that is all too short-lived.

209

Nerine undulata 'Alba'

This choice South African bulb, a member of the Flexuosa Group, is highly regarded for its delectable displays of white flowers late in the season. It is a plant for perfectly drained soil, where it should prove hardy; if you have heavy soil, grow it in a pot of gritty compost and overwinter in a cold greenhouse or cold frame. The leaves develop in summer, dark-green and strappy. They are followed in fall by tall stems bearing around a dozen pure-white flowers with delightful crinkled petals. Individual blooms are smaller than those of better-known *Nerine bowdenii*, but the effect is perhaps more elegant. Plant bulbs in summer with noses just above the ground. They are easiest kept on their own in a gravel border or rock garden—planting partners shade foliage, which reduces flowering, and harbor pests that damage the plant.

210

Kniphofia rooperi

If you believe the start of fall sees the end of spectacular flowers in the garden, this remarkable late-flowering red-hot poker will make you think again. A large, clump-forming herbaceous perennial, it develops a substantial mound of long, strappy, usually evergreen foliage. Then in late summer, stout, green, flowering stems emerge, bearing masses of downward-facing flowers, which open pinkish orange-red and fade to yellow, the heads rounded or egg-shaped. The display continues well into fall if the weather is mild and is perfect with the fiery tints of fall leaves. Once the flowers fade, stalks need cutting down. The foliage will suffer over winter and usually needs tidying in spring. Be prepared to water in a dry summer.

211

Crocus speciosus

Many species of crocus flower in fall rather than spring and this fine species is the best known. Its delicate buds arise leafless late in September or October, rather globular goblets held atop a tall, fragile, stemlike flower tube. The mauve petals have a silvery sheen outside but open to dark-veined, blue-purple flowers with feathery, orange-red anthers—a wonderful sight en masse, the flowers springing up among windfall apples perhaps or fall leaves. Indeed, the best place for this crocus is in rough grass, which will support the flowers—they can get top-heavy and easily topple after heavy rain. In sun and well-drained soil, it will naturalize well if undisturbed. The fine grassy leaves emerge after flowering and disappear in spring.

212
Clematis rehderiana

Among the most desirable of fall-flowering climbing plants, this delightful clematis is one to find a space for, as long as you do not mind its strong-growing, rambling habit. It is a leafy, bulky plant when established, its dark stems clothed with apple-green, toothed leaves. In late September, flower stems arise from leaf axils, bearing clusters of little, nodding, bell-shaped blooms. Each pale cream-yellow flower has four petals, the tips delightfully swept back. They have a gorgeous scent and the lovely display lasts for several weeks. Key is finding somewhere to grow it; it needs support but is too untidy for a neat trellis. Better to train it through a tree, large shrub, or up a wall. Prune back hard to around 2ft (60cm) each March.

COMMON NAME Nodding virgin's bower **HEIGHT AND SPREAD** Climbs to 20ft (6m) **FLOWERS** ¾in (2cm) bells carried in clusters in early to midfall **ASPECT/LIKES** Sun, but with feet cool and not too dry, good drainage, plenty of space **HARDINESS** Z 6-9

213
Buddleja × *weyeriana* 'Sungold'

HEIGHT AND SPREAD 10 x 6½ft (3 x 2m) **FLOWERS** Tiny, held in 8in (20cm) long clusters from late summer to early winter **ASPECT/LIKES** Open sunny site, any well-drained soil **HARDINESS** Z 5-9

I much prefer this lovely, usefully long-flowering hybrid buddleia to its orange-flowered parent *Buddleja globosa*, which, although briefly colorful, proves a coarse plant in the garden. Helpfully, it is also less vigorous than its other parent, familiar *B. davidii*, and benefits from a long flowering season, which can stretch on into December, with dead-heading and mild weather. It forms a rather open, deciduous shrub with broadly oval, silver-green foliage, new growth tipped from late summer onward by long, arching panicles of flowers arranged in ball-shaped heads. The blooms are yellow-orange with a darker eye, attractively tinged with mauve when in bud, which gives a subtle two-tone appearance. The plant seems as popular with butterflies and other pollinators as *B. davidii*. To get the best from it, prune back quite hard in spring.

214

Symphyotrichum turbinellum

This plant is a dramatic, end-of-season sight in the mixed borders in September and October, providing vast clouds of little, lavender-mauve, yellow-centered daisy flowers. Native to North America, it is an upright-growing, clump-forming herbaceous perennial. Its slender, dark-green stems bear blue-green, lance-shaped leaves and reach around 3ft (1m) or more at flowering time. The plant may need staking in the garden, especially if well fed, which makes it taller, but happily it does not seem to get affected by mildew, which can damage related plants. It is an outstanding partner for late-interest grasses, such as smaller *Miscanthus* (see p.160) or *Pennisetum* (see p.149), which like similarly open, sunny, well-drained conditions.

COMMON NAME Smooth violet prairie aster **HEIGHT AND SPREAD** 3 x 3ft (1 x 1m) **FLOWERS** ¾in (2cm), held in huge heads to around 2ft (60cm) in early to midfall **ASPECT/LIKES** Sunny, open, well-drained, moist site **HARDINESS** Z 4-8

215

Dianella tasmanica 'Emerald Arch'

Native to New Zealand, *Dianella* are evergreen herbaceous perennials that have in recent years become more widely grown, thanks in part to an increasing number of cultivars available at nurseries and garden centers. This lush, handsome selection has rich-green, glossy, arching foliage and looks rather like a miniature *Phormium*, growing to around 2ft (60cm) high and forming a clump that spreads gently at the root. In summer, spikes of quite attractive and unusual little flowers appear—they are pale blue with swept-back petals and golden anthers. These are followed in fall by arresting egg-shaped fruits the color of lapis lazuli, which dangle from stems amid the foliage. This is a great, quite easy plant for rather exotic-looking ground cover in the cool shade below deciduous trees, as long as there is some shelter and a reasonably moist soil. Prolonged freezing weather or drought will damage foliage, but it generally recovers.

HEIGHT AND SPREAD 2 x 3ft (60 x 100cm) **FLOWERS** ½in (1cm) across, held on a flowering stem in summer **ASPECT/LIKES** Part shade, shelter, cool moist soil **HARDINESS** Z 8-11

216

Vitis coignetiae

For spectacular fall color, this vigorous, large-leaved, climbing ornamental vine cannot be bettered. Use it to drape across a wall, garland large trees, train across and cascade down from a pergola, or soften architectural details of a building. In situations like this, the tropical-looking, 1ft (30cm) wide heart-shaped leaves can be easily admired. They are rich green, but turn to dazzling shades of pinkish-red, yellow-orange, and intense scarlet before falling—an incredible sight. Plants are lovely in spring, too, when the fresh silvery-green shoots elongate, tendrils attaching to wires or whatever support they can reach. In summer, little bunches of black grapes may form; these are best described as inedible. Plant somewhere reasonably sheltered in sun, but keep the vine clear of small or delicate trees and shrubs, as its vigor can be overpowering. The plant is not picky with regard to soil, but it must be well drained—winter waterlogging will kill even mature vines.

COMMON NAME Crimson glory vine **HEIGHT AND SPREAD** Climbs to 33ft (10m) **ASPECT/LIKES** Sun, well-drained soil, plenty of space to climb **HARDINESS** Z 6-9

217

Hylotelephium telephium 'Postman's Pride'

Herbaceous perennials do not come much easier to grow than *Hylotelephium*, succulent plants formerly known as *Sedum*. This striking selection is one of the most arresting. Forming a clump, it has fleshy foliage that is a remarkable dark bronze-purple, appearing almost black at times and impressive for months as it develops. In fall, it is topped by branched, fairly open, domed heads of soft-pink flowers that attract bees. It is great in a gravel garden, as the foliage needs a light backdrop to contrast with; seen against bare soil, it is invisible from a distance. Use it with silver-leaved plants—the metallic filigree of *Artemisia alba* 'Canescens' perhaps—or against variegation—*Sedum takesimense* ATLANTIS (see p.100), for instance.

219

Sesleria autumnalis

The great Dutch plantsman and garden designer Piet Oudolf has done so much to popularize plants that 20 years ago were almost unknown, especially those that work en masse in the European-style prairie plantings he pioneered. This wonderful, semievergreen grass is a fine example. I first met it in late summer at Hauser & Wirth Somerset, an art gallery graced by one of his gardens. There, I spied, growing in a broad drift beside fading heleniums and achilleas, a lowish grass with lime-green blades burnished with gold, an effect that intensifies through fall. The grass works well in traditional plantings, too, individual plants forming low mounds of growth, in summer topped by flower spikes. In fall, it can be teamed with asters and other late perennials.

218

Eucharis amazonica

I can't understand why this outstanding bulbous South American plant is not more often seen in homes, for it is easy to grow. Most of the year, it resembles an outsize hosta, with handsome, dark-green, oval foliage held upright, then arching out on long fleshy stems, the leaves incredibly glossy, as if they have just been varnished. It forms a clump of growth, from which the flowering stems arise during early fall. They usually carry 4–7 individual nodding flowers of great beauty. Some describe them as daffodil-like, owing to their cup-and-saucer form, but that is to understate their elegance. Each has six white petals and a central greenish chalice. They have a sweet perfume; the display lasts a couple of weeks.

220

Tetrastigma voinierianum

Sheer lust for life can be a highly attractive quality and few plants grow with quite as much vim as this tropical rainforest creeper. It produces huge, dark-green, palmate leaves that look a bit like those of a horse chestnut tree, held on felted stems with whiplike tendrils that attach to trellis or tree branches. The new growth is silvery green. The creeper can be grown well in the home for a while when young, trained up a tripod of tall canes, but it comes into its own where there is plenty of space, perhaps covering a room divider or conservatory wall or cascading from an indoor balcony. That said, it is tougher than supposed and worth experimenting with: I grow one in my outhouse, which is kept just frost free, and I have seen it outside year-round in London. The plant's common name comes from the tendency for stems to drop off for no apparent reason, like the tip of a lizard's tail.

217. HEIGHT AND SPREAD 24 x 8in (60 x 20cm) **FLOWERS** Tiny, held in 3in (8cm) wide heads in midfall **ASPECT/LIKES** Full sun, sharp drainage, fairly poor soil **HARDINESS** Z 5-9

218. COMMON NAME Amazon lily **HEIGHT AND SPREAD** 2¾ x 1¾ft (80 x 50cm) **FLOWERS** 4in (10cm) across, atop a flower stem, in midfall **ASPECT/LIKES** Bright windowsill away from direct sun, fairly warm spot, moist but not wet **HARDINESS** Z 10-11

219. COMMON NAME Autumn moor-grass **HEIGHT AND SPREAD** 1¾ x 1¾ft (50 x 50cm) **FLOWERS** Tiny, in a slender white head 1¼in (3cm) tall, held above foliage in summer **ASPECT/LIKES** Light shade, cool moist well-drained site **HARDINESS** Z 5-9

220. COMMON NAME Lizard plant **HEIGHT AND SPREAD** Climbs to 26ft (8m) or more if allowed **ASPECT/LIKES** Light shade, support, space, a large container kept not too dry **HARDINESS** Z 10-11

221. COMMON NAME Schreber's aster **HEIGHT AND SPREAD** 1¾ x 2ft (50 x 60cm) **FLOWERS** 1¼in (3cm) across, held in loose heads from mid- to late fall **ASPECT/LIKES** Shade or part sun, any soil **HARDINESS** Z 3-8

222. HEIGHT AND SPREAD 6½ x 2ft (200 x 60cm) **FLOWERS** Tiny, held in 16in (40cm) plumes above foliage in mid- to late fall, then silvery seed heads into winter **ASPECT/LIKES** Sun, open site, fertile well-drained soil, not too dry **HARDINESS** Z 5-9

223. HEIGHT AND SPREAD 1 x 1ft (30x30cm) in leaf **FLOWERS** Up to 4¾in (12cm) tall in midfall **ASPECT/LIKES** Sun or part shade, open site, fertile well-drained soil, not too dry **HARDINESS** Z 5-8

224. COMMON NAME Umbrella plant **HEIGHT AND SPREAD** 3 x 6½ft (1 x 2m) **FLOWERS** ½in (1cm) across, held in 4in (10cm) heads in spring **ASPECT/LIKES** Sun, shelter, continuously moist soil **HARDINESS** Z 5-7

221

Eurybia schreberi

Until fairly recently, this perennial was classified as an aster, but, whatever we choose to call it, this is a terrific, late-season, easy-to-grow plant for a shaded spot. For weeks in fall, masses of little, shining, white daisy flowers are produced, each with a gold center and held in loose clusters on slender, dark stems above attractive, still-fresh, pointed oval, rich-green leaves with serrated margins. The plant forms a fairly open clump, providing a drift of frothy flowers, and spreads well at the root. It shines even in quite dry shade below trees and remains fresh while most other plants have long finished—really useful in woodland plantings at this time of year. Care is simple—plants just eventually need cutting down after flowering.

222

Miscanthus sinensis var. *condensatus* 'Cosmopolitan'

An essential late-season grass, this is a plant that gets better as the growing season progresses. Like many other feather grasses, it is a large, clump-forming, herbaceous perennial, forming a fountain of foliage. In this case, it is boldly variegated, the broad, strap-shaped, green blades generously striped with white. It makes a tight, upright-growing plant, the foliage remaining in good shape to the ground, even when topped by showy, feathery, pink-tinged silver flower heads. These seem perfectly designed to catch the dew or frost and sparkle in the fall sun. One of the finest of all hardy variegated plants, it is superb in a white garden or border and will even stand alone as a specimen plant, or perhaps as a pair to frame a pathway or flight of garden steps.

223

Colchicum speciosum 'Album'

This gorgeous fall-flowering bulb is the best of its kind. Its pure-white chalices arise leafless on sturdy, pale-green tubes, contrasting with the falling leaves of the fall garden. They stand up well to wind and rain, and shine in the sun. The bulbs must be planted in late summer, around 6in (15cm) deep. Choose somewhere they will not be disturbed, perhaps in rough grass below trees or, if in a border, mark them well. The plants multiply and form clumps. The only downside is the foliage, which arises in spring and is attractive and glossy initially, but soon becomes disheveled and munched by slugs and snails. This is all forgiven, however, in fall; try teaming the flowers with black-leaved *Ophiopogon* or with fern fronds.

224

Darmera peltata

This bold herbaceous perennial is great in spring and summer, as well as fall. It thrives in bog gardens, on the margins of ponds, or colonizing stream banks, where plants form large clumps, with thick running rhizomes developing over the soil surface. In spring, the first signs of life are the flowers, which are small and pale pink but held aloft in showy dome-shaped heads atop 2ft (60cm) stalks. Then the leaves appear—exotic, glossy, and shaped like umbrellas with scalloped edges. They expand to 2ft (60cm) across, on 3ft (1m) stems, with the largest leaves in damp conditions. But the glory of this plant is in its decline into fall, when the foliage glows impressively in yellow, orange, and red. If space is an issue, go for *Darmera peltata* 'Nana,' which is less than half the size.

225

Miscanthus sinensis 'Yakushima Dwarf'

Feather grasses are outstanding fall-interest plants but can be large-growing and tricky to accommodate within small gardens. This diminutive, herbaceous perennial is a solution. Tightly clump-forming and growing to just 2¾ft (80cm) high, it has slender, arching, green blades topped by pinkish flower feathers in early fall. These gradually turn silvery and remain handsome well into winter, providing useful garden structure. It is an attractive border performer but can also do well in a container. It is not picky about soil, thriving even on heavy clay, as long as not waterlogged. Cut it all back hard to avoid unsightly buildup of old brush before the new shoots arise in late winter or you will have a far fiddlier task cutting each old stem individually to the ground.

COMMON NAME Dwarf Chinese silver grass **HEIGHT AND SPREAD** 2¾ x 2¾ft (80 x 80cm) **FLOWERS** Tiny, held in showy pink then silver plumes 6in (15cm) tall from early fall until midwinter **ASPECT/LIKES** Sunny open well-drained site **HARDINESS** Z 5-9

226

Chard Bright Lights

Edible, colorful, and easy to grow from seed sown in summer, this leaf beet is perfect if you want to have vegetables among your ornamental plants. In a protected site, plants will continue to crop through fall and winter, producing superbly colorful and tasty foliage. The main appeal is the colorful broad midribs of the puckered, dark-green leaves. They may be yellow, orange, red, or white (the hardiest) and look amazing backlit by the sun. The leaves are cooked and eaten like spinach, harvested one by one so plants continue to grow. Plants are best in sun, although they will stand part shade. Gradually thin out young plants as you go (use the leaves in salads), aiming to leave at least 8in (20cm) between plants by fall. Be generous with water and feeding—a mulch of garden compost around plants helps. In winter, cover with fleece on cold nights.

COMMON NAME Rainbow chard **HEIGHT AND SPREAD** 16 x 12in (40 x 30cm) **ASPECT/LIKES** Sun or part shade, open site **HARDINESS** Z 6-10

227

Aspidistra elatior 'Asahi'

Most people are familiar with *Aspidistra elatior* as near-indestructible inhabitants of countless gloomy Victorian parlors, with upright, dark-green, broadly strap-shaped leaves. Handsome enough, but in recent years, it has become apparent that this plant is a relatively plain member of the genus, as a wealth of exciting species and selections has become more widely grown. One of them is this superb, variegated, Japanese cultivar. The tips of its leaves look as if they have been spray-painted in white, the coloration extending down the midrib, fading into the usual dark green of the leaf to dramatic effect. It is lovely in a pot but will also grow well outside year-round if sheltered below an evergreen canopy. Full shade is vital, indoors or out, so a north-facing windowsill is ideal. Sharp drainage is also important, but don't let it get too dry or the lovely leaves will suffer.

228

Elegia capensis

A South African native from a group of grasses called "restios," this statuesque perennial produces impressive bamboolike upright stems to form a clump 6½ft (2m) or more high. Stems are segmented and, at each node, carry tiered whorls of soft, feathery, bright-green foliage, which emerges from conspicuous papery sheaths. Buff-colored, grasslike flower plumes appear in summer. In fall, after a season's growth, the plant looks superb, like no other that can be grown outdoors and worth going the extra mile to cultivate. It is, sadly, hardy only in the most sheltered gardens, but I do well with it in a large container, brought under cover in frosty periods. Moisture is key—plants hate to be dry and turn yellow if they go short. In summer, they need additional watering. New shoots appear from the base in spring, a good time to repot and cut away old stems.

229

Cyathea australis

This handsome Australian *Cyathea*, a cousin of better-known *Dicksonia antarctica*, is one that can be experimented with in mild gardens. Its appearance is luxuriant: the bright-green fronds are delicate and broad, held on a slender trunk, and look their best in fall after a good growing season. They have prickly bases and even on young plants can reach 6½ft (2m). The plant needs regular watering—daily in summer. Mine is in a large container, under cover for winter, although mature plants are hardy to 18°F (–8°C). The tricky part is tracking down a plant for sale that already has a trunk or finding space to grow on a young plant until you feel you can risk it outside.

230

Begonia 'Silver Spirit'

Among showy foliage houseplants, few can match begonias, which are particularly valuable in fall as we seek color from plants indoors. This selection is similar to those plants often referred to as "*Begonia rex,*" but this has a bushier, spreading habit. Dark stems carry large, spectacular leaves that are deeply and irregularly toothed. For the most part, they are silver, but at the heart of each is a bold, star-shaped, dark-purple patch, outlined with lighter purple; leaf edges are also purple. It is quite fast-growing and soon forms an impressive plant, so give it pride of place in a bright spot, in temperatures above 59°F (15°C). Plants grow well from leaf cuttings; you can then try it outdoors in summer pots, where the foliage can look most effective.

227. **COMMON NAME** Lime-striped cast iron plant **HEIGHT AND SPREAD** 2 x 2ft (60 x 60cm) **FLOWERS** Purple, star-shaped, ¾in (2cm) across, at soil level **ASPECT/LIKES** Full shade, shelter, well-drained soil **HARDINESS** Z 6-11

228. **COMMON NAME** Horsetail restio **HEIGHT AND SPREAD** 6½ x 3ft (2 x 1m) **FLOWERS** Small and brown, in 4in (10cm) spikes at stem tips in summer **ASPECT/LIKES** Full sun, moist well-drained soil, protection from winter cold **HARDINESS** Z 9-11

229. **COMMON NAME** Rough tree fern **HEIGHT AND SPREAD** 20 x 13ft (6 x 4m) **ASPECT/LIKES** Sheltered site away from cold winds, moist soil **HARDINESS** Z 9-11

230. **HEIGHT AND SPREAD** 2 x 1¼ft (60 x 40cm) **FLOWERS** Occasional pink bells 1¼in (3cm) long in summer **ASPECT/LIKES** Bright but not direct sun, away from radiators, plenty of space **HARDINESS** Z 10-11

231

Oxalis oregana

While some species of oxalis are troublesome weeds, others make appealing garden plants, and this ground-covering herbaceous perennial given to me by my former editor at *The Garden* magazine is one of the latter. The plant I grow is resolutely evergreen, but I believe deciduous kinds exist. Mine forms a thick carpet of cloverlike foliage that continues to look lush and green throughout fall. Each leaf is composed of three heart-shaped, dark-green leaflets, bright purple below and with a silvery central mark above, the foliage held on purple leaf stalks. Growth arises from rhizomes that cover the soil surface and, through summer, little white flowers sparkle amid the leaves. The plant would do well in a shaded border or below trees, perhaps with ferns, but I like it in a container, perfect under large potted shrubs, providing a lush froth of growth that spills out over the edges.

COMMON NAME Redwood sorrel **HEIGHT AND SPREAD** 8 x 24in (20 x 60cm) or more **FLOWERS** Occasional white flowers ¾–1¼in (2–3cm) wide in summer **ASPECT/LIKES** Part shade, moist humus-rich well-drained soil **HARDINESS** Z 7-9

"If you grow only one aster, this is probably the best to choose, for its superb displays of fall flowers."

232

Aster × *frikartii* 'Mönch'

If you grow only one aster, this is probably the best to choose, for its superb displays of fall flowers, ease of cultivation, and useful size. It is a fairly sturdy herbaceous perennial growing to just under 3ft (1m) tall, the well-branched, self-supporting stems gradually forming a broad clump. The daisylike flowers are profuse, opening from late September, the display improving until a vivid sheet of flowers forms. Individually, the rather graceful daisies are quite large, the petals mauve-blue around a golden button-like center, each lasting several weeks and attracting late pollinating insects, including butterflies. With a backdrop of fiery fall foliage and perhaps beside the last golden rudbeckias, they make a glorious sight. This selection is renowned for being free from mildew, a disease that can badly affect asters.

HEIGHT AND SPREAD 3 x 3ft (1 x 1m)
FLOWERS 3in (8cm) across, through mid- and late fall
ASPECT/LIKES Sunny open site, fertile soil, not too dry
HARDINESS Z 5-9

233

Cupressus cashmeriana

I fell in love with this beautiful tree as a boy on pilgrimages to London's Royal Botanic Gardens, Kew. In the mighty Temperate House soared surely the most elegant of conifers, its branches almost reaching the roof but positively dripping with delicate, flattened sprays of soft silvery-blue foliage in utterly glorious cascades of growth. I never then imagined that this endangered native of Bhutan and northeastern India would survive outdoors. But I bought a plant, which quickly and easily reached the roof of my little greenhouse, and had no choice but to risk it in the garden of the family house in Surrey. Surprisingly to me, it thrived, surviving even the cold winter of 2010 with little damage. I've yet to try it in my current garden, but I've now seen it outdoors elsewhere, where the trees are doing well. It is true that outdoor plants are less luxuriant and not as silvery blue in hue as those under glass, but they look good through fall and on until the first hard frosts. They make exciting trees for adventurous gardeners with a sunny, sheltered corner away from cold, drying winds in well-drained soil.

COMMON NAME Weeping cypress **HEIGHT AND SPREAD** 33 x 10ft (10 x 3m) outdoors **FLOWERS** Small pollen cones followed by oval seed cones 2in (5cm) long that stay on the plant for about two years **ASPECT/ LIKES** Sun, warm sheltered site, good drainage **HARDINESS** Z 9-11

234

Elaeagnus × *submacrophylla*

This large, useful evergreen is all too often relegated to municipal plantings but deserves better. To begin with, its oval, pointed foliage is far from ordinary—the young leaves in spring are beautifully metallic, almost like lightly tarnished silver, and are held on copper-colored stems. As they age, they become dark matte green speckled with pewter. New shoots can arise with great vigor; stems have spines that, in combination with the back-swept branches, help this plant hoist itself up through small trees. This wild habit can be embraced or retrained, for regular clipping transforms this shrub into a first-rate hedge. The best feature, though, is in fall, when little, white, bell-shaped flowers appear. They are not easy to spot, but the sweet scent is delicious and travels well on the air. Juicy, red berries follow, which you can add to fruit salads. Gold-variegated 'Gilt Edge' is another elaeagnus to consider, for its impressive winter foliage.

COMMON NAME Ebbinge's silverberry **HEIGHT AND SPREAD** 13 x 10ft (4 x 3m) **FLOWERS** ½in (1cm) long, sweetly scented, in fall **ASPECT/LIKES** Sun or part shade, any reasonable soil **HARDINESS** Z 7-10

235

Phlebodium aureum

COMMON NAME Golden polypody **HEIGHT AND SPREAD** 2¾ x 3ft (80 x 100cm) **ASPECT/LIKES** Bright room away from direct sun, not too wet **HARDINESS** Z 10-11

Until a few years ago, this unusual-looking fern was rarely seen, but in the past decade, it has become a popular houseplant—and for good reason. To begin with, it is easy to grow, tolerating a range of conditions found in our homes, including central heating. It grows from branching rhizomes that creep across the soil surface. These are, for want of a better word, furry, covered in dense golden hairs. From these sprout the upright, sea-green, lobed fronds, held aloft on short stems, the tone bluer if plants are in brighter light. On mature plants, fronds can be quite large (around 3ft/1m long) and look rather different, arching over elegantly. It can be grown in a pot or hanging basket. It likes moisture yet is forgiving of the odd missed watering. It also appreciates humidity, so does well in bathrooms, but again it can stand quite dry air too.

236

Arbutus unedo 'Atlantic'

This evergreen shrub or small tree is a valuable, refined garden plant with genuine year-round appeal, although it is best in fall when, rather unusually, it displays both colorful, ripe fruit and flowers at the same time. Slow and compact growing, it will in time form a tree with a dense rounded canopy around 10ft (3m) high. The sprays of white, bell-shaped flowers develop into bunches of rough-skinned, rounded, edible but tasteless fruit. They ripen from yellow to orange, eventually to bright red, the process taking a year. In time, plants also develop attractive, red bark, which is shown off perfectly by oval, lightly serrated, dark-green glossy leaves. My advice is to buy a young shrub and enjoy it in a container for a few years, planting it when reasonably mature and perhaps removing low branches for a treelike shape. It is generally easy and trouble-free.

COMMON NAME Strawberry tree **HEIGHT AND SPREAD** 10 x 10ft (3 x 3m) **FLOWERS** ¾in (2cm) long, held in clusters in fall **ASPECT/LIKES** Sun, open site, good drainage, great for coastal gardens **HARDINESS** Z 7-10

237

Euonymus alatus 'Compactus'

Bringing fall foliage color into a small garden can be tricky—the most spectacular tints often come from large-growing plants. However, this compact, mound-shaped *Euonymus* is fairly easy to accommodate and its foliage has among the most vivid fall color of all. Its appeal begins in spring: the young shoots with pointed, oval leaves are lush and glistening emerald green. But it is in fall that the fireworks begin, the leaves gradually turning to rich-scarlet tones. Eventually, the whole bush glows red before the leaves fall. The best colors are produced by plants in sunny open positions, but they will stand part shade. In summer, you could use a plant, such as a clematis, as a host for a climber that is not too vigorous.

COMMON NAME Winged spindle **HEIGHT AND SPREAD** 3 x 3ft (1 x 1m) **ASPECT/LIKES** Sun or part shade, any soil, not too wet or too dry **HARDINESS** Z 3-9

238

Decaisnea fargesii

COMMON NAME Dead man's fingers **HEIGHT AND SPREAD** 13 x 10ft (4 x 3m) **FLOWERS** 1¼in (3cm) across, green, held in a 4in (10cm) cluster in spring **ASPECT/LIKES** Part shade, fertile well-drained soil **HARDINESS** Z 4-8

This is the perfect deciduous shrub for Halloween, at which time it bears clusters of rather bizarre-looking fruit that give the plant its gruesome common name. Most of the year, however, it is quietly attractive, with bold pinnate leaves to around 32in (80cm) long held on upright, branching, suckering stems that form a multistemmed clump. New growth begins in spring and may need protecting from frosts in mid- to late spring. With it appear arching clusters of attractive, bright-green flowers. So far, so good. By fall, oddly ornamental, cylindrical fruits develop, held in clusters, each about the shape, size, and bruised-blue color of a (rather substantial) detached human finger. It gets worse: if you touch them, they are cold, with a soft, fleshlike texture. Best to put such thoughts out of your mind and enjoy them as blue seed pods hanging amid the butter-yellow tints the leaves acquire.

239

Rubus henryi

An unusual ornamental bramble grown for its foliage, this evergreen is a scrambling climber you can grow through large shrubs or small trees. It will scale a wall or fence but will need training and tying in to wires. The leaves are handsome—three-lobed and glossy, rich green on top, with a tarnished silver, felted reverse, held on slender barbed (as opposed to thorny) stems that are silver when young. These root as they touch the ground, but fear not—this plant is not especially vigorous. In summer, pinkish flowers appear that insects go crazy for. They are followed by small blackberries that are edible but not worth the bother. Stems grow to around 16ft (5m) through trees. Foliage is at its best cascading down, glistening and contrasting with fall tints of *Cercis* or maples, and is useful in winter when all else is bare. It thrives in even, dry shade but will flourish in sun and stands drought when established.

241

Chrysanthemum 'Innocence'

This chrysanthemum is a beauty. Upright, self-supporting stems form a rounded clump, topped by masses of long-lasting, yellow-centered daisy flowers of soft, clear pink—a delicate hue at this time of year. The display can last well into November and attracts late pollinating insects. If you like chrysanths a bit more compact, pinching out the tips in midsummer will create shorter, denser plants. Split and replant clumps every three years to maintain vigor. Pass on any surplus to friends—they will be delighted.

240

Clematis terniflora

This vigorous, late-flowering, deciduous clematis bursts into bloom in midfall, producing masses of little, starry, white flowers, each with four petals and a crown of anthers. In a sunny position, the frothy flowers can smother the plant, and the delicious, sweet almond scent can be detected from some distance. Give it well-drained soil and an open setting with as much sun as possible; it grows well enough in some shade, but flowering is reduced. It will scale a tree or cascade from a tall hedge; otherwise, grow up trellis. It may need restraint—prune in late winter before it starts to grow.

242

Sorbus cashmiriana

A delectable small tree appreciated for its impressive displays of white, marble-size fruits in fall, this mountain ash is worth going the extra mile to accommodate. In spring, it produces attractive, pink-tinged white flowers, which in time are followed by fruits that hang in clusters and last well on the tree, often into winter, glistening amid the deciduous foliage. In fall, the leaves develop lovely, reddish orange and yellow tints before falling. The tree is fairly upright growing, with an open habit, reaching around 13ft (4m) in 10 years. Plants do better in a border than grown as a specimen in a lawn, as roots hate compaction, and the base of the tree likes shade. The fruits show up best against a dark backdrop, perhaps tall conifers.

239. COMMON NAME Henry's raspberry **HEIGHT AND SPREAD** Climbs to 16ft (5m) **FLOWERS** Pinkish, bramble-like, ¾in (2cm) across, in summer **ASPECT/LIKES** Shade, somewhere to scramble, any reasonable soil **HARDINESS** Z 5-9

240. COMMON NAME Sweet autumn clematis **HEIGHT AND SPREAD** Climbs to 20ft (6m) **FLOWERS** ¾in (2cm) across, produced in multitudes in mid- to late fall **ASPECT/LIKES** Sunny, as warm a site as possible, good drainage **HARDINESS** Z 5-9

241. HEIGHT AND SPREAD 2¾ x 2ft (80 x 60cm) **FLOWERS** 2½in (6cm) across, produced in profusion from mid- to late fall **ASPECT/LIKES** Sun, open site, fertile soil **HARDINESS** Z 5-9

242. COMMON NAME Kashmir mountain ash **HEIGHT AND SPREAD** 13 x 10ft (4 x 3m) **FLOWERS** ½–¾in (1–2cm) across, held in clusters in spring **ASPECT/LIKES** Sun or part shade, shelter, fertile moist well-drained soil, not too dry **HARDINESS** Z 4-7

243

Goeppertia kegeljanii
Network

COMMON NAME Network calathea **HEIGHT AND SPREAD** 16 x 20in (40 x 50cm) **FLOWERS** 1¼in (3cm) across, held at soil level in early summer **ASPECT/LIKES** Bright windowsill away from direct sun and radiators **HARDINESS** Z 10-11

Also known as 'Pp0005,' this extremely handsome houseplant seems easy to please. Its main attraction is the wonderful leaves, which are rich green with a most unusual, fine, netlike, green-yellow patterning, best seen with the light shining through. They are also superbly glossy—especially the new leaves—tough and waxy, which explains why the plant is straightforward to keep. It slowly forms a clump, the oval, slightly rippled leaves arching outward on slender stems. Occasionally, little white flowers arise below the leaves, but these are easily missed. Avoid letting it get too dry, but equally never let it stand in water. It likes humidity, so stand the pot on moist pebbles and keep above 50°F (10°C). This plant is a relative newcomer at garden centers and has become quite popular.

244

Jubaea chilensis

This noble South American palm surprisingly, perhaps, has proved to be impressively hardy outdoors with me, standing the 2010 winter (wrapped in fleece), when temperatures dropped to around 10°F (–12°C). As a young plant, it is similar in appearance to Canary Island date palms, which are so often planted and then lost in the next colder-than-average winter. It very slowly forms an upright-growing shuttlecock of bright-green, feather-shaped leaves, the base gradually widening with age and eventually, after 15–20 years, a stout trunk begins to form. The plants look their best in October after a season's growth, the foliage still fresh and sprightly. Grow it in full sun in as warm a place as you can muster, in well-drained soil that does not get too dry.

COMMON NAME Chilean wine palm **HEIGHT AND SPREAD** 16 x 6½ft (5 x 2m) or more, but slow growing outdoors **FLOWERS** Small, yellow, held in clusters 3ft (1m) or so long (mature trees only) **ASPECT/LIKES** Full sun, warmth, shelter **HARDINESS** Z 8-11

245

Berberis wilsoniae

Too often associated with parking lots and municipal plantings, the genus *Berberis* includes some really outstanding garden shrubs, one of them being this lovely semievergreen species. Plants are quite variable and some sold with this name may be hybrids, but generally it forms a small and densely branched, mound-shaped, prickly shrub with little, blue-green oval foliage, the individual leaves usually shorter than the slender spines that armor its branches. In late summer, fairly insignificant clusters of yellow flowers open. A profusion of coral-colored berries follows and remains on the plant during October, clustered along arching stems as the foliage begins to color. The glowing display in shades of pinkish red is at its best backlit by the late-afternoon sun. The plant looks good growing on a bank or somewhere raised up, so it can catch the rays.

COMMON NAME Wilson's barberry **HEIGHT AND SPREAD** 3 x 5ft (1 x 1.5m) **FLOWERS** Small, yellow, held in clusters in late summer **ASPECT/LIKES** Sun or part shade, open site, any soil but not too dry or too wet **HARDINESS** Z 6-9

"A profusion of coral-colored berries follows and remains on the plant during October."

246. **COMMON NAME** False castor oil plant **HEIGHT AND SPREAD** 10 x 6½ft (3 x 2m) **FLOWERS** Tiny, held in 8in (20cm) long branched heads in fall **ASPECT/LIKES** Part shade, shelter, moist rich soil **HARDINESS** Z 8-10

247. **COMMON NAME** Giant chain fern **HEIGHT AND SPREAD** 3 x 6½ft (1 x 2m) **ASPECT/LIKES** Shade, shelter, moist well-drained soil **HARDINESS** Z 8-9

248. **HEIGHT AND SPREAD** 4 x 6½ft (1.2 x 2m), taller in flower **FLOWERS** Tubular, 1¼in (3cm) long, held on a 6ft (1.8m) stem in summer **ASPECT/LIKES** Sun or part shade, open fairly moist site, protection from coldest conditions **HARDINESS** Z 7-10

249. **HEIGHT AND SPREAD** 5 x 5ft (1.5 x 1.5m) **FLOWERS** ½in (1cm) across, held in 2in (5cm) clusters in summer **ASPECT/LIKES** Light shade, fertile well-drained soil, not too dry **HARDINESS** Z 7-9

246

Fatsia japonica

This superlative shrub provides architectural foliage, at its mature best after summer, as well as, frost permitting, displays of flowers. Basically a giant shrubby ivy, it forms a cluster of stout, upright, occasionally branching stems. The leaves are the main event: leathery, glossy green, and palmate, with 5–7 deep lobes, 1ft (30cm) across, held on long stalks. Then in fall, terminal clusters of cream, ivylike flowers appear. These may be followed by drooping clusters of black fruit after a mild winter. Plants are variable, with slightly differing leaf forms. They are also tough and tolerant of quite deep, dry shade. Hard frost can cause foliage to curl and hang forlornly—but don't panic; it generally recovers. Stems can be pruned if they get too tall. Alternatively, remove lower branches to make them more treelike, and plant shade-lovers below.

247

Woodwardia fimbriata

Many evergreen ferns are at their verdant best in fall, before being beaten down by winter weather. This unusual species is one of the finest of all hardy kinds for sheltered corners of the garden. It is a clump-forming species, the handsome, fresh, green fronds distinctly upright-growing at first, although arching out in time. They are impressively large, reaching 3ft (1m) or more in length and, given plenty of space, add a really exotic touch to plantings. The plant needs plenty of moisture and, being a fern, enjoys shade, perhaps below deciduous trees or in the lee of a cool wall. Winter—particularly heavy snow—may damage the fronds. Cut the most unsightly ones off once new fronds begin to unfurl in spring. The fern also grows well in a container so long as it is not allowed to dry out.

248

Phormium cookianum subsp. *hookeri* 'Tricolor'

The most elegant and handsome phormium of all, this is compact enough to fit into the average garden. Instead of forming a towering clump of erect, rapier-like leaves like many other selections, it adopts a more relaxed form. With broad, evergreen blades striped in green and cream and edged with red, the foliage of this plant arches over gracefully, forming a lush clump. In summer, dark-purple stems rise to around 6ft (1.8m), bearing on short branches greenish-yellow, tubular flowers—all quite ornamental. It is happy in coastal gardens but adapts well elsewhere, forming an impressive contrast with clipped evergreens and other shrubs, especially in fall and winter, when its foliage and shape are most valuable.

249

Aucuba japonica 'Rozannie'

This compact, tidy, evergreen shrub should be more popular, as it is a first-class plant for both its bold, glossy foliage and impressive displays of berries in fall and winter. Sometimes *Aucuba* are reviled (I think unfairly) for their yellow-spotted foliage, but this selection's is rich green, the leaves large, oval, and toothed, with a lovely healthy shine, especially in spring when the young growth is pale green at first. Clusters of brownish flowers follow. By fall, these develop into bright-red berries, produced in profusion amid the foliage—the fruit appearing even if plants are grown on their own, as flowers are self-fertile. The plant puts up with a lot of bad treatment, standing drought and deep shade, but it is so lovely in fall and winter that it deserves better.

250

Mahonia oiwakensis subsp. *lomariifolia*

For fine, evergreen foliage and displays of fall flowers, this mahonia is an impressive choice. An upright-growing, multistemmed shrub, it becomes dome-shaped and distinctly architectural with age, making an excellent specimen plant. Sturdy, stout stems bear rosettes of tough, sharply pointed foliage, each pinnate (featherlike) leaf to around 20in (50cm) long, forming a fabulous ruff atop each stem, lower leaves shed as the plant grows. In November, the plant is crowned by slender, erect clusters of flowers at the tips of each stem. Individual, cup-shaped blooms are golden yellow and have a light scent. The display lasts a few weeks and is followed by ornamental blue berries. Almost as lovely as the flowers are the spring shoots—the new foliage wonderfully soft and bronze tinted. Plants are easy to grow in well-drained soil, but if conditions are on the dry side, they are more inclined to drop foliage, resulting in slightly leggy growth—easily solved with occasional pruning to keep plants more compact. In spring, the multitude of old dead leaves below need clearing, an unpleasant task, given the foliage spines.

HEIGHT AND SPREAD 10 x 5ft (3 x 1.5m) **FLOWERS** ½in (1cm) across, held in tight clusters to 8in (20cm) long from late fall until early winter **ASPECT/LIKES** Sun or part shade, well-drained soil **HARDINESS** Z 7-10

251

Asplenium scolopendrium

One of the most instantly recognizable ferns, this is an essential garden plant for its marvelous lustrous foliage. It is a clump-forming perennial, more or less evergreen, although its foliage gets shabby by late winter, when it is best cropped off before new emerging fronds develop. In midspring, it is a glorious sight—long, lance-shaped, entire (as opposed to lacelike) fronds of the brightest green with an incredible shine, among the loveliest of the season's fresh foliage, and a great plant for contrasting with the more rounded foliage of, say, *Hosta* or *Brunnera*. By fall, it is at its mature peak—it glistens amid fallen leaves. It revels in shade, especially moist shade, but is very tolerant and stands drier conditions well, seldom needing extra water, except in the most parched places. Grow it below deciduous trees, beside a north-facing wall, in containers, or even as fall bedding in a window box.

COMMON NAME Hart's tongue fern **HEIGHT AND SPREAD** 1¾ x 2ft (50 x 60cm) **ASPECT/LIKES** Shade, moist well-drained soil **HARDINESS** Z 4-9

252

Rhamnus alaternus 'Argenteovariegata'

If you are looking for a large, quick-growing, dense evergreen with sparkling, silver-edged foliage, this could be the one for you. Plants form rounded, upright bushes that are excellent for screening. They have slightly sticky, small, oval, dark-green leaves with bold, rather irregular, cream margins, the overall effect at its best in fall after a year's growth. Plants flower in spring, the blooms yellowish and tiny and followed by small red fruit that slowly age to black. It is easy to grow as long as the site is not waterlogged and will stand exposed, windy sites particularly well and tolerates drought, when established. It is best kept away from the coldest areas, however, as severe frost will damage it. Plants can be trimmed in summer to keep them tidy. Remove any all-green branches, which can quickly overtake the variegated foliage.

253

Fuchsia magellanica

It may seem odd to suggest a fuchsia—albeit a hardy one—as a highlight of a month associated with the first cold weather. But these days, especially in town and city gardens, November proves fairly benign, allowing plants that once finished flowering in early fall to bloom on and on. In sheltered places, this deciduous, upright-growing shrub may reach 10ft (3m) but is often smaller. Flowering begins in early summer if last year's growth is retained—long, slender, red and purple, tubular blooms dangling from stems in great profusion. The show lasts all summer, but the cooler, wetter days of fall revitalize the show, and flowers drape the plant as never before, alongside long, dark-purple, edible fruits. Light ground frosts often cause no harm and it is not until the first air frost that the display ends. Give it a sunny, sheltered place and avoid pruning unless it gets too big or dead wood needs removing.

254

Dipsacus fullonum

Teasels are invasive if you don't watch out, yet I always make sure I have at least a plant or two. It is a biennial, completing its life cycle in two years and thrives in any situation, as long as it is not too shady or dry. In the first year, it forms an evergreen rosette of dark-green, overlapping leaves. In the second year, a barbed, branched, flowering stem rises to 6½ft (2m), the thistlelike heads of purple flowers attracting many pollinators in early summer. The stems remain impressively statuesque throughout fall and winter, usefully punctuating planting. As the heads dry, seeds form, and these attract delightful charms of goldfinches to feed on them. Plants seed very freely, but extracting the seedlings is easy.

255

Viburnum tinus

Often overlooked by plant snobs, this versatile evergreen is easy to grow. It thrives in any garden as long as it is not too dry or too wet, standing sun or shade, and forming a dense, rounded shrub with glossy, oval foliage. Plants are often trimmed back to keep them bushy but are more pleasing if the lower branches are removed and the plant is treated as a multistemmed tree. This way, you can also underplant it. It has a long flowering season, its heads of white or pink-tinted flowers opening at times in profusion. They are followed by blue berries. Plants are tough, standing coastal exposure, but can be damaged by cold. Watch for viburnum beetle, whose larvae damage spring foliage. Pick off the worst leaves.

252. **COMMON NAME** Italian buckthorn **HEIGHT AND SPREAD** 13 x 10ft (4 x 3m) **ASPECT/LIKES** Sun, well-drained soil, open site, not too cold **HARDINESS** Z 6-9

253. **COMMON NAME** Hummingbird fuchsia **HEIGHT AND SPREAD** 10 x 10ft (3 x 3m) **FLOWERS** Slender, to 1½in (4cm) long, from early summer until the first air frost **ASPECT/LIKES** Sun, shelter, good drainage **HARDINESS** Z 6-9

254. **COMMON NAME** Teasel **HEIGHT AND SPREAD** 6½ x 1¾ft (200 x 50cm) **FLOWERS** Tiny, violet, held in an 3in (8cm) head in early summer **ASPECT/LIKES** Sun, open site, poor soil **HARDINESS** Z 4-8

255. **COMMON NAME** Laurustinus **HEIGHT AND SPREAD** 13 x 10ft (4 x 3m) **FLOWERS** Small, held in 2in (5cm) heads, often in great profusion, from fall until spring **ASPECT/LIKES** Sun or shade, well-drained soil, shelter from extreme cold **HARDINESS** Z 7-8

256

Camellia sasanqua 'Narumigata'

Fall-flowering camellias—mostly selections of *Camellia sasanqua*, like this one—are still seldom grown but are among the most reliable and cheering of garden flowers at this time of year. This evergreen shrub produces fairly slender, upright-growing branches, with small, oval, dark-green foliage. The charming, cup-shaped flowers open from November and on into December; they are single and rather fragile, with golden stamens in the middle. The petals are white but marked seemingly randomly at the edges in strong pink. They are said to be scented, though I find it hard to detect anything I'd call perfume. Like all camellias, it needs fairly moist, well-drained, acidic soil, but selections from this species flower better in rather more sun than other camellias. It will adapt well to life in a container of acidic potting mix; choose a sheltered, ideally sunny corner, and ensure it is watered regularly.

HEIGHT AND SPREAD 10 x 6½ft (3 x 2m) **FLOWERS** 2½in (6cm) across, from late fall to early winter **ASPECT/LIKES** Light shade, shelter, well-drained acid soil **HARDINESS** Z 7-9

"The charming, cup-shaped flowers open from November and on into December."

257

Buxus sempervirens 'Elegantissima'

A lovely variegated shrub, silver box makes an elegant and eye-catching evergreen. Its small, dense, oval leaves are generously edged in cream, helping it appear rather less heavy than all-green selections of box, particularly in fall and winter, when it helpfully adds lightness and color, as well as structure. Use it perhaps clipped as balls or domes, to add structure in planting; plants look especially good repeated along a path to provide a sense of rhythm, while a pair can be used effectively on either side of a doorway, arch, or flight of steps. Like its plain-green cousin, it also thrives in containers if looked after and is indispensable for a smart patio or terrace. It will stand dry conditions for a while. Young growth can be damaged by late frost, and watch closely for both box moth caterpillar and the dreaded box blight. Pick off moth caterpillars by hand, and remove growth affected by blight completely. To prevent reinfection, practice careful hygiene subsequently by getting rid of any fallen leaves and clippings from around and below the plant.

COMMON NAME Silver box **HEIGHT AND SPREAD** Usually kept trimmed to 3 x 3ft (1 x 1m) **ASPECT/LIKES** Sun or shade, open site, well-drained soil **HARDINESS** Z 5-8

258

Phyllostachys aureosulcata f. *spectabilis*

Some gardeners like their bamboos big and bold, and this super plant will meet expectations. It is potentially a large, vigorous, running bamboo, spreading by underground rhizomes, usually not invasive, except in mild, moist conditions, but a plant that may need restraining by removing the running rhizomes each year. Its glossy culms (stems) are wonderfully golden-yellow with a green stripe, shining out in the fall garden. The lance-shaped, evergreen foliage is light and glossy. Key is summer heat and moisture. My plant is a division from a previous garden, where this bamboo grew slowly and formed a modest clump. Planted in the current garden by a south-facing wall in a place damp from the runoff from my outbuilding's roof, it has grown impressively. In a shaded, drier place, it would be a far smaller, tighter clump. Remove the lower branches to expose the stem color and thin out old dull culms annually.

COMMON NAME Showy yellow groove bamboo **HEIGHT AND SPREAD** 16 x 13ft (5 x 4m) or more **ASPECT/LIKES** Summer warmth, shelter, fairly moist soil **HARDINESS** Z 6-10

259

Trachycarpus wagnerianus

Introduced from cultivation in Japan more than a century ago, this palm has never been found in the wild anywhere in the world and has only recently become appreciated, with many growers now regarding it as the finest palm that can be reliably grown outdoors in mild climate. At first glance, it appears similar to the popular *Trachycarpus fortunei* (Chusan palm), with its fan-shaped leaves and slender, shaggy trunk, but look again and you will see important differences. It has a far tidier appearance, its leaves rather smaller and stiffer, held in a distinct upright stance, which makes the plant more compact and resistant to winds that reduce to tatters the fans of its better-known relative. In all, it looks better proportioned and more elegant and is especially impressive seen with a light dusting of frost, which highlights the divided foliage beautifully. After a few years, plants begin to form a trunk and bear pendant bunches of yellow flowers that develop from the crown. Give it a sheltered but fairly open sunny site. Young plants will thrive in containers for several years.

COMMON NAMES Waggy or Wagner's fan palm **HEIGHT AND SPREAD** 16 x 6½ft (5 x 2m) **FLOWERS** Tiny, yellow, held in branched clusters 16in (40cm) long in summer **ASPECT/LIKES** Sun, shelter, well-drained but moist soil **HARDINESS** Z 6-10

260

Euphorbia ceratocarpa

Native to southern Italy, this exceptional herbaceous perennial is evergreen and forms a shrubby plant, its leaves lance-shaped, bright green with a central silvery midrib, and held on upright slender pinkish stems. These are topped by delicate, long-lasting heads of bright, yellow-green flowers, which appear from late spring until December, later if winter is mild. Its displays in summer are the most showy, but its contribution to the garden late in the year more impressive. My plant has never needed watering, even in dry summers. It can be damaged by cold winters. Cut out dead stems in spring; new shoots arise from the base.

261

Ficus tikoua

This unusual fig is a ground-covering plant, most useful in fall for its overlapping green foliage. It hails from China and makes a handsome carpet of rather rough, oval, rich-green leaves held on woody stems that root in as they go. You can trim rogue stems to no ill effect and create interesting, dense cover below trees and shrubs. Winter normally knocks the plant back and defoliates it, but in milder years this seldom happens. Once established, it is vigorous and you need to watch its spread. I've tried to get it to grow as a self-clinging climber up a wall, like the smaller, more tender *Ficus pumila*, but my plant is having none of it. In the wild, it forms small red figs, but no sign of them here; you need male and female plants. It grows in sun or shade in any well-drained soil. It has never been affected by drought in my garden.

262

Rosa Summer Wine

Some roses are worth considering in the fall garden for their displays of hips; this fine climber, also known as 'Korizont,' is a good example. It is a lovely thing through summer, when it produces masses of scented single flowers with petals that are a rather unusual coral-pink, fading to yellow in the center. It is a strong, healthy rose, the glossy, dark-green foliage seldom troubled by disease. If you stop dead-heading in late summer, you will get to enjoy the displays of hips, which shine among the still-green leaves in November and remain on the plant after the foliage has fallen. They are quite large and glossy, bright red-orange, and held in conspicuous clusters that are so lovely you might want to cut them and enjoy them inside for a couple of weeks.

263

Polystichum munitum

Fans of the *Star Wars* movie *Return of the Jedi* may recall scenes set on the forest moon of Endor, with its towering trees and sea of huge ferns below. Filmed in California, the giant trees are coastal redwoods and the fern is this majestic species. It makes a wonderful, easily grown evergreen, slowly building into impressive mounds of dark-green fronds that can arch to 5ft (1.5m), given adequate moisture. When established, the plant is pretty robust, standing long spells of hot, dry weather well. In the cool, moist conditions of fall, it is at its best, before winter's cold and snow damage its appearance. In spring, clumps can be tidied as new fronds begin to emerge. Plant below deciduous trees and shrubs or beside a cool but sheltered wall.

260. COMMON NAME Horned spurge **HEIGHT AND SPREAD** 4 x 4ft (1.2 x 1.2m) **FLOWERS** ⅝in (1.5cm) across, held in 6in (15cm) wide heads from late spring until early winter **ASPECT/LIKES** Sun, shelter, well-drained soil **HARDINESS** Z 8-10

261. HEIGHT AND SPREAD 6in x 10ft (15 x 300cm) **ASPECT/LIKES** Sun or shade, shelter from cold **HARDINESS** Z 9-11

262. HEIGHT AND SPREAD Climbs to 10ft (3m) **FLOWERS** Semidouble (although they look single), 4in (10cm) across, produced in profusion throughout summer **ASPECT/LIKES** Sunny fence or pergola, well-drained soil **HARDINESS** Z 5-9

263. COMMON NAME Western sword fern **HEIGHT AND SPREAD** 5 x 5ft (1.5 x 1.5m) **ASPECT/LIKES** Cool shade, moist well-drained soil **HARDINESS** Z 5-9

<u>264</u>

Blechnum chilense

Another evergreen fern making my November selection, this majestic South American species is a distinctive plant with a really exotic look. In mild, moist places, it makes remarkable, dense clumps to 5ft (1.5m) tall, spreading widely from rhizomatous roots. Its sturdy, dark-green, almost prickly fronds composed of leathery leaflets with undulating margins are most valuable for their impressive appearance in fall. It looks superb below tree ferns. Young fronds are often pink flushed before turning glossy bright green. In my dry garden, it is far smaller: even by a sheltered, north-facing wall with extra water in summer, it is only around 2ft (60cm) tall with a couple of rosettes, but still impressive. It is not entirely hardy and can be damaged by snow, but after a spring clean up, new growth soon regenerates the plant. A thick mulch in early spring helps ensure lush growth.

COMMON NAME Chilean hard fern **HEIGHT AND SPREAD** 5 x 6½ft (1.5 x 2m) **FLOWERS** None **ASPECT/LIKES** Shade, shelter from cold winds, well-drained consistently moist soil **HARDINESS** Z 7-9

265

Arum pictum

I don't grow as many alpine plants as I'd like, but this Mediterranean arum is a real gem. It starts into growth in midfall, the shoots unrolling to reveal fantastically glossy, rounded heart-shaped leaves. These are dark green with a reddish edge; in some plants, foliage develops conspicuous silvery veins. Plants grow from tuberous roots and form a clump, the foliage reaching 16in (40cm). After a couple of years, you may notice pointed, reddish shoots pushing through the soil before or at the same time as the leaves. These develop into maroon flowers, each with a darker central spadix (spike of minute flowers). They are interesting rather than beautiful and give off a nasty pong if you put your nose up close to them. Leaves shine through winter before fading in late spring. Plants must have a sunny, sharply drained site and are best kept in a raised bed or trough of gritty soil, although they will also thrive at the edge of a sunny, well-drained border.

HEIGHT AND SPREAD 16 x 16in (40 x 40cm) **FLOWERS** Around 6in (15cm) tall in fall **ASPECT/LIKES** Full sun, very well-drained site **HARDINESS** Z 6-9

266

Nandina domestica

Sacred bamboo is a shrub that seems to have it all: handsome, evergreen foliage; a neat, upright, architectural form; sprays of pretty, little, white, summer flowers; followed, if you are lucky, by showy, long-lasting, orange-red berries; and then—to top it off—impressive fall foliage tints. Yes, even on an evergreen. Plants form a tight thicket of upright, unbranched stems to 5ft (1.5m), the wonderful, fernlike leaves composed of pointed, rounded leaflets to around 1ft (30cm) long, sometimes more. There is a slight caveat: for some reason, plants usually survive rather than thrive. Shelter seems to be key. Moisture, summer heat, and wind protection are also important. There are several named selections, some adding purple young growth to the plant's virtues. Best known is 'Fire Power,' a dwarf plant I have mixed feelings about. Its fiery foliage is incredible in fall, but the leaves look deformed and the elegance of the plant is quite lost. Again, it is tricky to keep looking happy.

COMMON NAME Sacred bamboo **HEIGHT AND SPREAD** 5 x 5ft (1.5 x 1.5m) **FLOWERS** ½in (1cm) across, held in a cone-shaped head 6in (15cm) long in summer **ASPECT/LIKES** Light shade, shelter **HARDINESS** Z 6-11

267

Hedera helix 'Buttercup'

This is an old ivy cultivar but one that has never been bettered for its evergreen—or evergolden—foliage. It is still not that often seen, for it needs some care to get well established. In many respects, it is like any other common ivy, except for the fact that its leaves, especially when young, are a wonderful pale yellow. They are really incredible when seen on a well-grown, mature plant, although they age gradually to lime-green. Plants need a sunny place to produce the most vibrant color and usually look best scaling a wall or tree trunk, but this ivy can also eventually make good ground cover. A bit of coaxing is needed to get it to attach to a vertical surface, but continual contact with the wall or fence is important if the plant is to self-cling with its little aerial roots. Plant in improved soil in a fairly sheltered spot.

HEIGHT AND SPREAD Climbs to 13ft (4m) **FLOWERS** Small and green, held in 1¼in (3cm) rounded heads on mature growth in fall **ASPECT/LIKES** Part shade or sun, a surface to cling to, decent soil **HARDINESS** Z 5-10

268

Sarcococca wallichii

COMMON NAME Wallich's sweet box
HEIGHT AND SPREAD 3 x 3ft (1 x 1m)
FLOWERS Small, held in ¾in (2cm) clusters in late fall and early winter **ASPECT/LIKES** Cool shade, shelter, moist well-drained soil
HARDINESS Z 8-10

Most commonly grown sarcococcas flower freely in late winter and early spring, but this rather more unusual species is earlier, providing its lovely scent in late fall. Native to Nepal, it is a clump-forming, evergreen shrub, with upright then arching stems well furnished with shining, rich-green foliage. The long, oval, pointed leaves are larger than in many more familiar species, such as *Sarcococca confusa*. This is also a larger, more open plant, the green stems reaching around 3ft (1m) tall; in all, quite strong growing when established. The sweetly scented, white starry flowers are held in clusters in leaf axils and, although tiny and pretty insignificant, they certainly pack a punch to the nose, the sweet perfume carrying on the air, quite a surprise in November. Plant it somewhere sheltered, probably in the lee of deciduous trees.

269

Schefflera taiwaniana

This extraordinary, evergreen shrub or small tree does well in drier areas. Its arresting palmate leaves can be 8in (20cm) across, held on initially upright leaf stems. New growth arising from stem tips in spring is superbly silvery and at its most dramatic when fully developed in fall. It develops stout, occasionally branched stems, forming a large, impressive, usually multistemmed shrub with a rounded crown. Give it a sheltered, partly shaded site tucked below deciduous trees, near a wall perhaps out of drying winds.

HEIGHT AND SPREAD 13 x 6½ft (4 x 2m) **FLOWERS** ½in (1cm), green-white, carried in 8in (20cm) across clusters on mature plants in summer **ASPECT/LIKES** Part shade, shelter, protection from extreme cold, fertile well-drained moist soil **HARDINESS** Z 8-10

270

Carex oshimensis 'Everillo'

HEIGHT AND SPREAD 1 x 2¾ft (30 x 80cm) **ASPECT/LIKES** Part shade, well-drained soil, not too dry **HARDINESS** Z 5-9

For fall and winter color, this evergreen sedge makes a terrific investment. Quick growing, it forms a large mound of grassy leaves to 20in (50cm) long, erect at first then arching gracefully. In summer, plants are lime-green, but in winter they take on an impressive golden tint—spectacular in a shaded position. It is a plant that suits a container almost better than the open ground: its leaf blades are so long, they cascade beautifully over the sides of a pot or, better still, an urn elevated on a pedestal. It colors up best in sun, so by keeping it in a container you can move it about to suit. It is easy to grow if kept fairly moist—keep an eye on this in summer. Mature plants hold on to old foliage; trim them in spring. Split plants that are too large at the same time.

271

Luma apiculata 'Glanleam Gold'

This cheery, evergreen, Chilean myrtle has several great qualities that make it a terrific garden shrub or small tree. Upright growing, the ascending branches are densely clothed with small, oval, dark-green leaves that have creamy-gold edges—most impressive in fall and winter. When shoots are young in spring, the foliage also has an appealing pinkish tinge, while in summer white, four-petaled flowers appear in quantity, followed by edible, black fruits. Young plants are bushy and can be lightly trimmed to keep them compact—they will even make a reasonable hedge. However, grown this way, you miss out on another of this plant's great characteristics—its cinnamon-colored bark, which peels away at times, leaving creamy patches—a lovely sight in any season. Grow in some shelter, as it is not entirely hardy, choosing not too dry a position. It will do well in a container for a while.

COMMON NAME Chilean myrtle **HEIGHT AND SPREAD** 13 x 6½ft (4 x 2m) **FLOWERS** ¾in (2cm) across in summer **ASPECT/LIKES** Sun or part shade, shelter, moist well-drained soil, shelter from cold **HARDINESS** Z 8-10

272. COMMON NAME Rimu **HEIGHT AND SPREAD** 2¾ x 6½ft (75 x 200cm), more in time **ASPECT/LIKES** Cool light shade, shelter, well-drained moist acid soil, best under glass in winter **HARDINESS** Z 8-11

273. COMMON NAME Cabbage palm **HEIGHT AND SPREAD** 10 x 5ft (3 x 1.5m) **FLOWERS** Rare, individually tiny, held in a branched 2¾ft (80cm) long spike **ASPECT/LIKES** Sun, open but warm site **HARDINESS** Z 9-11

274. COMMON NAME Silver spear **HEIGHT AND SPREAD** 4 x 2¾ft (120 x 80cm) **FLOWERS** Tiny, insignificant, held in a spike, hidden by foliage **ASPECT/LIKES** Sun or part shade, shelter from cold, moist well-drained soil **HARDINESS** Z 8-9

275. COMMON NAMES Paper-bearing borinda or blue bamboo **HEIGHT AND SPREAD** 20 x 6½ft (6 x 2m) **ASPECT/LIKES** Shelter from drying winds, consistently moist soil **HARDINESS** Z 8-9

272

Dacrydium cupressinum

Conifers do not come much more desirable than this elegant New Zealander, which is a plant to try in a cool conservatory, although it will grow outdoors in mild areas. In the wild, it reaches a vast size, but the slow-growing, graceful youngsters we see here are different. They form a delicate-looking, weeping tree, dripping slender branchlets with bristly, scalelike leaves arching out to 2ft (60cm), young growth pale green at the tips. It's a nice thing in fall, when its spring and summer growth has matured and can be admired. Grow in a container of well-drained, acidic compost and keep moist and cool in a lightly shaded place. Stand out in summer in a sheltered position, but move under glass in winter. When it reaches the roof, it may be time to try outdoors, in a semishaded spot away from drying winds; just keep your fingers crossed.

273

Cordyline australis 'Torbay Dazzler'

There can be something a bit bargain-basement about cordylines—they are so ubiquitous, it can be hard to see them for the terrific foliage plants they are, adding a feel of the tropics to gardens. This selection deserves special treatment, for, when mature, it is impressive. Strappy green leaves at first form a simple rosette, lavishly edged and striped with cream, boldest in full sun. The bases of leaves are often flushed pink. As the plant matures, it develops a stout trunk and palmlike appearance, the leaves forming a rounded head of colorful foliage that stands out particularly well in fall. It needs a warm sunny place, sheltered from frost, as it can be killed in winter if its growing point freezes. The best plants are often in towns, where they dodge frost, or by the coast, where they excel.

274

Astelia chathamica

With impressively bold, sharply defined foliage that looks almost as if it's been crafted from sheet metal, *Astelia* are particularly useful in fall and winter because of their evergreen nature. A genus of herbaceous perennials, they are native to the southern hemisphere and can grow on tree branches as epiphytes—something worth trying in the garden. This one comes from the Chatham Islands, east of New Zealand. It forms a clump of upright then arching, bladelike leaves, with clean edges pointed at the tips. Plants seem to be lusher in shade and more silvery in sun. Winter can knock them back, but they normally recover. Consider growing them in containers, which they seem to enjoy, so you can move them under cover if need be.

275

Borinda papyrifera

The idea of a blue-stemmed bamboo may seem far fetched, but this is a super plant. Native to parts of China, it is clump forming, so well behaved. New culms (stems) arise bolt upright, clothed in large papery sheaths. They are a gorgeous soft powder-blue and remain so for a couple of years before aging to tan as they develop more foliage—leaves lance-shaped and rich green—and adopt an arching, graceful habit. I like the plant best in fall when the current season's growth is fresh yet mature. Still rare, it is sometimes available from specialty nurseries. There are several clones, some with bluer culms than others.

winter

276

Miscanthus transmorrisonensis

Usefully evergreen, as well as handsome and upstanding, this structural grass is a plant that really comes to the fore in the time between leaf fall and midwinter, when it still looks tidy and verdant and is topped by interesting seed heads. It is not quite as tall as many other feather grasses, reaching around 4ft (1.2m), rather more when in flower, the rich-green, quite slender foliage itself rather shorter. In summer, one-sided flower dusters arise, held well above the foliage. They are produced most freely after a good summer. Pink-tinged at first, they become pale buff as they age and turn to rather fluffy, long-lasting seed heads. Sometimes the plant self-seeds around a bit and will form quite a wide clump. The evergreen foliage does begin to yellow a little by the end of winter. I find this grass does rather well in a pot.

COMMON NAME Evergreen eulalia **HEIGHT AND SPREAD** 4 x 2¾ft (120 x 80cm) **FLOWERS** Tiny, held in 4in (10cm) long plumes in summer **ASPECT/LIKES** Sun, shelter, well-drained soil **HARDINESS** Z 6-9

"This structural grass is a plant that really comes to the fore in the time between leaf fall and midwinter."

277

Mahonia gracilipes

You can't have enough mahonias in fall and winter, for their evergreen architectural foliage and, often, illuminating displays of flowers. This species is rather different. For a start, it flowers in August or September, with long, slender clusters of red and yellow flowers appearing from shoot tips—pretty but not spectacular. They are followed by blue berries. When these are lost in fall, an unusual but showy feature takes over, as the flower stems turn bright coral pink, the color lingering through winter. The plant is fairly upright at first, then becomes more spreading, forming a dome-shaped shrub. Shoots carry arching, pinnate leaves to 2ft (60cm), the oval pointed leaflets lightly toothed and slightly prickly. The surprise comes when you turn these over—underneath, they are dazzling white, although this fades on old leaves. New shoots in the spring are pink flushed and easily damaged by frost or wind, so give the plant shelter.

HEIGHT AND SPREAD 4½ x 3ft (1.4 x 1m) **FLOWERS** ½in (1cm) across, held in 8in (20cm) clusters in late summer or early fall **ASPECT/LIKES** Light shade, shelter, well-drained soil **HARDINESS** Z 7-10

278

Aucuba japonica 'Picturata'

HEIGHT AND SPREAD 8 x 8ft (2.5 x 2.5m) **FLOWERS** ½in (1cm) across, held in a 4in (10cm) panicle in summer **ASPECT/LIKES** Light shade, any well-drained soil **HARDINESS** Z 7-10

This uncommon spotted laurel has evergreen leaves that are not only speckled as usual but also have a large, showy, golden heart, making it a really glowing contribution to the fall and winter garden. In time it forms a dense, dome-shaped shrub. The large, leathery, oval leaves have dark-green margins speckled with the same yellow that fills each leaf's central marking. In summer, panicles of dull-brown flowers appear. There seem to be both male and female plants of this selection in cultivation. Only females bear red berries, but they are very much of secondary interest to the foliage. It is a great choice for a shaded position, where it can prove illuminating and is best with some protection from cold drying winds. Watch out for and remove shoots with leaves bearing only spots—these can soon take over the whole plant.

279. **HEIGHT AND SPREAD** 8 x 24in (20 x 60cm), taller in flower **FLOWERS** ¾in (2cm) bells, held atop 12in (30cm) stems in spring **ASPECT/LIKES** Light shade, perhaps with morning sun, fertile well-drained soil **HARDINESS** Z 3-8

280. **COMMON NAME** Polypody **HEIGHT AND SPREAD** 8 x 24in (20 x 60cm) **ASPECT/LIKES** Shade, moist well-drained soil, although it will stand drier conditions **HARDINESS** Z 6-8

281. **HEIGHT AND SPREAD** 6½–10ft (2–3m) **FLOWERS** ½in (1cm) wide, held in 8in (20cm) clusters in early winter **ASPECT/LIKES** Sheltered warm site with some sun, any well-drained soil **HARDINESS** Z 5-9

282. **HEIGHT AND SPREAD** 6½ x 5ft (2 x 1.5m) **FLOWERS** Insignificant **ASPECT/LIKES** Sun or light shade, summer heat, well-drained soil **HARDINESS** Z 5-8

279

Bergenia cordifolia 'Tubby Andrews'

I have a bit of a fondness for variegated plants. I'm also quite keen on *Bergenia*, so perhaps it is only natural that I should enjoy growing this choice selection. It is a super plant, with large, broadly oval, leathery, green foliage generously marbled with cream. It is at its best in early winter, when the leaves develop appealing pinkish tinges. Hard winter weather will damage it more than most green-leaved selections, but in a mild year it stays impressive until spring, when it sends up reddish stems topped by heads of pink bells. It needs more pampering than other bergenias, so give it a decent spot in light shade in well-drained, improved soil. I grow it in a pot, dividing and replanting it every 2–3 years in late spring. Watch out for shoots that have reverted and turned plain green—and simply cut them off.

280

Polypodium vulgare

Common polypody is an evergreen fern of great ornamental use in gardens, thanks to the diversity found among its many selections, most of which are at their verdant best in fall and early winter. They are readily accommodated because they are compact and are also easy to cultivate. All grow from a creeping rhizome, which usually spreads across the soil surface, but which in this species also helps anchor the plant to other surfaces—in wetter parts, it grows on tree branches or stone walls. Triangular, leathery fronds arise to around 8in (20cm) long, more in some selections. It is slow growing, forming low rafts of growth, perfect at the front of shaded borders or for growing below bamboo, but it could be attached to a tree or in a shaded rockery. Plants go through a shabby stage in early summer as fresh growth replaces old fronds. These detach freely and can be combed out.

281

Mahonia napaulensis 'Maharajah'

A splendid mahonia for early winter interest, this plant is in many ways similar to commonly grown selections of *Mahonia* x *media*, with its stout, upright, evergreen growth. Yet subtle differences make this plant distinct. Its foliage is more dramatic: the large leaves composed of around six pairs of spiny, quite narrow leaflets are rich, glossy green, and bold in outline. Then in December, from tips of stems come masses of spreading, erect, showy clusters of clear-yellow flowers that are sweetly scented. It is a super specimen shrub for a sheltered corner that ideally gets some sun for part of the day.

282

Ilex × *meserveae* Blue Princess

If you fancy something different, this so-called blue holly, also known as 'Conapri,' is a good evergreen with foliage whose subtle, metallic-blue sheen is at its most intense in early winter. It forms a bushy, pyramid-shaped plant, densely furnished with quite oval leaves on the smaller side. The toothed foliage, held on purple-tinged stems, is also less prickly. A great bonus is the bright-red, glossy berries this female clone produces in fall, most generous if a male holly is planted nearby, and especially nice in a wreath. It stands dry spells once established but is not a plant to keep for long in a pot.

283

Luzula sylvatica 'Aurea'

A member of the rush family, this useful, evergreen perennial is grown for its splendid, golden foliage, which is at its brightest during fall and winter. A fairly low-growing, ground-covering plant, it forms dense, spreading clumps composed of individual rosettes of foliage, the grasslike leaves broad, smooth, and arching. Its bright-yellow tone is most vivid when the plant is in good light, although it is vigorous enough to thrive in shaded areas, too, where the foliage is closer to lime green—still an illuminating feature. In summer, little stems of brownish flowers arise to around 1ft (30cm). Easy to grow, it also stands periods of drought well and makes a good choice for quite dry shade, even under evergreens if watered until established. To keep it looking good, it sometimes needs a bit of cleaning up—old dead rosettes removed and faded foliage cleared out.

HEIGHT AND SPREAD 8 x 20in (20 x 50cm) **FLOWERS** Tiny, brown, held on 1ft (30cm) stems in summer **ASPECT/LIKES** Summer shade, reasonable soil **HARDINESS** Z 4-9

284

Clematis cirrhosa 'Wisley Cream'

Flowers in the garden in early winter are few and far between, so plants that produce them reliably are to be cherished. This climbing evergreen is among the most useful, deserving a place on a sheltered wall or fence or scrambling through a small tree. It is a fragile-looking plant, especially when young, with slender but surprisingly sturdy climbing stems. These bear small, toothed, glossy-green leaves, which attach to trellis, wires, or twigs. Then, one late-fall day, the first swags of flowers appear—glowing, greenish-ivory bells composed of four petals that flare open as they age, a heart-warming sight and one that will be repeated in the months to come. The trick is to plant it somewhere you can look up into the flowers, which is why it works well scrambling through a tree.

COMMON NAME Winter clematis **HEIGHT AND SPREAD** Climbs to 10ft (3m) **FLOWERS** Bell-shaped, 1¼in (3cm) long, from late fall until midspring **ASPECT/LIKES** Sunny sheltered wall, warmth, well-drained soil **HARDINESS** Z 7-11

285

Rhododendron simsii hybrids

COMMON NAME Pot azalea **HEIGHT AND SPREAD** 1 x 1¼ft (30 x 40cm), but larger if kept year to year **FLOWERS** 2in (5cm) across, usually double, from early winter until midspring **ASPECT/LIKES** Cool bright position, never dry **HARDINESS** Z 8-10

These beautiful flowering plants are available in the stores in December. It is worth buying them early, while still in perfect condition. Low-growing, tender evergreen shrubs, they produce masses of large, frilly, upward-facing blooms in shades of pink, purple, or white; plants sold in heavy bud may be bicolored. They hate the conditions in our centrally heated homes, so choose a sunny windowsill, away from radiators, in your coolest room. A porch or chilly bathroom is ideal. Plants must never even begin to dry out—the first tell-tale sign is flowers starting to flop. Watered regularly, plants bloom for six months, with displays finishing in midspring. Try keeping your plant another year by putting it in a shady spot outdoors for summer; repot into acidic potting mix and feed regularly. Then bring under cover before the frosts. It needs a cool position—ideally a frost-free greenhouse, where it can form new flower buds for the following year.

286

Kale 'Cavolo Nero'

Black kale, sometimes called black cabbage, is a plant I enjoy both for its tasty leaves and handsome appearance. The plant forms wonderful, architectural rosettes of long, slender, waxy leaves that are heavily puckered. When dark gray-green in winter, they are at their most beautiful, particularly with frost on them, and by summer have become a glowing blue-green. Plants form a central stem, with the leaves radiating out from it. The idea is to harvest lower leaves as you need them. You have to keep on top of this, as they get bitter with age. I treat some plants as ornamentals, leaving them to produce clouds of pretty, pale-yellow, bee-attracting flowers in spring. Sow seed in late summer for a fall crop. Plants will often overwinter for an early spring harvest.

287

Ajuga reptans 'Golden Glow'

Plants that grow tightly over the soil provide useful contrast. If they are evergreen and have colorful foliage, too, their value increases. Many *Ajuga* offer these virtues, but this selection is especially cheering. Its foliage is gray-green with an irregular yellow-cream margin. In cool weather, the new leaves are blushing pink. The resulting tapestry effect is further topped off by spires of blue, bee-attracting flowers in spring, but it is in winter that its foliage really injects unexpected brightness. A slow-growing plant, it needs decent conditions to thrive. Avoid planting in hot sun—plants will dry out and burn. They are often sold as fall container plants, good for spilling over the edges of a pot or window box.

288

Euonymus fortunei 'Kewensis'

Given free rein, this hardy evergreen shrub can create striking effects in the garden, which are most easily admired in winter. It is best described as a ground-covering plant, its slender, low-growing, creeping stems bearing tiny, oval, dark-green leaves. These form a dense, deep mat of branches so tough that you can walk on it with no fear of harm. The plant will smother anything in its path. If it reaches a tree trunk or wall, it will act as a climber, slowly clambering up and over. Its party piece develops gradually, too: the plant forms pyramids of growth, such that the ground cover it creates is not flat but distinctly wavy. To do this, it needs plenty of space. It will grow in dry shade below trees but is most dramatic in a better, open site.

289

Ardisia crenata

If you fancy an unusual festive house plant, try coral berry. A tender, compact evergreen, it has dark-green, waxy foliage, each oval leaf with a wavy edge. Plants usually have a single stem and are sold at Christmas bearing crops of showy berries, normally red but sometimes pink, white, or yellow, lasting a couple of months. Buy promptly, as plants decline in quality fast if not looked after. They have specific needs. Position in bright light, with a couple of hours of winter sun, and keep moist but not wet—plants hate both drying out and standing in water. Keep away from radiators. When summer comes, stand your plant in a shaded place outdoors and keep cool. Sprays of small, white flowers will appear, developing into berries. As long as no frost is forecast, your plant can stay outdoors until November—a cool spell will help the berry displays.

286. **COMMON NAME** Black kale **HEIGHT AND SPREAD** 5 x 3ft (1.5 x 1m) **FLOWERS** ¾in (2cm) across, held in a cloudlike head in spring **ASPECT/LIKES** Sun, shelter, well-drained soil **HARDINESS** Z 5-9

287. **HEIGHT AND SPREAD** 4 x 12in (10 x 30cm) **FLOWERS** Small, blue, held in 4in (10cm) tall spires in spring **ASPECT/LIKES** Open cool place, moist well-drained soil **HARDINESS** Z 3-9

288. **HEIGHT AND SPREAD** 2 x 10ft (60 x 300cm) **ASPECT/LIKES** Open site; good, light, reasonable soil **HARDINESS** Z 5-8

289. **COMMON NAME** Coral berry **HEIGHT AND SPREAD** 3 x 1¾ft (100 x 50cm) as a house plant **FLOWERS** ¾in (2cm) across, held in a cluster in summer **ASPECT/LIKES** Bright windowsill, cool moist conditions **HARDINESS** Z 8-10

290

Anemanthele lessoniana

This useful, easy, and handsome perennial is a plant that looks highly effective year-round because, unlike most other ornamental grasses, it is evergreen. I enjoy it most at the end of the season, for its warming tones and dynamic nature. It is quick growing, forming a fairly open clump around 3ft (1m) tall, with its slender blades gracefully arching outward and shifting beautifully in any breeze. Foliage is green in spring as it emerges, then later cloudlike, pink-tinged, flower heads develop, all the while foliage becoming tinted with orange and red until it reaches its peak in late fall and winter. The plant's open structure means that, if several plants are grown in a drift, it can be interplanted. Try it in a sunny spot with *Allium hollandicum* 'Purple Sensation' (see p.61) or *Galtonia candicans*. Although it is not long lived—clumps looking good for 3–4 years before they decline—the plants set seed, and you will find youngsters popping up all over the place, especially if grown in gravel. A comb through in spring keeps plants looking good.

COMMON NAME Pheasant grass **HEIGHT AND SPREAD** 3 x 2ft (100 x 60cm) **FLOWERS** Minute, held in open cloud-like heads from late summer **ASPECT/LIKES** Sun or part shade, open site, moist free-draining soil **HARDINESS** Z 8-10

291

Eucalyptus gunnii

Cider gums make beautiful, quick-growing, broad-leaved evergreen trees with glittering foliage and a lovely resinous scent. Their spectacular peeling bark is at its best in the winter sun. The only drawback is that the trees often outgrow even quite large gardens. The alternative is to grow the tree as a coppice (when stems are cut almost to the ground) or pollard (when plants are cut to short stems). Both approaches have the benefit of not only keeping the plant within bounds but also forcing it to produce its handsome, rounded, bluer foliage, rather than the sea-green, sickle-shaped, adult leaves and starry white flowers. Plants grown this way are also less prone to wind rock, common with gum trees, and, once established, will put on 3–6ft (90–180cm) of annual growth, which will look impressive in fall and winter. Stems will need cutting each year in early spring, and a good mulch with garden compost helps keep them going. The foliage is useful in winter flower arrangements.

COMMON NAME Cider gum **HEIGHT AND SPREAD** 6½ x 6½ft (2 x 2m) as a coppice; 20x12m (65x39ft) as a tree **FLOWERS** 1¼in (3cm) across, on mature growth, in early and midsummer **ASPECT/LIKES** Sun, protection from high winds, well-drained soil **HARDINESS** Z 8-10

292. COMMON NAME Chinese bramble **HEIGHT AND SPREAD** 1¾ x 16ft (0.5 x 5m) or more **FLOWERS** ¾in (2cm) across, in summer **ASPECT/ LIKES** Shade, well-drained soil **HARDINESS** Z 6-9

293. COMMON NAME Wandering Chilean iris **HEIGHT AND SPREAD** 1 x 2ft (30 x 60cm) **FLOWERS** 1¼in (3cm) across, in a cluster below leaves in spring **ASPECT/LIKES** Sun, open site, well-drained soil **HARDINESS** Z 8-11

294. COMMON NAME Japanese privet **HEIGHT AND SPREAD** 5 x 3ft (1.5 x 1m) **FLOWERS** Tiny, held in 1½in (4cm) panicles in summer **ASPECT/LIKES** Sun, open site, fertile well-drained soil, not too dry **HARDINESS** Z 8-10

295. COMMON NAME Stinking hellebore **HEIGHT AND SPREAD** 16 x 12in (40 x 30cm) **FLOWERS** 1½in (4cm) across, held in a cluster in late winter **ASPECT/ LIKES** Shade, shelter, moist fertile soil **HARDINESS** Z 6-7

292

Rubus tricolor

More often a denizen of neglected parking lot landscaping than a cherished garden plant, this tough, normally evergreen ground coverer nonetheless has appeal. Although a bramble, it isn't prickly; ruby-red bristles cover its arching, slender stems. These bear textured, rich-green foliage with silver-green undersides and are most appealing wet and shining after rain or dusted with frost. In summer, occasional small white flowers appear, followed by edible, raspberry-like fruits. The bramble forms dense cover and is vigorous, stems rooting as they go, so plant it in a shaded corner to suppress weeds or to cover dry, root-filled soil—somewhere it can spread without smothering other plants. If it goes too far, cut it back; new growth will be fresh and attractive with reddish bristles. A cold winter can defoliate the plant, but it will recover.

293

Libertia peregrinans 'Gold Leaf'

As soon as this interesting selection of *Libertia* appeared, I was hooked. It is an evergreen perennial with pointed, lance-shaped leaves held stiffly upright in tight tufts. For much of the year, they are orange-tinged olive-green, but in winter, they turn golden-orange, which looks especially attractive in glancing sunlight. Ideal at the front of borders, the plant has a slightly odd growth pattern, forming a running clump, so you get numerous tight tufts with gaps between. This habit lends itself perfectly to interplanting with bulbs, winter heathers, or *Ophiopogon*. In spring, little stems bear white, irislike flowers. I find it does not enjoy summer drought, despite its appearance.

294

Ligustrum japonicum 'Rotundifolium'

I love this privet, which comes into its own in fall and winter, when its super-glossy foliage and compact form can be readily admired. A tough, hardy, easy-to-grow plant, standing a range of conditions, it will thrive for years in a container, too. It forms an upright, evergreen shrub, the branches densely clothed with broadly oval leaves of darkest green that look as if they are made of wax or even plastic. In the winter garden, plants lend a sculptural quality, looking almost like miniature versions of full-size trees, although they are particularly slow growing. New shoots in spring are paler and bronze-flushed, while in summer, white, privet-scented flowers may appear, followed by blackish berries.

295

Helleborus foetidus 'Gold Bullion'

With its beautiful, glowing, fingerlike foliage, followed by displays of yellow-green, bell-shaped flowers, this evergreen perennial makes a really striking sight in fall and winter. Its leaves can give off a pungent odor if bruised—hence its common name. It grows best in shade; in sun, foliage can burn. Plants are fairly bushy, forming a leafy, upright-growing, reddish stem, with palmate, finely divided foliage. For most of the year, it is lime green, but with the winter cold, the yellow hue intensifies considerably, making it perfect for illuminating a shaded corner, especially if a small group of plants is grown together. Flowers set seed freely; some plants will be yellow, while a proportion will be yellow and green.

296

Helleborus niger

Irresistible in the depths of winter for its large, shining, white, outward-facing flowers held above compact clumps of rich, evergreen foliage, the Christmas rose is a perennial long-cherished by gardeners and found in any garden center at this time of year. The flowers are usually composed of five pointed petals, although double-flowered selections exist too. In the center of each bloom sits a crown of showy golden stamens. Flowers are held on short, stout stems to around 8in (20cm) tall and appear from December to the first days of spring. The individual blooms are remarkably weather resistant and long lasting, gradually aging to green. This is a plant I have more success with in a pot. Planted, clumps seem to decline rapidly and disappear after a couple of years. I think it is down to my sandy soil. Ideally, it wants a rich, leafy, moist place. Clay soil can suit it as long as the drainage is good. Some winter sunshine is also beneficial. In pots, plants may thrive for longer. My best and oldest plant is a self-sown seedling growing in a clump of *Haberlea rhodopensis*.

COMMON NAME Christmas rose **HEIGHT AND SPREAD** 1¾ x 1¾ft (50 x 50cm) **FLOWERS** 3in (8cm) across, from early winter to spring **ASPECT/LIKES** Light shade with some winter sun, rich moist well-drained soil **HARDINESS** Z 3-8

297

Wollemia nobilis

I chose this incredible Australian conifer for early winter partly because it looks good now, but mostly because it makes a terrific and generous Christmas gift for keen gardeners. The story of this tree's survival is fascinating. Discovered as recently as 1994 growing in a canyon not far from Sydney, it is a living fossil, with fewer than 40 individual trees known in the wild. Populations are at severe risk of extinction from forest fires and other threats, but the species is now safe in gardens around the world. This conifer looks like nothing else, with flat, leathery, lance-shaped, olive-green leaves arranged around stems held in two or—on mature trees—four ranks. The new growth is soft and an attractive bright green. Trees are fairly slender, initially with a single trunk and side branches that bear male or female cones on the same plant. In time, plants develop odd, chocolate puffed rice cereal–like bark and additional trunks. While not entirely hardy, they seem tougher than was initially thought. Plant it somewhere sheltered in a bright position in well-drained soil. You may like to grow young plants in containers before planting.

COMMON NAME Wollemi pine **HEIGHT AND SPREAD** 80 x 26ft (25 x 8m) **FLOWERS** Round female cones 4in (10cm) across, cylindrical male cones 4¾in (12cm) long, in summer **ASPECT/LIKES** Shade, shelter, moist site with good drainage **HARDINESS** Z 9-11

298

Schlumbergera × *buckleyi*

Two different *Schlumbergera* are known as Christmas cacti. This is my preferred choice. Forming arching then pendent growth, its segmented stems bear at their tips beautiful dangling flowers of almost fluorescent pink in winter. It is an easy plant to grow—perfect for an indoor hanging planter or pot on a stand—and one that is often passed as cuttings between friends. I don't think I've ever seen it for sale, yet it is a common and long-lived house plant. The other Christmas cactus, *Schlumbergera truncata*, sometimes known as Thanksgiving cactus, is the one sold in stores at this time of year. Its upright stems with toothy segments bear upward-facing blooms in shades of white, pink, yellow, or red. Both plants like a bright position near a windowsill but away from direct sun. They can be watered freely but must never stand in water.

299

Juniperus rigida subsp. *conferta*

This distinctive ground-covering conifer is native to parts of Japan and Russia, where it grows on the seashore. It is a plant I admire for the way it brings interesting texture and color to plantings, especially in winter, although it looks attractively fresh year-round. The creeping stems form ground cover that looks soft and frothy from a distance, almost like turf. Close up, the needlelike foliage is prickly and has a blue-green hue. It is held on reddish stems that lie flat on the ground and spill attractively over retaining walls or around rocks and cobbles. It is super in gravel gardens, forming a flat, weed-suppressing carpet that contrasts well with rounded or upright forms. There is also a yellow-leaved selection, 'All Gold,' which is worth trying.

300

Pittosporum tenuifolium 'Warnham Gold'

For injecting a touch of evergreen sunshine into winter gardens, this terrific shrub has much to recommend it, yet you don't see it too often. It forms a dense bushy plant. Its glossy, oval leaves with undulating margins are held on dark twiggy stems. Young foliage emerges lime green in late spring, but, as leaves age, they get more yellow. Also in spring come the flowers; these are curious rather than beautiful—little black bells that smell of honey. The plant can be trimmed directly after flowering to keep its shape or to form a loose topiary form. Keep away from cold drying winds, although it is quite at home with coastal exposure. It will grow in some shade, where the foliage color sings out.

301

Solanum pseudocapsicum

Versatile and vibrant, this highly useful plant can be used indoors or out in mild winters, providing lovely displays of ornamental berries in shades of yellow and orange for weeks on end. A shrubby evergreen plant, it has dark-green, pointed, oval leaves held on slender twiggy stems. In late summer, small, white, starry flowers appear, followed by yellow fruits that swiftly age to orange. The foliage has an odd pungent odor. Indoors, the plant is great as festive decoration, although with milder winters it is more often seen in outdoor container displays. It is pretty tough, surviving light frost. Try planting it by a warm wall in spring, where plants may grow for several years, becoming covered in berries and reaching perhaps 3ft (1m) across. The berries are toxic.

298. COMMON NAME Christmas cactus **HEIGHT AND SPREAD** 1 x 2¾ft (30 x 80cm) **FLOWERS** 2½in (6cm) long in early winter **ASPECT/LIKES** Bright windowsill out of direct sun, above 50°F (10°C), don't allow to stand in water **HARDINESS** Z 10-12

299. COMMON NAME Coastal juniper **HEIGHT AND SPREAD** 8in x 10ft (20 x 300cm) **ASPECT/LIKES** Sun, open site, well-drained soil **HARDINESS** Z 6-7

300. HEIGHT AND SPREAD 8 x 5ft (2.5x1.5m); trim to keep smaller **FLOWERS** Bells, ¾in (2cm) across, in spring **ASPECT/LIKES** Shelter, well-drained site **HARDINESS** Z 9-10

301. COMMON NAME Winter cherry **HEIGHT AND SPREAD** 2 x 3ft (60 x 100cm) **FLOWERS** ¾in (2cm) across, in late summer **ASPECT/LIKES** Cool bright windowsill (indoors); sun, shelter, well-drained site, near frost-free in winter **HARDINESS** Z 10-12

302

Viburnum × *bodnantense* 'Dawn'

One of the best-known winter-flowering shrubs, this deciduous plant often produces its first flushes of sweetly scented pink flowers before the end of the year. If the weather is mild, this can even be before its oval, deeply veined, green leaves fall—a taster of what is to follow in the coming 2–3 months. A large-growing, multistemmed shrub with distinctly upright branches that then arch outward, it is a vigorous plant and needs plenty of space. The beautiful tubular flowers are held in clusters and are dark pink in bud, opening to clear pink—a genuine revelation on any dark, gloomy winter's day. Light frost has little effect on flowers, but days of freezing weather can kill them; fear not, as more flushes will follow until spring. Thanks to the plant's vigor, you can cut a few stems to enjoy indoors once plants establish.

COMMON NAME Arrow wood **HEIGHT AND SPREAD** 10 x 6½ft (3 x 2m) **FLOWERS** Tubular, held in clusters to 2in (5cm) across from early to late winter **ASPECT/LIKES** Sun, open site, well-drained soil **HARDINESS** Z 5-7

303

Iris foetidissima

An essential perennial for winter, this iris is one of the toughest and easiest of garden evergreens, ideal for dry shade where little else will thrive. It forms a clump of dark-green, leathery, initially erect then arching sword-shaped foliage. In late spring, spikes of somber flowers appear—quite variable, usually murky purple or mauve but sometimes pale yellow, and often missed amid the profusion elsewhere. These are followed by large green pods that swell through summer and fall, eventually splitting open in early winter to reveal a showy display of seeds. These are usually bright orange, although in some rare selections they can be yellow or even white. There are also variegated cultivars with white-striped leaves. These choice selections want a decent shaded place, but the common orange-seeded plant will flourish even in the dry shade below conifers. The snag is that plants are short lived, owing to rust, which weakens clumps, and a leaf-mining pest that makes foliage unsightly. Fortunately, seeds germinate freely and young plants soon replace ailing veterans.

COMMON NAME Gladwin iris **HEIGHT AND SPREAD** 1¾ x 2ft (50 x 60cm) **FLOWERS** 2½in (6cm) across, in late spring **ASPECT/LIKES** Shade, shelter, moist well-drained soil **HARDINESS** Z 6-9

304

Ilex aquifolium 'Handsworth New Silver'

I have a vivid memory of a front garden I visited one Christmas while caroling many years ago. In it was a perfectly trimmed, variegated holly, a 10ft (3m) tall pyramid that had been strung with white fairy lights, showing off its bold, cream-edged foliage to outstanding effect. A good choice of holly for just this purpose would be this fine selection. It is a female plant that bears good crops of red berries, in addition to its long, handsome, dark-green, spine-edged leaves, each with a broad silver margin. It looks great all year round, especially once established. You can grow small plants for a few years in containers, but hollies are generally not long-term pot plants.

COMMON NAME Holly **HEIGHT AND SPREAD** 26 x 10ft (8 x 3m); trim to keep smaller **FLOWERS** Tiny, held in clusters in spring **ASPECT/LIKES** Sun, open site, decent drainage **HARDINESS** Z 5-9

305

Zamioculcas zamiifolia Raven

COMMON NAME Jet black raven **HEIGHT AND SPREAD** 3 x 2ft (100 x 60cm) **FLOWERS** Rare; green, 2in (5cm) tall, any time **ASPECT/LIKES** Bright position away from direct sun, above 59°F (15°C), allow to dry between waterings **HARDINESS** Z 9-10

The foliage of this impressive-looking house plant, also known as 'Dowon,' comes pretty near to black, giving a gleaming, exotic look that is most welcome in winter when other foliage house plants can start to dull. I always feel *Zamioculcas*, with their long pinnate leaves reaching 3ft (1m) long, emerging from what appears initially to be a sort of rosette, bear a strong resemblance to primitive cycad plants. But closer inspection reveals that the leaves grow from a thick rhizome and produce arum flowers. The individual leaflets are oval, as shiny as patent leather, and arranged alternately up the fleshy, central midrib. In this easy-to-care-for cultivar, they are darkest purple-green, although when they initially emerge, the leaves are bright green, forming a nice contrast with the older foliage.

306

Acorus gramineus 'Ōgon'

Evergreen herbaceous perennials don't get much more useful than this plant, for its brilliant foliage contribution to gardens and container displays in winter. It's a fairly common thing, often sold as a fall and winter seasonal plant at garden centers and nurseries and, therefore, easy to overlook. Despite its grassy appearance, it is not a true grass but a member of a genus in its own family, related to aroids. The plant forms low, fanlike clumps of arching, yellow-and-green variegated leaves, each blade quite leathery and tough. It is perfect for underplanting *Cornus* stems or growing below witch hazels, especially if the site is consistently moist and quite shaded, where it will make bright, weed-suppressing ground cover. In drier places, the plant may suffer in summer heat without watering. Alternatively, use it to bring color and elegance to container displays, tucked in with winter heathers, evergreen ferns, and hellebores. It does well in a pot.

COMMON NAME Slender sweet flag **HEIGHT AND SPREAD** 1 x 1¾ft (30 x 50cm) **ASPECT/LIKES** Part shade, moist open site **HARDINESS** Z 6-9

307

Rubus thibetanus

In my imagination, the brambles that grew up around Sleeping Beauty's castle after she pricked her finger were something like this plant, for it has a slightly sinister appearance in winter, with spectral, white, fiercely barbed, upright then arching canes. But in the right place, it is spectacular during the winter months, especially glimpsed glittering with frost and perhaps underplanted with black *Ophiopogon*. It is a vigorous, dense, deciduous, clump-forming plant, its leaves silvery and fernlike. Its summer flowers are white and attractive to pollinators. The ends of the arching canes root when they reach the ground, so it needs watching carefully in a border, although it is less of a menace than similar *Rubus cockburnianus*. Young canes are the whitest; older ones gradually turn brown and need cutting out at ground level, which helps open up the clump nicely. This is a job I aim to do in fall; gloves are essential.

COMMON NAME Ghost bramble **HEIGHT AND SPREAD** 6½ x 10ft (2 x 3m) **FLOWERS** ¾in (2cm) across, in summer **ASPECT/LIKES** Sun or part shade, open site **HARDINESS** Z 5-9

308

Arum italicum subsp. *italicum* 'Marmoratum'

With beautiful, silver-veined, dark-green, shining leaves that emerge from below ground in midfall, just as virtually everything else in the garden is in decline, this vigorous, tuberous perennial is an essential, easily grown plant. It forms handsome ground cover, ideal for a shaded position, although it grows perfectly well in sun, too. The foliage is at its glossy best in winter and combines brilliantly with the first snowdrops or perhaps evergreen ferns. In late spring, green arum flowers appear. By this time, the leaves are starting to look shabby, but no matter, as by then other plants will have hidden them from view. Then, in late summer, once the leaves have died away, comes a surprise—showy spikes of bright-orange berries, which can create quite an arresting show beside pink-flowered colchicum. Seeds within the berries will germinate freely, which may frustrate tidy gardeners, of which I am not one.

COMMON NAME Italian arum **HEIGHT AND SPREAD** 1¾ x 1¾ft (50 x 50cm) **FLOWERS** Arums, 6–8in (15–20cm) high, in spring **ASPECT/LIKES** Sun or shade, fertile soil not too dry **HARDINESS** Z 5-9

309. COMMON NAME Rocky Mountain bristlecone pine **HEIGHT AND SPREAD** 20 x 13ft (6x4m) after about 50 years **FLOWERS** 3½in (9cm) long cones that remain on the tree for months **ASPECT/LIKES** Sun, open site, well-drained soil **HARDINESS** Z 3-7

310. HEIGHT AND SPREAD 5 x 6½ft (1.5 x 2m) if coppiced **FLOWERS** Small, held in heads 1¼in (3cm) across, in summer **ASPECT/LIKES** Sun, open site, moist soil **HARDINESS** Z 4-7

311. COMMON NAME Emerald tree **HEIGHT AND SPREAD** 6½ x 5ft (2 x 1.5m) indoors **FLOWERS** 3in (8cm) long, but it doesn't flower indoors **ASPECT/LIKES** Bright position, don't allow to stand in water **HARDINESS** Z 10-12

312. COMMON NAME Makura grass **HEIGHT AND SPREAD** 2¾ x 4½ft (80 x 140cm) **FLOWERS** Tiny, held in 1¼in (3cm) long sprays amid leaves in summer **ASPECT/LIKES** Sun, open site, fairly moist soil, shelter from winter cold **HARDINESS** Z 6-10

309

Pinus aristata

Knowing that in this conifer's wild home, the Rocky Mountains of Colorado, this pine can live for more than 2,000 years makes planting it feel like quite a responsibility. A compact, quietly attractive tree, at its most useful in the garden through winter, it has short, blue-green needles densely covering the branches, which look lovely dusted with frost or strung with dewy cobwebs. At first glance, needles appear to be suffering from an outbreak of dandruff, with little white flecks sticking to them. This is actually resin and a characteristic of the species. Plants start shrubby and are distinctly slow growing; mine certainly cannot be called a tree yet, but must be at least 20 years old, having been kept for the first part of its life in a container. It was happy enough, but this tree prefers being planted.

310

Cornus sanguinea 'Midwinter Fire'

Among selections of dogwood grown for the colors of their winter stems, this is the one I return to. It is well named; I remember being stopped in my tracks one bitter January morning by a plant lit perfectly by the low sun. The fiery effect is created by the two-tone qualities of the stems; yellowish-orange for the most part, but turning red toward stem tips. The colors are best on young stems, so grow it as a coppice, removing half of the stems at ground level early each spring. Once established, it is vigorous and forms a thicket of growth. Its foliage and heads of white, summer flowers are unremarkable, although the leaves turn a nice orange-yellow before falling. Plant it somewhere the winter sun can ignite those branches for all to marvel at.

311

Radermachera sinica

After it has been cleared of Christmas clutter, the house can feel rather empty, a void I often fill with a new plant. This handsome character is one of my favorites, with glossy, divided leaves composed of diamond-shaped leaflets. In subtropical Asia, it is a tree, so the plants we buy are effectively mere seedlings. They are compact and bushy, to begin with, but after a few years they develop a more open, treelike habit. The conditions must be consistent—moist not wet and in bright but not full sun. Leaves yellow and drop if you do something wrong. It is hardier than supposed and has been known to grow outside to tree-sized proportions in central London, even producing white, trumpet-shaped flowers.

312

Carex secta

I can't understand why this noble sedge from New Zealand is not more often seen. With its super-shiny, slender, grasslike, rich-green foliage glinting in the winter light, it makes a large, handsome fountain of growth. Each arching blade can measure 3ft (1m) in length and the plant eventually forms a sizable tussock. It retains faded foliage, so established plants have a shaggy strawlike skirt, with the new growth erupting from the top. With age, the skirt becomes almost a short trunk, giving the plant an unusual appearance. In summer, sprays of tiny cream flowers are produced on arching stems. Tough and adaptable, it seems to thrive when growing beside water and, in time, needs plenty of space.

313

Acer griseum

This fine maple, a native of China, is one of the most aesthetically valuable trees for relatively small gardens, particularly for gardeners wanting year-round appeal. It is grown mainly for its paper bark, which peels partially away from the trunk and main branches, often in quite large, coppery orange sheets. Mature trees give the best show, but young ones also begin to peel once they reach five or so years old. Plant your tree somewhere the sun can illuminate the translucent peelings, setting the whole thing aglow. The effect is most remarkable in winter. In spring, emerging growth may be tinged red, while in fall the foliage develops dramatic orange, pink, and red tints before falling—a terrific sight. Those who worry about garden trees getting too big need not be concerned—this acer is relatively slow and compact growing.

314

Juniperus recurva var. *coxii*

I often wish I had more space in my garden for trees. If I did, one of the first I'd plant again would be this elegant Himalayan conifer, with its weeping growth habit. Unlike some conifers, it does not get that large, so it's suitable for many gardens. It is particularly attractive when young, forming a dense conical tree, its cascading branches dripping with dark, blue-green, needlelike foliage. It is lovely year-round, but when I grew it in my last garden, I appreciated its evergreen beauty most in winter. Plant as a specimen in a lawn or in the middle of an island bed to show off its shape. With the years, this tree develops middle-age spread, becoming more open in habit, with a rounded crown and a clearer trunk that shows off its peeling bark. It is a good alternative to lovely but tender *Cupressus cashmeriana* (see p.166).

315

Hedera pastuchovii 'Ann Ala'

We have wonderful plantsman Roy Lancaster to thank for introducing this superb ivy, which he collected from the ancient forests above the Caspian Sea, in Iran, in 1972 and named after a friend who'd helped arrange his trip. He selected this plant for its pointed, spear-shaped leaves. Naturally variable in outline, they are apple green in color when young, then glossy and rich green when mature, shining all winter long. Roy's own plant covers part of a shady house wall. I rooted a little piece and my plant now clings to a wall at the back of my south-facing border, its foliage making a great foil to plants in front. It seems as easily pleased as other ivies, growing in sun or quite deep shade, but it deserves a decent place.

316

Microbiota decussata

I'm fond of this curious conifer. It is handsome but unshowy, with fernlike sprays of rich emerald-green foliage held on slightly red-tinted branches. It makes good and consistently low ground cover in a more elegant fashion than many other prostrate conifers. It looks great tumbling down a shady bank or creeping across gravel. But it saves its party trick for winter, when, as the cold weather begins to bite, its foliage changes color dramatically to a lovely, warm, reddish bronze. Native to far-eastern Russia, it is pretty hardy but does not like too much competition. It stands some drought when established, but don't let young plants get dry in summer. I've seen images of it growing in the wild with *Bergenia*. Try it with *Bergenia* 'Admiral' (see p.231) for a naturally inspired combination.

313. COMMON NAME Paperbark maple **HEIGHT AND SPREAD** 39 x 26ft (12x8m) after 50 years **FLOWERS** Tiny, green, on drooping stems in spring **ASPECT/LIKES** Sunny open site, avoid dry situations **HARDINESS** Z 4-8

314. COMMON NAME Drooping conifer **HEIGHT AND SPREAD** 33 x 8ft (10 x 2.5m) **FLOWERS** Small, oval pollen cones in spring **ASPECT/LIKES** Shelter from cold winds, well-drained soil, not too dry **HARDINESS** Z 7

315. HEIGHT AND SPREAD Climbs to 13ft (4m) **FLOWERS** 1¼in (3cm) heads of green flowers on mature growth in fall **ASPECT/LIKES** Shade or part shade, somewhere to climb **HARDINESS** Z 4-8

316. COMMON NAME Siberian cypress **HEIGHT AND SPREAD** 1¼ x 5ft (40 x 150cm) **ASPECT/LIKES** Sun, open site, decent well-drained soil, not too dry **HARDINESS** Z 3-7

317

Pinus mugo 'Ophir'

It comes as a surprise to some people that conifers can be among the most colorful plants, particularly in winter. This fine dwarf pine is an example. For much of the year, its little needles are warm green, but with the onset of cool weather, they develop ever-stronger yellow tints that intensify as the cold begins to bite, eventually giving the plant a striking golden glow. It is a dense, compact-growing plant—keep it as a bushy dome of growth, or leg it up (cut off the lower branches) to form a small tree. Once it reaches the desired size, you can prune it: simply use shears to trim new growth in early summer. You can also keep it in a pot—I did with mine for years before I planted it.

HEIGHT AND SPREAD 6 x 6½ft (1.8 x 2m) **FLOWERS** Cones in late spring, which stay on the plant for months **ASPECT/LIKES** Sun, open site, any reasonably well-drained soil **HARDINESS** Z 2-7

COMMON NAME Persian ivy **HEIGHT AND SPREAD** Climbs to 26ft (8m) **FLOWERS** Tiny, held in round heads 2in (5cm) across in fall **ASPECT/LIKES** Sun or shade, not picky **HARDINESS** Z 5-10

318

Hedera colchica 'Sulphur Heart'

This bold ivy is undeniably attractive, with large, glossy, pointed, roughly heart-shaped, overlapping leaves of rich green, the centers of which are splashed with lime-green and gold. It is self-clinging and will soon hide an ugly fence or wall. I used it once to clad the trunk of an old apple tree. It made a super feature, especially in winter, when the large colorful leaves caught the sun. It needs controlling, however. Prevent it from spreading too far into the canopy of trees and competing with them (think of the ivy as a skirt rather than a onesie). This plant will also grow horizontally for thick, luxuriant, weed-proof ground cover in the driest shade across root-filled soil.

319

Salix gracilistyla 'Mount Aso'

When I first saw a photograph of this amazing pussy willow, I thought it had been artificially colored. But, no, in mid- to late winter, its bare, slender branches are indeed covered for weeks with lovely, fluffy, vivid red-pink catkins, which seem to emerge from nowhere just after the first hint of mild weather. Later, catkins turn yellowish, as pollen is produced, and then in spring, narrow silvery green foliage develops. Grown originally for the cut-flower trade, it is a recent introduction outdoors but is now an essential plant for the winter garden, simply because there is nothing else like it. I've not had mine long, but I'll keep it as a coppice, cutting a third of the oldest stems back hard each year just after flowering. Unpruned, it can get quite large, although it is less vigorous than some other willows. Mature plants can be plundered for flower arrangements without too much concern.

COMMON NAME Japanese pink pussy willow **HEIGHT AND SPREAD** 10 x 10ft (3 x 3m) **FLOWERS** Catkins 1¼in (3cm) long, in mid- to late winter **ASPECT/LIKES** Sun, open site, reasonably moist soil, not too dry **HARDINESS** Z 4-9

320

Hyacinthus orientalis

Even positive-minded gardeners must admit that there are times in midwinter when they can't wait for spring. A great tonic is the sight and scent of a bowl of flowering hyacinths. If you buy a pot of three bulbs, you are usually limited to blue-, white-, or pink-flowered selections, so I get two pots and replant a mix of colors into a larger ornamental bowl, using bulb fiber, perhaps topped off with polished pebbles or some florist's moss. If you buy dry bulbs in fall, a more exciting range of colors is available. I like yellow 'City of Haarlem' (*pictured, right*) planted with 'Delft Blue,' and orange 'Gipsy Queen' with grape-purple 'Woodstock.' The show is at its best in the week before blooms open fully. When the flowers loll about awkwardly, I cut them and place in a vase, where they last a week or so longer. Then I pop the bulbs into a cold frame, replanting outdoors in fall. They continue to flower for years in the garden.

321

Erica arborea var. *alpina* f. *aureifolia* 'Albert's Gold'

Tree heathers such as this are seldom planted, which is a great pity, as they have useful qualities of texture, color, and form, especially combined with other plants. From a distance, they resemble some conifers, but with a grace all of their own. Forming an upright beacon of gold, this plant is impressive in winter, its soft, tactile growth and rounded, billowing shape contrasting beautifully with bold- or dark-leaved plants. Try it beside *Viburnum davidii* or a purple phormium. It also looks great with standing stems of miscanthus and other grasses. The gold is brightest in spring as new growth begins after the honey-scented flowers have faded. Plants grow well for several years in a container, allowing you to move them about through the year to form interesting associations with other potted plants. Just don't let them dry out.

322

Danae racemosa

With lustrous, rich-green, lance-shaped foliage held on arching, canelike stems that rise directly from the ground, this lovely evergreen shrub thrives easily in quite deep, even fairly dry shade, where it slowly spreads at the root to form a handsome, rather open clump. On sunny winter days, the whole plant seems almost to sparkle and, while I've never noticed the tiny, green, spring flowers on mine, they must appear, as in summer, stems are spangled with red berries. I've seen people trim stems back, but this ruins the plant's graceful appearance. Instead, remove old stems at the base after 3–4 years once the leaves start to yellow, and give it an annual mulch of well-rotted manure. Foliage apparently lasts well in a vase, but plants are so slow growing it's a shame to cut it.

323

Murdannia loriformis Bright Star

If you are looking for an indoor plant to cheer you in winter, this could be it. Also known as 'Ppimur004,' it is a sophisticated member of the *Tradescantia* family and a newcomer on the house-plant scene. Its appearance is striking: tight rosettes of lance-shaped, fleshy, undulating leaves are lustrous silver-blue in the center, with a contrasting green margin. After a while, the rosettes develop into short stems that spill out nicely over the edges of the pot. The plant also produces tiny blooms, which need snipping off as they begin to look unsightly. Grow it in a broad bowl, perhaps as a table centerpiece in a bright place. It won't resent the odd missed watering.

320. **COMMON NAME** Hyacinth **HEIGHT AND SPREAD** 10in (25cm) in flower **FLOWERS** ¾in (2cm) across in a 10in (25cm) spike, any time between early winter and early spring **ASPECT/LIKES** Cool sunny windowsill **HARDINESS** Z 4-8

321. **COMMON NAME** Tree heather **HEIGHT AND SPREAD** 6½ x 6½ft (2 x 2m) **FLOWERS** ½in (1cm) across, held in 12in (30cm) plumes in mid- to late spring **ASPECT/LIKES** Sun, open site, moist free-draining acid soil **HARDINESS** Z 7-10

322. **COMMON NAME** Alexandrian laurel **HEIGHT AND SPREAD** 3 x 4½ft (1 x 1.4m) **FLOWERS** Tiny, held in a 1¼in (3cm) cluster in spring **ASPECT/LIKES** Shade, shelter, not too dry **HARDINESS** Z 7-9

323. **HEIGHT AND SPREAD** 8 x 12in (20 x 30cm) **FLOWERS** Minute, white, held in 8in (20cm) spikes above foliage in summer **ASPECT/LIKES** Bright but not sunny place, keep fairly moist **HARDINESS** Z 9-11

324

Ophiopogon planiscapus 'Kokuryu'

Not a grass, but a member of the lily family, this distinctive, ground-covering, evergreen perennial is indispensable. It is as useful at the front of shady borders as it is for underplanting specimen shrubs, but, above all, for providing contrast. It looks terrific with silvery *Brunnera macrophylla* 'Jack Frost,' overlaid with fallen fall leaves (especially those of Japanese maples), or beside pale flowers—try it near snowdrops. To me, the inky black, grasslike leaves are perhaps best seen lightly edged with frost, making this plant great for a winter garden. It spreads in a controlled way at the root; bits are easily detached and replanted. In summer, little pink-tinged white flowers appear, followed by glossy black berries. Seeds easily germinate, but a high proportion of seedlings will be green leaved. These need to be removed or the clump's appearance is spoiled. I plant the green-leaved ones together elsewhere—they are still useful as quite dense ground cover.

COMMON NAME Black mondo grass **HEIGHT AND SPREAD** 3 x 4ft (1x1.2m) **FLOWERS** ½in (1cm), held on a 2½in (6cm) stem in summer **ASPECT/LIKES** Sun or shade, fertile soil, not too dry **HARDINESS** Z 6-9

325

Nephrolepis exaltata 'Bostoniensis'

COMMON NAME Boston fern **HEIGHT AND SPREAD** 3 x 4ft (1 x 1.2m) **ASPECT/LIKES** Bright but not sunny spot, consistent conditions with no changes in light, temperature, or watering **HARDINESS** Z 9-11

A happy Boston fern makes a knockout house plant. The rich-green, arching, slightly ruffled fronds are best appreciated raised up, cascading from a stand or hanging basket, and make a heart-warming sight on a winter day. On mature ferns, the fronds reach almost 3ft (1m) long. Healthy plants also produce slender green runners, which in the wild help them spread across forest floors or even on tree branches. Despite their great beauty, I seldom see really well-grown Boston ferns. Yellowing, falling leaves are early signs that something is not right. Usually it's the watering—potting mix should never be dry, but the plant must not stand in water either, particularly in winter. Choose somewhere bright but not too sunny—a humid bathroom is ideal. Get the basics right and these are easy-to-keep plants.

326

Jasminum nudiflorum

This is probably the best-known winter-flowering climber and it's certainly the toughest. It produces flushes of yellow flowers that emerge like sparks of sunshine from bare branches during the darkest days of the year. If individual flowers are killed by hard frost, more soon emerge, and then in spring, fresh green foliage appears. How you grow it is a matter of personal taste. I have trained mine neatly along wires against a north-facing shed, where the flowers show up well against the black-painted wood. I remove odd dead sprigs each spring. Meanwhile, in a front garden near me, there is a huge one cascading over a wall in full sun, growing more as a relaxed, mound-shaped shrub than a climber. Although unkempt, it's covered in blooms all winter, putting mine, quite frankly, to shame in the flower-power stakes. But I'm not sure I could live with the space it takes up grown this way. Perhaps in the right place ... The plant will also grow in a container, at least for a while, but is happier in the ground.

COMMON NAME Winter jasmine **HEIGHT AND SPREAD** Scrambles to 14½ft (4.5m) **FLOWERS** 1in (2.5cm) long, in flushes through winter **ASPECT/LIKES** Sun or shade, somewhere to scramble, well-drained soil **HARDINESS** Z 6-9

327

Narcissus 'Bridal Crown'

Bulbs are essential flowering plants for the house in winter and this exquisite narcissus is one of the best. If I remember in time, I buy dry bulbs and plant them in late fall in bulb fiber in an old Delft bowl, keeping them somewhere cool and dark. But often I forget. Happily, early in the year garden centers offer them potted up beside daffodils for outdoor use, although these will flower later. Simply replant in a nice pot, pushing in a few birch twigs to help support the stems, which grow quickly. Flowering is profuse—pretty, creamy white, double blooms, each with a yellow eye, opening in clusters atop elongating stems. The scent is strong and sweet, with none of the nasty drain smell I often detect with *Narcissus papyraceus* (paperwhites), and the display lasts at least two weeks. Stems collapse toward the end, so I pop the remaining blooms in a vase and shove the bulbs in a cold frame to dry off. You can then try them in the garden in a sunny warm spot or replant for indoor use again. I get a decent show in the second year.

HEIGHT AND SPREAD 20in (50cm) tall indoors **FLOWERS** 1½in (4cm) across, held in a 2¾in (7cm) cluster from midwinter to early spring **ASPECT/LIKES** Sunny but cool windowsill **HARDINESS** Z 3-9

"Lit by the glancing rays of the winter sun, the whole plant glows in a magical fashion."

<u>328</u>

Rubus phoenicolasius

I first saw this lovely plant in the Winter Garden at Cambridge University Botanic Garden and have loved it ever since. Some might dismiss it as little more than a bramble, but in place of fierce barbs on its arching canes, dense rust-colored bristles sprout evenly up the stems. It is deciduous, so this characteristic is most evident after the leaves have fallen: lit by the glancing rays of the winter sun, the whole plant glows in a magical fashion. It's easy to grow in any reasonable soil in a fairly open place where it can form a well-behaved thicket. I find it less vigorous than many other *Rubus*. The young stems are most appealing, so old canes need cutting out from the base in early spring. At around the same time, its quite attractive, pale-green leaves appear. Better still, after its white, bramblelike flowers fade, crops of edible, raspberry-like fruit appear—a tasty little treat to enjoy while gardening nearby.

COMMON NAME Japanese wineberry **HEIGHT AND SPREAD** 6½ x 13ft (2 x 4m) **FLOWERS** ¾in (2cm) across, in early summer **ASPECT/LIKES** Sun or part shade, fertile well-drained soil, not too dry **HARDINESS** Z 4-8

329

Helleborus thibetanus

Looking almost like a large wood anemone, this diminutive hellebore is a favorite of mine. Its nodding, white, pink-veined flowers appear in January, followed by handsome, glossy, divided foliage. Best treated as an alpine, it needs sharp drainage and sun to thrive. I keep some plants in deep terracotta pots; others grow in my little rock garden. I remember the excitement this newly introduced plant caused when it was first available in the plant center (these beauties are still seldom seen for sale). I bought one, but the leaves soon withered and the plant appeared dead. Disgruntled, I tossed what remained away. Stupid of me, for this hellebore is summer dormant; its leaves start to yellow in May. Plants may well set seed, which germinates easily and is worth sowing.

COMMON NAME Tibetan hellebore **HEIGHT AND SPREAD** 6–8 x 6in (15–20 x 15cm) **FLOWERS** 1¼in (3cm) across, in midwinter **ASPECT/LIKES** Open airy quite sunny site, sharp drainage, not too dry **HARDINESS** Z 5-8

330

Eranthis hyemalis

Few sights are more welcome than the massed, yellow, cup-shaped flowers of these little charmers, which open as a precursor to spring-bulb displays, seemingly breaking winter's frigid grasp. What they like best is a moist place in short grass, ideally under deciduous trees. Here, they can naturalize, undisturbed by fork and spade and untroubled by other plants, although they seem to enjoy the company of snowdrops and other early flowers such as crocus. The blooms sit atop a ruff of green leaves on short stems, briefly forming ground cover. They last a couple of weeks, but by early summer, most traces of the plant have gone. They are best planted after flowering while still in leaf; the dry tubers sometimes sold seldom amount to much.

COMMON NAME Winter aconite **HEIGHT AND SPREAD** 4in x 6½–10ft (10 x 200–300cm) **FLOWERS** ¾in (2cm) across, in midwinter **ASPECT/LIKES** Undisturbed place in moist deciduous shade **HARDINESS** Z 4-7

331

Bergenia 'Admiral'

HEIGHT AND SPREAD 1 x 1¾ft (30 x 50cm) **FLOWERS** Bells, ½in (1cm) across, held atop 1ft (30cm) stems in spring **ASPECT/LIKES** Sun, open site, well-drained soil **HARDINESS** Z 3-8

Bergenias are "Marmite" plants—people seem to either like them or loathe them. I'm certainly in the former camp, although my garden is not suited to displaying them well. I can't really see what there is to dislike about *Bergenia* 'Admiral.' Like all the best selections, it has bold leaves that develop interesting coloration in winter; in their case, they go plummy red with a metallic sheen with the first frosts. In spring, tall, lipstick-red stems carry clusters of quite bright-pink flowers well above the ground-covering foliage, which, although still burnished, will have begun to return to its usual, rich, glossy green. Bergenias are pretty easy to grow, but look and do best with a bit of space—spilling over the edge of a border, cascading down a bank, or forming a raft of growth in a gravel garden, as this selection does at Beth Chatto's Plants & Gardens, where I first saw it.

332

Chimonanthus praecox

If I had to choose my favorite floral scents, I think the perfume produced by wintersweet flowers through January would top the list. I adore it, but it is hard to describe. It's warm and spicy, and I certainly detect the scent of cloves, a touch of citrus and a sweet hint of honey perhaps, maybe with a slightly medicinal edge. And the joy of wintersweet is that you don't need to put your nose into a flower to enjoy it—on a warm day, the perfume carries freely on the air. A cut stem, with just a few open flowers, will scent a room. The nodding blooms of this large, deciduous shrub open from bare stems and are curious rather than beautiful. Their yellowish, almost translucent, pointed outer petals surround a purple-stained center. The oval, pointed leaves develop later and turn a nice, butter-yellow before falling in fall. The plant gets pride of place in my garden and often sets seed, which germinates easily, I find.

COMMON NAME Wintersweet **HEIGHT AND SPREAD** 13 x 6½ft (4 x 2.5m) **FLOWERS** 1¼in (3cm) long, on bare stems, in midwinter **ASPECT/LIKES** A position in full sun, ideally by a warm wall **HARDINESS** Z 7-9

333

Skimmia japonica 'Marlot'

Some plants that might be passed by in borders make great features displayed in a pot. This variegated skimmia is one example. Its leathery, evergreen, lance-shaped leaves are long and slender and, when mature, are marbled gray-green, save for an irregular, thin, cream margin. The plant is compact-growing, in time forming a handsome dome, at its best early in the year, when upright panicles of flower buds arise at the tips of shoots. These are richly pink flushed and tone beautifully with the foliage. They open into scented, cream-colored flowers later in the spring. Skimmias have male and female (as well as hermaphrodite) plants. This is a male selection and won't bear ornamental fruit. Keep your plant somewhere cool but bright and open for summer. Don't let it get too dry or too wet and give it the odd feed to keep its foliage tip-top. Then, when winter arrives, allot it a plum position.

HEIGHT AND SPREAD 2 x 2ft (60 x 60cm) **FLOWERS** Tiny, held in 2½in (6cm) long heads in spring **ASPECT/LIKES** Sun or part shade, well-drained soil, not too dry **HARDINESS** Z 6-8

334

Galanthus elwesii var. *monostictus*

If there is one plant that I enjoy seeing more than any other each year, it is this wonderful snowdrop. Indeed, it almost makes me look forward to winter. I find it one of the earliest of the season's snowdrops, pushing through the soil before New Year in a mild season. Large, sturdy, vigorous, and dependable, it has leaves that are lush, broad, and a beautiful silvery gray. The nodding, well-proportioned flowers start to open before foliage fully develops and last several weeks, especially if the weather is cool rather than cold. This is an impressive snowdrop—visitors always want to know which it is—and, above all, so obliging. With no pampering, a single bulb bulks up into a clump within three years in the right spot and soon you'll have a little drift. It is perfect at the edge of a border or in front of a sunny hedge.

335

Philodendron hederaceum 'Brasil'

This striking and fairly recently introduced house plant has arresting, dark-green, heart-shaped leaves daubed irregularly with both paler green and bright lime-green, almost as if painted on with a brush. It can be grown either as a trailer, perhaps cascading down from a shelf or in a hanging basket, or upright, trained on a moss pole for support. It is a colorful plant, cheering in winter and pretty easygoing. Good indirect light is best, with enough water to prevent it from drying out. It also likes the occasional misting over, especially if the central heating is on, which will prevent the air from getting too dry. The fascination is that you can never tell what a new leaf will look like; my plant features a few all-green leaves, some with a slender lime stripe, and others that are much more luxuriantly marked. Sometimes half of the leaf is dark green, the other lime-green.

336

Asplenium nidus

It's a familiar enough house plant, but this lovely fern is particularly special when grown well. Its fronds are a superbly glossy bright green, each with a contrasting black central midrib. Broad, delicately veined, and wavy edged, they form an ever-increasing shuttlecock of foliage. The attraction for me is to watch the pale, tightly coiled, young fronds gradually unravel like a slow-motion version of one of those paper party blowers. My fern is on a stand near a window but away from direct sun, in a cool bathroom, where the winter sun shines through its translucent leaves beautifully. Plants get big eventually. There are now also crinkly leaved selections, such as 'Crispy Wave,' which don't appeal to me so much.

337

Cyclamen persicum hybrids

Native to the Middle East, the true species of this elegant cyclamen is seldom seen for sale, but extensive breeding means its cultivars are sold by their thousands as seasonal plants in fall. Flowers come in shades of red, purple, pink, or white. The key is to choose one with scented blooms, for some now have no perfume. Outdoors, plants provide a good show until frosted; indoors, mine will flower nonstop for six months until spring, as long as it has good light, a cool location, and is kept moist. Eventually, it will die down; the tuber can either be kept and regrown in late summer or simply discarded. Either way, I can't think of a flowering plant that gives better value for money.

334. COMMON NAME One-spotted Elwes's snowdrop **HEIGHT AND SPREAD** 10 x 12in (25 x 30cm) clump **FLOWERS** 1¼in (3cm) long, in early to midwinter **ASPECT/LIKES** Some sun in winter, semishade in summer, well-drained soil **HARDINESS** Z 3-8

335. HEIGHT AND SPREAD 5 x 1¾ft (150 x 50cm) **ASPECT/LIKES** Bright but not sunny spot, above 50°F (10°C) **HARDINESS** Z 9-11

336. COMMON NAME Bird's nest fern **HEIGHT AND SPREAD** 4 x 3ft (1.2 x 1m) **ASPECT/LIKES** Bright position away from direct sun, above 50°F (10°C), moist but not wet **HARDINESS** Z 10-11

337. COMMON NAME Pot cyclamen **HEIGHT AND SPREAD** Variable: 8–20 x 6–16in (20–50 x 15–40cm) **FLOWERS** 1¼–2in (3–5cm), from fall to spring **ASPECT/LIKES** Cool sunny airy windowsill or sunny spot protected from frost and heavy rain **HARDINESS** Z 9-11

338

Acacia dealbata

If you're out and about in London in winter, the chances are you'll spot one of these trees somewhere in full flower: the frothy clouds of golden-yellow, puff-ball blooms are hard to ignore. Not fully hardy, but thriving in our increasingly mild winters in many urban areas, this evergreen is remarkably quick growing and can form a sizable tree, so allow space and be prepared to prune it regularly to keep it in bounds. One in my parents' garden astonished winter visitors for years, but I'd planted it against a neighbor's fence, which it began to damage, so it eventually had to be removed. The winter flowers smother the tree and last for several weeks as long as days are reasonably mild. They have a sweet scent that carries on the air. The wonderfully delicate, silvery green, fernlike foliage is another draw. When established, it usefully shrugs off drought.

COMMON NAMES Silver wattle, mimosa **HEIGHT AND SPREAD** 39 x 13ft (12 x 4m) **FLOWERS** Held in clusters 4in (10cm) long in late winter and early spring **ASPECT/ LIKES** Sun, shelter from cold winds **HARDINESS** Z 7-10

"The winter flowers smother the tree and last for several weeks as long as days are reasonably mild."

339

Clematis napaulensis

I've grown this unusual climber since I first met it. It is summer dormant, losing all its leaves in late spring. In fall and winter, however, it is a gem. Little ferny leaves appear on bare stems in November, lovely and fresh, just as other leaves are falling. Then in winter come the flowers—creamy bells with showy, purple-tipped stamens that emerge from their skirts and look rather like tassels. They are abundant, putting on quite a show, although hard frost kills both blooms and foliage. After the flowers fade, you get loads of fluffy seed heads. Grow the plant up something else (I have one draped over a *Cupressus sempervirens*). Alone on a wall, its unsightly summer behavior is too obvious.

HEIGHT AND SPREAD Climbs to 26ft (8m) **FLOWERS** 1in (2.5cm) long, in late winter **ASPECT/LIKES** Sun, shelter, good drainage **HARDINESS** Z 9-11

340

Iris unguicularis

COMMON NAME Algerian iris **HEIGHT AND SPREAD** 1 x 1¼ft (30 x 40cm) **FLOWERS** 2in (5cm) across, from midwinter until early spring **ASPECT/LIKES** Sun, well-drained soil **HARDINESS** Z 7-9

One of the highlights of winter in the garden is seeing this delightful perennial burst into bloom. For much of the year, it is not much to look at—a clump of strap-shaped leaves, often browning at the edges. But, then, one mild day in winter, it will catch you quite unawares, flaunting its delicate flowers, usually purple marked with yellow and white. These arise on short tubes from the base of the plant among the leaves. Individual blooms are short lived and easily damaged by rough weather, but more will arise when conditions improve. There are some lovely selections: 'Walter Butt' has large blooms of palest mauve; 'Mary Barnard' is rich purple; 'Alba' is white; and 'Peloponnese Snow' is white and purple. They take drought and poor stony soil in their stride and perform well at the base of a sunny wall. I've had good results raising plants from seed.

341

Hamamelis × *intermedia* 'Pallida'

Regardless of when they bloom, few plants can match the impression that a well-grown example of this fine shrub or small tree can make when seen at its best in late winter. I recall one that was smothered with flowers and underplanted with *Galanthus* 'Magnet,' its clear yellow flowers scenting the air with a zesty perfume. For years, I grew mine fairly well in a container, but eventually I planted it and it took off, forming a wide, spreading, open shrub. Plants need reasonable amounts of water in summer to set decent flower buds, so don't let them get too dry. In fall, the leaves almost match the color of the flowers, turning buttery yellow and making quite a show. Most witch hazel cultivars are grafted, so keep an eye out for suckers arising from the rootstock and remove them promptly.

COMMON NAME Witch hazel **HEIGHT AND SPREAD** 10 x 10ft (3 x 3m) **FLOWERS** 1½in (4cm), in late winter **ASPECT/LIKES** Sun or part shade, fertile well-drained soil, not too dry **HARDINESS** Z 5-9

342

Galanthus 'Trumps'

The name of this fine snowdrop often raises a smirk on the faces of those unfamiliar with the game of bridge. The word "trumps," of course, refers to the heart-shaped, green markings on the outer petals of the blooms. Reliably flowering in early February, this selection also proves easy to grow, bulking up into a decent clump in just a few years. The flowers really are lovely, dangling from quite tall stems and opening before the gray-green foliage fully develops. The inner petals are marked boldly with green, but in this selection, it is the outer petals that really impress. These open widely and are resplendent with showy, inverted-heart-shaped markings toward the tips. The effect is particularly striking when the plants are grown near more traditional snowdrops. Give them the conditions they need and just let them go about their business.

HEIGHT AND SPREAD 6in (15cm) high **FLOWERS** ¾in (2cm), in late winter **ASPECT/LIKES** Some sun in winter, semishade in summer, undisturbed site, fertile well-drained soil, not too dry **HARDINESS** Z 3-8

343. HEIGHT AND SPREAD 1¾ x 1¼ft (50 x 40cm) **FLOWERS** 2½in (6cm) across, opening in midwinter and lasting into spring **ASPECT/LIKES** Shade from summer sun, fertile well-drained soil **HARDINESS** Z 6-9

344. COMMON NAME Witch hazel **HEIGHT AND SPREAD** 10 x 10ft (3 x 3m) **FLOWERS** 1½in (4cm) across, from late winter until early spring **ASPECT/LIKES** Sun or part shade, fertile well-drained soil, not too dry **HARDINESS** Z 5-9

345. HEIGHT AND SPREAD 8 x 4in (20 x 10cm) **FLOWERS** 1½in (4cm) wide, from midwinter until early spring **ASPECT/LIKES** Part shade, fertile well-drained soil **HARDINESS** Z 3-8

346. COMMON NAME Eastern cyclamen **HEIGHT AND SPREAD** 4 x 6in (10 x 15cm) **FLOWERS** ¾in (2cm) across, from late winter until early spring **ASPECT/LIKES** Sun or part shade, well-drained soil **HARDINESS** Z 4-8

343

Helleborus Walberton's Rosemary

This sensational evergreen perennial, also known as 'Walhero,' is a hybrid between *Helleborus niger* (see p.208) and *Helleborus* x *hybridus* (see p.246) and combines the January flowering of the former with the habit, vigor, and colorful flowers of the latter. The blooms are open and star-shaped, rather like those of *H. niger*, but atop taller, slender stems and with a more delicate appearance. They are also a superb, clear rose-pink, the petals greenish toward the central crown of golden stamens. Flowers arise before new foliage and plants form decent clumps, bearing masses of blooms that last in beauty for weeks. Mulch annually with garden compost, taking care not to spread it over the crown of the plant, as this can damage emerging foliage. Water in dry spells.

344

Hamamelis x *intermedia* 'Orange Peel'

This lovely witch hazel flowers reliably early from February, when its spidery blooms appear on bare stems. They consist of curled, glowing-orange petals that look and give off a scent just like the pieces of citrus zest that you might scrape off a grater and pop into a cake. The display lasts in beauty for several weeks; hard frost never dulls the show. As a bonus, this selection also has leaves that turn yellow and orange in fall. A rather upright shrub when young, it can form a small rounded tree, if you have space. If not, prune after flowering, cutting last year's branches back to a couple of buds. New stems then arise in spring and flower the following winter. Witch hazels grow well in light shade in fertile, well-drained soil. It need not be acidic, but avoid dry, shallow chalk.

345

Narcissus 'Cedric Morris'

This is one of the most charming of all bulbs, a tiny golden daffodil so perfectly miniaturized, it would fit into the garden of a doll's house. It is best grown in a low pot in an airy unheated glasshouse or cold frame, although it can do well outdoors in a bright, well-drained place, perhaps a pocket in a rock garden or at the edge of a woodland border. Plantswoman Beth Chatto introduced it to me. The plant she gave me perished—because I planted it in sun, which attracted narcissus fly; a place in some shade helps prevent this. It starts to flower early, often in January or even late December, and then on and off until March. It looks remarkable among snowdrops.

346

Cyclamen coum

With pretty, little, heart-shaped leaves that are variably but beautifully patterned in silver and green, and masses of dainty, white or purple-pink flowers that last into spring, this low, ground-covering plant is a garden essential. It grows from a tuber that slowly increases in size over the years, producing ever more flowers, while also seeding freely around. Grow in sun or shade in well-drained soil and it should thrive and naturalize as long as tubers are not disturbed. This can be an issue once leaves die off in summer; little is more infuriating than finding a tuber impaled on your hand fork. It is a classic partner for snowdrops, but avoid growing next to larger, fall-flowering *Cyclamen hederifolium*, which can take over.

347

Lonicera × purpusii 'Winter Beauty'

Honeysuckles that start to flower during our coldest months are shrubs rather than climbers. Easiest and most reliable is this first-rate plant, which for weeks bears masses of sweetly scented, white flowers, the perfume of which carries well on the air on sunny days. Flowers generally survive light frosts but may be damaged in extreme cold; even then, further flushes develop once milder conditions return. It flowers best in a sunny, fairly open position. Some winter cold benefits the display, as it encourages the foliage to fall—blooms stand out better on bare stems. Prune after flowering, when around a quarter of stems can be thinned out. Replacement shoots often arise right from the base of the plant.

COMMON NAME Winter honeysuckle **HEIGHT AND SPREAD** 8 x 8ft (2.5 x 2.5m) **FLOWERS** ¾in (2cm), from late winter until early spring **ASPECT/LIKES** Sun or part shade, well-drained soil **HARDINESS** Z 4-10

348

Galanthus elwesii 'Grumpy'

HEIGHT AND SPREAD 6in (15cm) high **FLOWERS** ¾in (2cm) long, in late winter **ASPECT/LIKES** Some sun in winter, semishade in summer, undisturbed site, well-drained soil, not too dry **HARDINESS** Z 3-8

Snowdrops are so popular, hundreds of cultivars are grown, often with beguiling names and collected by enthusiasts willing to part with eye-watering sums for a single bulb of a sought-after kind. It's hard not to get swept up in the excitement and this particularly characterful snowdrop is irresistible. From a distance, it is little different from typical plants of *Galanthus elwesii*, with broad, gray-green foliage, topped by large white drops. But, in the world of snowdrops, the devil is in the detail. Look closely and peeking out from between the larger outer petals is a mournful little face, with green markings on the inner petals resembling two eyes and a downturned mouth. You just have to give it a home. Find it fertile, free-draining soil with some sun in winter in a place that does not get too dry in summer and 'Grumpy' will be happy—even if he doesn't show it.

349

Lonicera standishii var. *lancifolia* 'Budapest'

This choice and easily grown, winter-flowering honeysuckle has appealing displays of sweetly scented, pink-flushed cream flowers that appear for up to a month from midwinter onward, often attracting the odd early bee. The perfume has a rather lemony quality and carries well on milder days. Frost may brown individual blooms, but more soon open. The plant makes a rather upright-growing but fairly compact, well-behaved shrub with quite handsome, slender, pointed foliage, which look its best in spring, when the young shoots are bronze-flushed and glossy. By early winter, the leaves are beginning to fall and numerous flower buds form in pairs from leaf axils up more or less bare stems. Prune out a few older branches as needed in spring if the plant becomes congested.

HEIGHT AND SPREAD 8 x 8ft (2.5 x 2.5m) **FLOWERS** ¾in (2cm), from mid- to late winter **ASPECT/LIKES** Sun or part shade, well-drained soil **HARDINESS** Z 6-9

350

Galanthus 'Augustus'

I grow around 30 different snowdrops; this distinctive selection is among my favorites and was named for the great plantsman and bulb expert E. A. Bowles, one of my gardening heroes. It is a most reliable cultivar, with good vigor, and bulking up well. I also find it to be one of the more long-lasting in flower, the blooms remaining in beauty for a couple of weeks or more into late winter in cool weather. Elegantly pear-shaped when in bud, the flowers are quite rounded, with outer petals that are white with a textured, almost seersucker finish to them. They are complemented by unusually handsome foliage—lush, broad, gray-green, rather glistening leaves with a generous, central, silver stripe. Give plants a place with some sun in winter and part shade in summer you will soon have a decent clump.

HEIGHT AND SPREAD 4in (10cm) high **FLOWERS** ¾in (2cm) long, from late winter until early spring **ASPECT/LIKES** Sun or part shade, undisturbed site, fertile well-drained soil, not too dry **HARDINESS** Z 3-8

351

Hippeastrum papilio

Many people will be familiar with the hippeastrum bulbs given as Christmas gifts, which a few weeks after planting bear flamboyant blooms, usually in shades of red, pink, or white, to brighten our homes in winter. Worth seeking out is this marvelous species, which in the wild in southern Brazil (where it is endangered) grows on tree branches. It is evergreen and so, unlike showy hybrid hippeastrum, does not go through a period of dormancy, which may make it a better long-term houseplant. The main attraction is the astonishingly beautiful flowers, which are apple green and boldly striped in wine-red to dramatic effect. The blooms arise on stout stems rather shorter than hybrid hippeastrum, and they do not open flat but rather hold their petals in the stance of a resting butterfly, adding a delicate touch. It is easy to grow on a sunny windowsill or in a conservatory. It stands cool night temperatures and swiftly forms offset bulbs, which can either be detached and grown or left to form a handsome pot full.

COMMON NAME Butterfly amaryllis
HEIGHT AND SPREAD 1¾ x 1ft (50 x 30cm)
FLOWERS 4¾in (12cm) across, in late winter
ASPECT/LIKES Sunny windowsill or conservatory, well-drained compost
HARDINESS Z 8-10

<u>352</u>

Daphne bholua 'Jaqueline Postill'

It is hard to overstate the brilliance of this remarkable plant. If it flowered in summer, it would rank as one of the finest, scented, flowering shrubs, but the fact that it produces its delectable display in winter places it among the most valuable of all garden plants. A large, upright-growing evergreen, it likes a fairly sheltered space. It does well under deciduous trees and will perform admirably against a wall, but it wants good soil that does not get too dry. The rich-green leaves are elliptical and form an excellent foil for the clusters of small, starry, four-petaled, pink and white, rather waxy flowers, which appear in profusion for weeks and resist frost well. The perfume is powerful and deliciously sweet and can be detected some distance from the plant. Mine grows by the front door and I often hear passersby remark on it. It readily produces new shoots from the root. These can be detached and grown. In summer, leaves are sometimes eaten by snails, but otherwise, the plant has proved trouble-free.

HEIGHT AND SPREAD 8 x 5ft (2.5 x 1.5m) **FLOWERS** ⅝in (1.5cm) across, held in a 2in (5cm) cluster from late winter until early spring **ASPECT/ LIKES** Sun or part shade, shelter from cold winds, well-drained soil, not too dry **HARDINESS** Z 7-10

353

Galanthus 'Primrose Warburg'

Selections of so-called "yellow" snowdrops are growing in number, with enthusiasts introducing more each year. Flowers are for the most part still white, but the green markings are replaced by yellow ones. This particular drop is named after a well-known collector and is, for good reason, among the most popular. When a galanthophile friend gave me a single bulb, I nervously planted it (yellow snowdrops once had a reputation for lacking vigor), but I needn't have worried. In a couple of years, it had multiplied into a clump with perhaps 15 flowers. The yellow markings are surprisingly noticeable—when the flowers are seen en masse, the clump almost seems to glow in my winter garden. I'm told that yellow snowdrops like a slightly sunnier place than their kin; mine thrive at the front of an open, north-facing border.

354

Helleborus × *hybridus*

It is hard to know where to begin with Lenten roses, for these virtuous, evergreen perennials are essential in any garden enjoyed year-round. The beautiful nodding flowers are infinitely variable in a vast range of colors, from black to slate-gray (almost blue), purple, red, pink, peach, green, yellow, and white. Some also have contrasting petal edges. Many are spotted inside, a few have star-shaped flowers, some are semidouble ("anemone-flowered") and others fully double. All are beautiful. Flowers arise on stout stalks and last in beauty for months. Hard frost may flatten and even freeze blooms to the ground, but they find the vim to stand upright again. They seed with great abandon and do best with an annual mulch around (not over) crowns. Snip off old leaves in winter as flower stems arise—this displays flowers better and puts mice off nibbling the buds.

355

Lonicera elisae

This charming, winter-flowering honeysuckle was introduced from China. For some reason, it is still seldom seen, but it thrives against a sheltered, north-facing wall in my garden and has proved to be easy and rewarding to grow. It forms an upright, fairly compact shrub. In spring, the quite hairy new growth is attractively purple tinted, but it is in mid- to late winter that the plant comes alive—paired, delicate, ivory-white, pink-flushed, rather tubular flowers appear, hanging down from the branches. Individually, each looks rather like a little trumpet. These last several weeks and can provide quite an impressive display on mature plants. They are often followed later in the year by red berries.

356

Petasites fragrans

You might think a plant that bears heads of purple and cream, heliotrope-scented flowers in the depths of winter would be popular, but many people will shudder to see me discuss what can be an invasive weed. Yet I am fond of this low-growing, ground-covering, semievergreen perennial. My own plant came from a piece I pulled out of a garden near my student digs. I had wondered what the vanilla-like scent in the winter air could be and my nose led me to spikes of blooms rising through a carpet of bold, rounded leaves. The plant spreads via running roots and will quickly overtake a border, so it must be grown with caution. Cold knocks it back, but it always regrows; kept in dry shade as ground cover, where little else will thrive, it is far less vigorous.

353. **HEIGHT AND SPREAD** 6in (15cm) high **FLOWERS** ¾in (2cm), in late winter **ASPECT/LIKES** Some sun in winter, semishade in summer, undisturbed site, well-drained soil, not too dry **HARDINESS** Z 3-8

354. **COMMON NAME** Lenten rose **HEIGHT AND SPREAD** 1¾ x 1¾ft (50 x 50cm) **FLOWERS** Up to 2½in (6cm) across, from early winter until midspring **ASPECT/LIKES** Part shade, fertile well-drained soil, not too dry or too wet **HARDINESS** Z 6-9

355. **COMMON NAME** Elisa's honeysuckle **HEIGHT AND SPREAD** 8 x 6½ft (2.5 x 2m) **FLOWERS** 1in (2.5cm) long, in mid- to late winter **ASPECT/LIKES** Sun or part shade, shelter from wind, well-drained soil **HARDINESS** Z 6-9

356. **COMMON NAME** Winter heliotrope **HEIGHT AND SPREAD** 1 x 6½ft (30 x 200cm) **FLOWERS** ¾in (2cm) across, held in an 3in (8cm) cluster in mid- to late winter **ASPECT/LIKES** Sun or shade, any soil **HARDINESS** Z 4-8

357

Leucojum vernum

Appearing from February, spring snowflakes are often mistaken for snowdrops, although, on closer inspection, the more substantial flowers are quite different. Each is broadly bell-shaped, composed of six equal petals with a pointed, usually green (sometimes yellow) marked tip. They dangle snowdrop-fashion from short stems, often opening before the strap-shaped, glossy green leaves fully emerge. Bulbs slowly build into clumps and are plants of great beauty yet seldom seen. They are good for attracting early pollinating insects. Grow them undisturbed in rich soil below deciduous trees or shrubs. Choose somewhere that will remain cool and moist in summer, although sun at flowering time is ideal. They look lovely beside evergreen ferns or winter aconites, but their impact is rather lessened in association with snowdrops. Mark the bulbs' positions with a label—they are too precious to risk damage from a trowel later in the year.

COMMON NAME Winter snowflake **HEIGHT AND SPREAD** 8 x 4in (20 x 10cm) **FLOWERS** 1in (2.5cm) across, from late winter until early spring **ASPECT/ LIKES** Sun or part shade, fertile moist soil **HARDINESS** Z 4-8

358

Sycopsis sinensis

This handsome Chinese member of the witch hazel family flowers well in winter, so it is curious that these hardy plants are seldom seen. A potentially large, semievergreen shrub or small tree, it bears numerous clusters of brushlike blooms that, at first glance, look orange, but in fact are yellow with red anthers. As the flowers age, the anthers elongate. The display is quite showy, the flowers appearing amid elegant, quite glossy, pointed, oval foliage. It seems an easy plant to keep. Young examples can be grown for a few years in a pot, making them simple to display with other winter-interest plants when they're in flower. Allow a bit of space when planting—although quite upright when young, plants become spreading once mature.

HEIGHT AND SPREAD 26 x 13ft (8 x 4m) **FLOWERS** Held in ¾in (2cm) clusters in late winter **ASPECT/LIKES** Sun or part shade, shelter, moist well-drained acidic/neutral soil **HARDINESS** Z 8-10

359

Crocus corsicus

COMMON NAME Corsican crocus **HEIGHT AND SPREAD** 3in (8cm) high **FLOWERS** 2in (5cm) tall, held atop a short tube in late winter **ASPECT/LIKES** Sun, undisturbed site, well-drained soil **HARDINESS** Z 4-9

Few gardeners know of this crocus, but in my garden this little beauty is the first of the year to flower and often takes me unawares. The dainty, rather slender flowers pop open on the first sunny day toward the end of February, reassuring me that spring is almost here. The chalices of pinkish purple petals contrast with central orange stamens, while the external surface of the outer three petals is boldly feathered in dark purple and pale mauve. If you can get your nose down low enough, the flowers also have a sweet scent. The plant will naturalize in a well-drained, sunny site if undisturbed. My clump of corms does well in sun in a well-drained gravel garden just in front of a clipped box cube. It has very narrow, silver-striped, grassy leaves, which arise just after the flower bud makes itself seen and which die down by late spring.

360. **HEIGHT AND SPREAD** 6in (15cm) high foliage **FLOWERS** 2¾in (7cm) tall, in late winter **ASPECT/LIKES** Sun, open undisturbed site, well-drained soil **HARDINESS** Z 5-8

361. **COMMON NAME** Common correa **HEIGHT AND SPREAD** 5 x 5ft (1.5 x 1.5m) **FLOWERS** ¾in (2cm) long, from midfall until midspring **ASPECT/LIKES** Sun, shelter, well-drained soil **HARDINESS** Z 9-11

362. **COMMON NAME** Winter box **HEIGHT AND SPREAD** 2¼ x 2¼ft (70 x 70cm) **FLOWERS** Held in ⅝in (1.5cm) clusters in late winter **ASPECT/LIKES** Sun or part shade, shelter, any good soil, not too dry **HARDINESS** Z 6-8

363. **COMMON NAME** Three-colored Sieber's crocus **HEIGHT AND SPREAD** 3in (8cm) high **FLOWERS** 1½in (4cm) tall, held atop a short tube in late winter **ASPECT/LIKES** Sun, open site, well-drained soil **HARDINESS** Z 3-8

360

Iris 'Katharine Hodgkin'

This well-known cultivar is probably the most popular of all early bulbous irises, and, with its delicate, beautifully patterned flowers, it is irresistible. The inner upright petals are pale blue, while the outer ones are infused with yellow and also spotted and striped in navy blue. They open a few centimeters above the soil surface, the buds appearing before the grassy foliage arises. They last well, though wet and windy conditions will spoil the show. Plants may endure from year to year and even multiply, forming low rafts of flowers, so long as they remain undisturbed and untroubled by competition. They need excellent drainage—conditions sometimes possible in a gravel garden. The alternative is to grow them in shallow terracotta pots of enriched, sandy potting mix, probably replanting and largely replacing them each year.

361

Correa reflexa

Unless you live in an unusually mild district, you will probably need to devote your sunniest, most sheltered corner to this small Australian shrub, but the outlay of a plum position is worth it for the displays of exotic, pink, tubular flowers, each petal with a green, back-swept tip. The flowers appear sporadically from midfall and on into spring, and dangle amid small, rounded, evergreen leaves held on slender stems. These are easy and quick-growing plants, resisting summer heat and drought well, making them good candidates for growing at the foot of a sunny wall, perhaps below climbing plants or taller wall-trained shrubs. If hard frost is forecast, protect plants with straw and fleece; in cold areas, the shrub can be kept in a container and protected in a cool glasshouse or conservatory to get it through spells of freezing weather.

362

Sarcococca hookeriana Winter Gem

This handsome, compact evergreen, also known as 'Pmoore03,' teams glossy foliage with a dense habit, forming a rounded clump, with new shoots arising from the base. The leaves are long, pointed, and oval, each slightly arched with a gleaming sheen. But the highlight is in late winter, when the tufts of white flowers appear, opening from red-pink buds. These are showier than most *Sarcococca* but with much the same sweet scent that carries on the air. Use it as an understory plant below trees or taller shrubs or as an evergreen anchor in a mixed border. It is pretty tough, standing shade and spells of summer drought when established, but it repays the trouble of giving it a decent spot. It will also grow well in a large container.

363

Crocus sieberi subsp. *sublimis* 'Tricolor'

If you are looking for winter flowers with impact, this crocus is among the most striking. Despite their diminutive size, the blooms are very eye-catching. The top half of each petal is rich purple, below which is a band of white, with a center that is egg-yolk orange. The color is just as good on the outside of the flower as it is on the inside, so, when the sun goes in and blooms close, it still looks impressive. Plant in a drift in a sunny, well-drained, open site, such as the front of a border, in a rock garden, or even below roses. The grassy leaves are of little bother and can be pulled away once yellow in late spring. The key thing is to remember where you have planted your crocus to avoid accidental disturbance.

364
Iris lazica

Although rather later-flowering than similar *Iris unguicularis* (see p.237), this handsome, evergreen perennial has the benefit of being a rather tidier plant, with broader, sturdier, erect foliage. It is perhaps less free-flowering, with a shorter season, but the blooms arising on short tubes from the base of the clump are still most attractive. They are a glowing lavender-blue, with showy bright-yellow markings on the lower petals. The other bonus is that this species also grows well in light shade and prefers some moisture at the root, bulking up quickly. This makes it an easy and adaptable candidate for planting in borders and forming effective associations with other low-growing plants, such as winter-flowering heathers, black *Ophiopogon* (see p.226), or interplanted between clumps of heucheras. Plants form large clumps with an open center; these can be divided and sections replanted in spring.

COMMON NAME Lazistan iris **HEIGHT AND SPREAD** 1 x 2ft (30 x 60cm) **FLOWERS** 6in (15cm) tall, 3in (8cm) across, in late winter **ASPECT/LIKES** Sun or part shade, any reasonable soil **HARDINESS** Z 8-10

365
Clematis urophylla 'Winter Beauty'

Some plants are worth going the extra mile for; of the few winter-flowering clematis, this is arguably the most beautiful, bearing clusters of pure-white, dangling, bell-shaped flowers, each with four petals that terminate in an elegant back-swept tip. These surround a central boss of creamy stamens and hang amid the plant's shiny evergreen foliage, looking as if they have been crafted from wax. The only slight snag is that this climber is not especially hardy and demands a sheltered place out of cold winds, ideally on trellis up a sunny wall. Such is its beauty in flower, however, that a valuable site like this is worth giving up: when happy, it grows vigorously and seems to shrug off at least light frosts well. When planting it by a wall, remember that roots need regular watering until well established. If you live in a cold or exposed area, it can also be grown in a cool greenhouse or conservatory but will need a decent-size container and plenty of air in summer.

HEIGHT AND SPREAD Climbs to 10ft (3m) **FLOWERS** 1in (2.5cm) long, in late winter **ASPECT/LIKES** Sun, shelter from cold winds, somewhere to climb, well-drained soil **HARDINESS** Z 7-9

“Thoughtfully planted, a garden will add new delights every day, regardless of the season.”

Plants A–Z

About the author After completing a horticulture degree at Wye College in Kent, Philip Clayton headed to the Royal Horticultural Society (RHS) Garden at Wisley in Surrey as a student. In 2002, he joined the RHS's *The Garden* magazine, through which he met many of the UK's foremost nurserymen and plantsmen and visited the country's great gardens and plant collections. In 2004, he was named Journalist of the Year by the Garden Media Guild. By 2006, he'd started work on his own urban plot in Peterborough, now overflowing with exciting plants. In 2016, he became deputy editor of *The Garden*; from 2022, he began a freelance garden writing career.

Follow Philip on Twitter **@clayton_philip**.

Author acknowledgments This book is dedicated to my parents, especially my father, Alan Clayton, who died of COVID-19 just as I started writing. My garden helped sustain me through those days that followed. My thanks go to Rae Spencer-Jones at the RHS, and Chris Young, Amy Slack, Vicky Read, and Mikey Fullalove for their guidance and perseverance. I'd like to also thank my dear friend Deborah Parker for her encouragement, and my wonderful Rob for his love and understanding. A final salute must go to those great experts Roy Lancaster, David Jewell, Ian Hodgson, and Graham Rice who I feel so fortunate to call friends, the late Christopher Lloyd who opened my eyes to the many possibilities gardening allows, and the innumerable gardeners and nurserymen and -women who've inspired along the road.

Publisher acknowledgments DK would like to thank John Tullock for consulting on the US edition; and Francesco Piscitelli for proofreading.

Picture credits

The publisher would like to thank the following for their kind permission to reproduce their photographs:
(Key: a-above; b-below/bottom; c-center; f-far; l-left; r-right; t-top)

Alamy Stock Photo: 86–87, Avalon.red 78br, 187bl, Botanic World 203bl, Botany vision 143, Luis Echeverri 147b, Josie Elias 74bl, Florapix 89bl, 211tl, Deborah Vernon 122–124t; **Laurie Gray Bounsall:** 121br; **Philip Clayton:** 12tl, 12tr, 15bl, 19br, 21tl, 23bl, 31tr, 38bl, 47br, 50tr, 52-53tc, 53bl, 55tl, 57tr, 59br, 60br, 71cla, 71ca, 71cra, 73br, 76tr, 78tl, 93tr, 96br, 99bl, 103tl, 110, 121tl, 121tr, 123bl, 137bl, 138br, 157br, 171tl, 174tr, 176, 181bl, 185tr, 189bl, 190bl, 195cl, 195r, 198tl, 198tr, 198bl, 203tr, 225br, 233, 235tr, 237tr, 250tr, 252; **Dorling Kindersley:** Avon Bulbs / Mark Winwood 244tr, RHS Wisley / Mark Winwood 2br, 33bl, 61, 66tr, 133cr, 145bl, 150bl, 247tr, 250br; **Fairyscapedaylilies.com:** Charmaine Payne 93bl; **GAP Photos:** 27, 35tl, 50br, 113tl, Matt Anker 168–169t, 211tr, Lee Avison 38tr, Adrian Bloom 200br, 218tl, Richard Bloom 2tl, 26bl, 38tl, 164–165bc, 192br, Christina Bollen 150tl, Mark Bolton 31bl, 64br, 191bl, 247tl, Jonathan Buckley 16tl, 32bl, 37bl, 45, 59tl, 69tl, 91, 114-115bc, 145tl, 152–153tc, 179tl, 188, 192bl, 196, 227, 230–231tl, 232, Jonathan Buckley – Design: John Massey, Ashwood Nurseries 185br, Jonathan Buckley – Design: Sarah Raven, Perch Hill 75, 103br, Chris Burrows 82br, Torie Chugg 133l, 145tr, 150tr, 214-215tc, Marg Cousens 85br, Sarah Cuttle 44tl, Jacqui Dracup 32–33tc, Carole Drake 47tl, 119tr, 142, 209, 222tr, 229bl, 240tr, Geoff du Feu 129bl, Heather Edwards 35bl, 64bl, 68tr, 99tr, 171tr, 203tl, 206tl, Ron Evans 105tl, Liz Every 28tr, FhF Greenmedia 22–23tc, 135br, Clare Gainey 12br, Tim Gainey 240tl, John Glover 108tr, 116tl, 149tl, 189tr, 235br, Bjorn Hansson 59bl, 148–149b, Marcus Harpur 59tr, 192tl, Marcus Harpur – Fullers Mill, Suffolk 35tr, Charles Hawes 113br, Sue Heath 96bl, 197tr, Neil Holmes 197bl, Michael Howes – RHS Garden Hyde Hall 206tr, Martin Hughes-Jones 15tl, 16br, 19tl, 35br, 52bl, 56, 104tr, 113tr, 119bl, 127tr, 138tl, 148tr, 155, 169bl, 171bl, 180–181tc, 185tl, 192tr, 200–201t, 211bl, 213tl, 218br, 225tr, 236, 248–249tl, Jason Ingram – Pan Global Plants – Nick Macer 136br, J S Sira 80tl, 99br, 133r, 171br, Adrian James 90, 163bl, Ernie Janes 11, 12bl, 15br, 116tr, 247br, Dianna Jazwinski 48bl, 216, Andrea Jones 64tl, 164tr, Lynn Keddie 40bl, 150br, 179br, Geoff Kidd 38br, 198br, Joanna Kossak 36–37tc, 145br, 158tr, 186–187tc, Jenny Lilly 154, 231bl, Caroline Mardon 101br, Jonathan Need 44br, 163tr, 242bl, Clive Nichols 28bl, 66–67bc, Clive Nichols – Designer: Dominique Lafourcade 20–21b, Clive Nichols – Great Fosters, Surrey 64tr, Nova Photo Graphik 20tr, 42–43bc, 135bl, 146–147tc, 157tl, 166, 168br, 174br, 203br, 214bl, 215bl, 218bl, 225tl, 249bl, Anna Omiotek-Tott 113bl, 163br, 182bl, Sharon Pearson 17, Abigail Rex 89br, 157bl, Fiona Rice 185bl, Howard Rice 2bl, 47tr, 49bl, 95bl, 107, 108bl, 116br, 125, 157tr, 173, 208bl, 230br, 247bl, 253, Howard Rice – Garden: Cambridge Botanic Gardens 212–213b, Howard Rice – The Winter Garden, Cambridge Botanic Gardens 221tl, Jan Smith 63, Nicola Stocken 28tl, 158br, Friedrich Strauss 108br, 201bl, John Swithinbank 211br, Tommy Tonsberg 89tr, Visions 73tr, 74tr, 118, 121bl, 167bl, Visions Premium 83bl, 100, 139, 235bl, 250bl, Evgeniya Vlasova 28br, Rob Whitworth 55tr, 55br, 78tr, 160, 235tl, 243bl, Doreen Wynja 78bl, Dave Zubraski 179bl; **Garden Exposures Photo Library:** Andrea Jones 2tr, 111, 122br, 221bl; **Garden World Images:** 87bl, 106, Oscar D'arcy 73tl, 140, Flowerphotos / Jonathan Buckley 158bl, Trevor Sims 127br, 174bl; **The Garden Collection:** FP / Andrew Lawson 99tl, FP / Arnaud Descat 104–105b, 127bl, FP / Bildagentur Beck 82–83t, FP / Christine Ann Föll 80br, FP / David Dixon 84, FP / Frédéric Tournay 94–95tc, 167tr, 172br, FP / JS Sira 103tr, 114tr, FP / Martin Hughes-Jones 103bl, 108tl, 116bl, 161, 190–191tc, FP / Nathalie Pasquel 76–77b; **GardenPhotos.com:** judywhite 47bl; **Getty Images / iStock:** Francisco Herrera 172tl; **Jason Ingram:** 4–5, 10bl, 15tr, 19tr, 19bl, 30, 41, 42tr, 48–49tc, 50tl, 50bl, 55bl, 57bl, 60tl, 62, 68–69b, 73bl, 77tl, 81tl, 89tl, 94bl, 124, 128-129tc, 130bl, 131, 136-137t, 141, 153bl, 177, 183, 205, 206bl, 217, 218tr, 221tr, 221br, 222–223b, 225bl, 226tr, 228–229c, 237bl, 238–239tl, 239bl, 240br, 244bl, 245, 248br, 250tl; **Roy Lancaster:** 163tl; **Marianne Majerus Garden Images:** RHS Garden Wisley / Marianne Majerus 135tl, Glen Chantry, Essex / Marianne Majerus 206br, 240bl, Marianne Majerus 92, 96tl, 96tr; **Clive Nichols:** 127tl, 158tl

Cover images: Front: Philip Clayton; Dorling Kindersley: RHS Wisley / Mark Winwood; Back: Philip Clayton; Dorling Kindersley: RHS Wisley / Mark Winwood.